Jeffrey M. Berry

Lobbying for the People

The Political Behavior of Public Interest Groups

PRINCETON UNIVERSITY PRESS
Princeton, New Jersey

Copyright © 1977 by Princeton University Press

Published by Princeton University Press,
Princeton, New Jersey

In the United Kingdom: Princeton University Press,
Guildford, Surrey

ALL RIGHTS RESERVED

Library of Congress Cataloging in Publication Data
will be found on the last printed page of this book

Printed in the United States of America by
Princeton University Press, Princeton, New Jersey

To My Parents

CONTENTS

TABLES AND FIGURES

ACKNOWLEDGMENTS

DURING the years it has taken to complete this study, I have been helped by many different people in many different ways. I would first like to thank the Brookings Institution, and its Director of Governmental Studies, Gilbert Y. Steiner. I was the recipient of a Brookings Research Fellowship during 1973-1974, and I am grateful for the support they gave me. Brookings bears no responsibility for the final product. I would also like to thank the Tufts University Faculty Awards Committee for a timely grant that aided me in the last stages of this project.

In completing the two case studies that comprise Chapters V and VI of this book, I was fortunate to be able to work with a group of very understanding and patient public interest activists. Lewis Regenstein and Marian Newman of the Fund for Animals, and Rosalie Riechman, Bill Samuel, and Marti Powers of the Women's International League for Peace and Freedom permitted me to observe the workings of public interest groups at first hand as a participant observer. Their cooperation is deeply appreciated, and I am indebted to them for teaching me so much about public interest lobbying. Cleveland Amory, President of the Fund for Animals, and Dorothy Steffens, Executive Director of the Women's International League for Peace and Freedom, were kind enough to allow me to spend the day at their offices in New York and Philadelphia talking to them and their co-workers.

For their advice, assistance, or critical reading of my manuscript, I would like to thank Anne Costain, Douglas Costain, Daniel Fiorino, William Frasure, G. David Garson, Jerry Goldman, Susan King, Mordecai Lee, Theodore Macaluso, Barry Mitnick, James Nathanson, James Qualls, Francis Rourke, Paul Sabatier, Thomas Wolanin, and Graham Wootton. At Princeton University Press, Sanford

Thatcher was a thoughtful and supportive editor. I would especially like to thank Robert Peabody and Milton Cummings for their help throughout the course of this study. They gave generously of their time, and I profited greatly from the many suggestions they made.

Vicki Nixon, Rosa Cook, Miriam Berry (no relation), and Deborah Manning provided skillful typing assistance in the preparation of my manuscript. I thank them all for their tireless and reliable work.

My wife, Lori, was a constant source of support and encouragement. My biggest debt is to her.

Medford, Massachusetts
August 1976

LIST OF ABBREVIATIONS AND ACRONYMS

ACA	Americans for Constitutional Action
ACLU	American Civil Liberties Union
ADA	Americans for Democratic Action
AEC	Atomic Energy Commission
ALACP	American League to Abolish Capital Punishment
CAB	Civil Aeronautics Board
CHL	Committee for Humane Legislation
CIA	Central Intelligence Agency
EPA	Environmental Protection Agency
FAA	Federal Aviation Administration
FCC	Federal Communications Commission
FPC	Federal Power Commission
FTC	Federal Trade Commission
IRS	Internal Revenue Service
MCPL	Members of Congress for Peace Through Law
NCC	National Council of Churches
NCEC	National Committee for an Effective Congress
NEPA	National Environmental Policy Act
NRDC	Natural Resources Defense Council
OUTS	Open Up The System
PIRGs	Public Interest Research Groups
WILPF	Women's International League for Peace and Freedom

LOBBYING FOR THE PEOPLE

CHAPTER I

Introduction

DURING the past decade, advocacy organizations commonly known as "public interest groups" have become increasingly prominent in American society and politics. These groups are not a new form of political organization; they have existed far back into our history. There does, however, seem to be a new awareness of the activities of public interest groups. Through the lobbying efforts and accompanying publicity generated by Ralph Nader and organizations such as Common Cause and the Sierra Club, a greater recognition of the work of these groups has emerged. There is little question that in recent years public interest groups have gained a growing acceptance as legitimate representatives of significant constituencies or "interests" within the polity.

It is important to try to learn about public interest groups (to be defined shortly) and their political behavior. An understanding of the operation of such organizations can contribute to our knowledge of how citizens communicate with their leaders. In broad terms, how is public opinion aggregated and preferences expressed in the day-to-day political world? Public interest groups offer individuals one means of participating collectively in politics for the purpose of trying to influence public policy outcomes. The endeavors of these organizations to "lobby" the institutions of government are the culmination of this collective action.

Public interest groups are, of course, just one of the channels through which politically concerned people direct their time, money, and psychological involvement. However, unlike political parties or labor unions, for example, little is known about the organizational and political behavior of public interest groups. Despite an extensive literature on interest groups generally, public interest and other types of citizen groups have received scant attention. It would be a dubious assumption to believe that public interest groups are largely similar to the farm, labor, and business organizations that have been traditionally emphasized in interest group research.[1] Public interest groups can be distinguished not only by the causes they espouse, but also by the motivational basis of their memberships and the internal structure of their organizations.

The present study is based primarily on a survey of lobbyists of national public interest groups in Washington, D.C., during the fall, winter, and spring of 1972-1973. This work examines the development and maintenance of public interest groups, their resources, the recruitment and background of their lobbyists, their decision-making structures, and their strategies and tactics of lobbying. The goals of this research are twofold. The first objective is to expand the basic knowledge on public interest groups and to integrate the findings into the larger body of literature on interest groups. To this end, numerous comparisons will be made between public and private interest groups. The data on public interest groups collected here will be used in many instances to test some of the prevailing thinking on the internal operation and lobbying practices of the broader universe of interest groups. What are the generalizations that public interest groups "violate," and how do their patterns of behavior qualify the findings of other studies on interest groups?

The second objective is to take the research data a step further to place it in a conceptual framework for under-

[1] For a concise summary of the literature since 1951, see David Truman's "Introduction to the Second Edition," in *The Governmental Process*, 2nd ed. (New York: Alfred A. Knopf, 1971), pp. xvii-xlviii. For an earlier overview of the field, see Henry W. Ehrmann, ed., *Interest Groups on Four Continents* (Pittsburgh, Pa.: University of Pittsburgh Press, 1958).

standing interest group decision making. The focus of this framework is on the process by which public interest groups reach decisions concerning their issue priorities and their lobbying tactics. The purpose is to explain how a public interest group makes the choices that determine the nature of the communication between the organization and the government.

The emphasis of this study on the choice of issues and lobbying tactics by public interest groups is based on a simple premise. The act of lobbying is, in very general terms, an act of representation. Like the votes of members of Congress, however, the strategic decisions of lobbyists are not simply mirror images of constituency preferences. An interest group is an intermediary between citizens and government, and it is the task of the organization to convert what it perceives to be the desires of its constituents into specific policies and goals. The choice of issues by the organization is the conversion process by which constituency preferences are ordered. The choice of tactics is the process by which resources and policy objective are converted into specific acts of interest articulation and representation.

In trying to develop a framework or model of public interest group decision making, there was a presupposition that there are a variety of factors, or variables, that help to explain the lobbying activity of interest groups. The quality of the interaction between the lobbyist and government officials is not exclusively dependent on the skill of the lobbyists, or the amount of resources they have available, or the attitudes of officials toward lobbyists. The organizational determinants of lobbying decisions are a complex array of variables that individually and collectively lead each group to choose its issues and methods of influence. It is hoped that this study offers some understanding of how these variables affect the advocacy work of public interest groups.

PUBLIC INTEREST GROUPS: AN OPERATIONAL
DEFINITION

"The public interest" is a much abused as well as downright ambiguous expression. All governmental policy makers, no doubt, consider their decisions to be in the "public
interest." Yet those same policy makers may decide between
the desires of competing interest groups that both claim to
be acting in the public interest. For example, in the case of
the controversy over the building of the trans-Alaska oil
pipeline, who was acting in the public interest: the environmental groups who used litigation in an attempt to stop the
pipeline and save pristine wilderness, or the oil industry
which was trying to meet the ever-growing demands of
consumers? Stephen K. Bailey's observation that "The
phrase 'the public interest' is the decision maker's anchor
rationalization for policy-caused pain"[2] must surely be applicable to the deliberations of Interior Department and
White House officials who had to mediate between the
conflicting interests.

Political scientists have been no more unanimous in defining exactly what constitutes the public interest than have
the politicians who use it for their "anchor." Students of
political philosophy have struggled endlessly with the problem of whether or not there is an all-encompassing, defina-
ble public interest. As Frank Sorauf writes:

> Clearly, no scholarly consensus exists on the public in-
> terest, nor does agreement appear to be in the offing. Not
> only do scholars disagree on the defining of the public
> interest, they disagree as well about what they are trying
> to define: a goal, a process, or a myth.[3]

[2] Stephen K. Bailey, "The Public Interest: Some Operational Dilem-
mas," in Carl J. Friedrich, ed., *The Public Interest* (New York:
Atherton, 1962), p. 97.
[3] Frank J. Sorauf, "The Conceptual Muddle," in Friedrich, *The
Public Interest*, p. 185.

This study will not attempt to resolve the debate over whether there is, or is not, an identifiable public interest.[4] Rather, a much narrower goal is sought. The purpose here is only to construct an operational definition of a public interest group. In labeling certain organizations as public interest, it should be clear there is no intention of implying that only these groups hold objectives that coincide with a national or universal public interest.

Because the public interest is such an amorphous concept, it may seem self-defeating to use it at all. The simple fact is that both the media and the organizations themselves are using the expression "public interest group" with increasing frequency. It is most meaningful, therefore, to take what is common usage and to construct a precise definition that will make reasonable sense to both political elites and political scientists alike.

For the purposes of this study, *a public interest group is one that seeks a collective good, the achievement of which will not selectively and materially benefit the membership or activists of the organization.* It is important to stress that there are two components of this definition that must be used in evaluating a given interest group. One criterion is the goods or objectives sought by the group. The second basis for judgment is the characteristics of the people seeking those objectives.[5]

[4] See, generally, Frank J. Sorauf, "The Public Interest Reconsidered," *Journal of Politics*, vol. 19 (November 1957), pp. 616-639; Glendon Schubert, *The Public Interest* (Glencoe, Ill.: The Free Press, 1960); Virginia Held, *The Public Interest and Individual Interests* (New York: Basic Books, 1970); Clarke E. Cochran, "Political Science and the 'Public Interest,'" *Journal of Politics*, vol. 36 (May 1974), pp. 327-355; and Barry M. Mitnick, "A Typology of Conceptions of the Public Interest," *Administration & Society*, vol. 8 (May 1976), pp. 5-28.

[5] This definition is similar to the one Paul Dawson is using in his research on public interest groups. He states that "public interest groups are membership based organizations that seek collective goods that are not of exclusive benefit to their members." See "On Making Public Policy More Public: The Role of Public Interest Groups,"

The term "collective good" is used here to refer to any public policy whose benefits may be shared equally by all people, independent of their membership or support of a given group.[6] Some obvious examples of collective goods are clean air and world peace. Many goods are not, however, inherently collective or exclusive. What is a collective good to one group may be an exclusive or private good to another. In drawing his distinction between public interests and private interests, E. E. Schattschneider uses the example of the American League to Abolish Capital Punishment (ALACP). Because ALACP's members were not those facing death sentences, Schattschneider concludes that they were seeking a collective or "public" good; specifically, they sought a more humane system of justice.[7]

Schattschneider neglected to consider an alternative capital punishment group that could form. Prisoners on death row could organize and hire lawyers to fight against the death penalty. The good that the prisoners seek, namely, the right to continue living, is an exclusive and material good. Even though both ALACP and the hypothetical prisoners' group desire the same goal, the achievement of that goal will affect them very differently.

In analyzing a group's public or private status, it must be determined if any material goods they seek will have a *differential* impact on the membership or financial supporters. A material good is one that pertains to the physical, as opposed to the intellectual or spiritual, well-being of an individual. Usually, material goods are thought of in eco-

paper delivered at the annual meeting of the American Political Science Association, New Orleans, Louisiana, September 1973, p. 2. For an alternative approach, see Paul Lutzker, *The Politics of Public Interest Groups: Common Cause in Action* (unpublished Ph.D. dissertation, The Johns Hopkins University, 1973), pp. 6-20.

[6] The term "collective good" is defined in a different manner by Mancur Olson, Jr. See *The Logic of Collective Action* (New York: Schocken, 1968), pp. 14-16.

[7] E. E. Schattschneider, *The Semisovereign People* (New York: Holt, Rinehart and Winston, 1960), pp. 25-26.

nomic terms, such as policies that affect wages, welfare benefits, or ability to compete in the marketplace.[8] If a public interest group pursues material goods, the benefits must not selectively reward its own members.

The Children's Foundation is an example of a public interest group that does seek material benefits for certain people. The organization works for the full implementation of laws designed to feed children in poverty areas. The membership of the group is not made up of poor people who have ill-fed children. The middle-class staff of the Children's Foundation is supported entirely by grants from philanthropic foundations. The Children's Foundation works for material goods for others, but the staff and sponsors are in no way selectively benefited by achieving those goods.[9]

A few additional distinctions need to be made in defining public interest groups. Organizations that receive their funding from governmental sources, such as some legal aid or community action groups, which might otherwise qualify as public interest, are not considered within the scope of the definition. Groups supported by the government operate under a much different set of constraints and should be studied from a different perspective. A problem does arise in that many privately funded groups also receive some money from the government. No organization that receives 20% or more of its funds from the government shall be considered as a public interest group. Any figure is admittedly arbitrary, but the less than 20% division assures a high degree of independence on the part of the public interest groups in choosing their advocacy actions.

It should also be noted that many private interest groups will, at times, lobby for the same collective goods that public interest groups seek.[10] This study is limited to those

[8] As in the rather extreme case of the hypothetical prisoners' group, a noneconomic material good might be one that involves the health or safety of individuals.

[9] In this case the collective good sought by the sponsors of the group is a just society in which no child goes hungry.

[10] Mancur Olson explains the lobbying of large economic groups

organizations whose *primary* purpose is the pursuit of collective goods that will not selectively and materially reward their members. Public interest groups may not conduct any significant amount of lobbying for private or exclusive goods in addition to their public interest work.[11] For example, even though the AFL-CIO may, at times, seek collective goods that will not selectively and materially reward its members, the fact that it engages in substantial private interest lobbying excludes it under the definition.[12]

The concept of "interest group" needs some further clarification before the definition of a public interest group is complete. The groups that are included in this study are advocacy organizations; in David Truman's words, they "make claims" upon other groups or institutions.[13] In sum, an organization is an interest group if it is actively trying to influence the distribution of political goods. Quite often the names of various groups are misleading; many advocacy organizations entitle themselves as research centers or institutes. An authentic research center—such as the Brookings Institution—may produce research that is of real use to policy makers, but as long as they do not, as an organization, take issue positions and do not attempt to bring

---

for collective goods as a "by-product" of other activities that serve as the basis of organization. See *The Logic of Collective Action*, pp. 132-167.

[11] The qualifier "significant amount of lobbying" for private goods is necessary because so many of the groups have lobbied on legislation that affects their tax status—surely a private interest matter. There seems to be little justification for excluding groups for lobbying on tax matters, because changes in the law could easily kill these organizations by cutting off sources of funding. The Internal Revenue Service also makes this distinction and allows groups that may not otherwise legally engage in lobbying to try to influence legislation that affects the existence of the organization and its tax status. See *Law and Taxation* (Washington, D.C.: Conservation Foundation, 1970), p. 26.

[12] Mark Nadel makes a similar differentiation between primary (public interest) consumer groups and secondary (by-product) consumer groups. See *The Politics of Consumer Protection* (Indianapolis, Ind.: Bobbs-Merrill, 1971), p. 157.

[13] *The Governmental Process*, p. 33.

about the adoption of the policy preferences of their staff, they are not an interest group. Many public interest groups contend that they only do research, but by their actions in calling press conferences, leaking information to the press, and contacting sympathetic people in the bureaucracy and on Capitol Hill, they qualify as advocacy groups.[14]

To avoid confusion, a more precise definition of advocacy or lobbying is necessary. Lester Milbrath's definition can serve this purpose. In Milbrath's words, "lobbying is *the stimulation and transmission of a communication, by someone other than a citizen acting on his own behalf, directed at a governmental decision-maker with the hope of influencing his decision.*"[15] A communication itself does not have to be overtly persuasive in nature; it can be technical information or a research report. It is the inferred intent of the communicator that is crucial to the definition.

DATA COLLECTION

A number of earlier studies have used surveys of lobbyists as a data base. Most notably, Lester Milbrath's *The Washington Lobbyists*,[16] Walter DeVries' *The Michigan Lobbyist*,[17] and Harmon Zeigler and Michael Baer's *Lobbying*,[18] all utilized original surveys of lobbyists as a primary

[14] Obviously, decisions on advocacy/nonadvocacy status have to be made on a case-by-case basis. One problem that arises is that many groups do both research and advocacy and, thus, there needs to be a guideline to distinguish the amount of advocacy necessary to qualify as a lobby. Those groups for which lobbying is considered to be part of their ongoing organizational purpose—regardless of whether or not it is their major task—qualified as interest groups. Those groups for which a lobbying effort is really an aberration, and where there is no anticipation of a continued lobbying role, were not included under the definition.

[15] Lester W. Milbrath, *The Washington Lobbyists* (Chicago: Rand McNally, 1963), p. 8.

[16] *Ibid.*

[17] Walter D. DeVries, *The Michigan Lobbyist* (unpublished Ph.D. dissertation, Michigan State University, 1960).

[18] Harmon Zeigler and Michael Baer, *Lobbying* (Belmont, Calif.: Wadsworth, 1969).

data source. Almost all of the lobbyists interviewed for these studies worked for organizations that would be considered private interest under the definition being used here. To replicate the above studies, by substituting the public interest lobbyists for the samples of mostly private interest lobbyists, would surely bring forth interesting results. Some of the questions in the public interest interview schedule were drawn up with an eye toward comparison in the subsequent analysis. The present study, however, moves into a number of areas not covered, or not dealt with in sufficient depth, in these previous works. Consequently, direct comparisons with these earlier studies are made only in certain parts of this book.

Another major difference in the public interest group survey is that the research for this study was not restricted to legislative lobbying. Milbrath, DeVries, and Zeigler and Baer all chose their interviewees from lists of lobbyists registered with the Congress (Milbrath) or a state legislature (DeVries, and Zeigler and Baer). They thereby excluded those lobbyists and organizations that try to influence public policy, but concentrate their efforts on an institution of government other than the legislative branch. As Lewis Anthony Dexter observes, *"there is no reason for most Washington representatives to spend the bulk of their time on legislative lobbying."*[19] It should also be noted that, at least for the U.S. Congress, the filings of registered lobbyists do not form an accurate compendium of those who actually do legislative lobbying. Under the current lobbying laws, many interest group representatives who do advocacy work before the Congress are not, in practice, required to register.[20] Although all but a handful of the public interest

[19] Lewis Anthony Dexter, *How Organizations Are Represented in Washington* (Indianapolis, Ind.: Bobbs-Merrill, 1969), p. 7.

[20] Although the case may be different in the various states, the filings of lobbyists who register with the Congress are a rather biased list of those who actually do legislative lobbying. The U.S. Supreme Court has held that only those whose principal purpose is the influencing of legislation must file (if they plan to communicate di-

groups in the sample have some contact with the Congress, only about a third of them were found to have registered lobbyists.[21]

Because the lists of lobbyists registered with the Congress could not be used, and because there are no existing lists of public interest groups, part of the task of the survey was simply to identify the relevant organizations. This involved not only locating potential groups, but also determining whether they did, in fact, fit the operational definition. Creating such a list of public interest groups was no simple matter. With the exception of those groups associated with Ralph Nader, and a few other well-known organizations such as Common Cause and the American Civil Liberties Union, public interest groups do not receive adequate attention from the media. It was quite difficult to find information about low-visibility groups such as the Citizens Advocate Center, the Media Access Project, and Defenders of Wildlife. Nevertheless, through a constant scanning of newspapers and periodicals, and through conversations with activists in the field, a large number of public interest groups were identified, one by one.

Interviews were ultimately conducted at 83 public interest organizations that qualified under the definition. All these organizations had an office in Washington, D.C., and all were "national" in their orientation. Groups dealing with the problems of the District of Columbia or its suburbs were excluded. Although there were no uninterviewed groups left on the self-constructed list, there is no claim that this study contains a census of all public interest groups in Washington. There certainly exist groups that were simply overlooked, or were wrongly disqualified on the basis of

---

rectly with members of Congress). This loophole skews the lists toward lawyers on retainer, who tend to be scrupulous in observing the law. See *United States v. Harriss*, 347 U.S. 612 (1954).

[21] This low number for the public interest groups included in the sample is also explained by the tax status held by many. See Chapter III.

faulty or incomplete information. In spite of any unconscious biases that may have been present, however, it must be concluded that this survey represents an extremely high percentage—surely above 80%—of the true number of public interest groups that existed at the time of the interviewing (September 1972 to June 1973).

The sample of public interest groups can be broken down into a number of broad categories. For purposes of analysis, the public interest groups are classified by subject matter and basis of organization as environmental, general politics,[22] consumer, church, poverty-civil rights, and peace-arms. In addition, there are eight organizations in the sample that cannot be placed in any of the above categories. Most of these "miscellaneous" groups overlap two or more of the categories to a degree that it would be inaccurate to place them in one or the other. (See Table I-1.)

TABLE I-1

Organizational Classification

Environmental	25%	(21)
General Politics	13%	(11)
Consumer	16%	(13)
Church	11%	(9)
Civil Rights–Poverty	6%	(5)
Peace–Arms	19%	(16)
Miscellaneous	10%	(8)
	100%	(N=83)

A standardized interview format was used to interview staff lobbyists in each of the 83 public interest groups. To obtain a more accurate sample of public interest lobbyists for the discussion of their personal attributes, more than a single interview was conducted at the larger organizations.

[22] The general politics category includes those groups that are clearly organized on a traditional left-right basis, or that work on issues concerning governmental reform.

If a group had more than 10 professional staff members, one supplementary interview was conducted; and if there were more than 20 professional staffers, two supplementary interviews were done. Throughout this study, all statistics that reflect organizational characteristics are based on the responses from the primary interviews.

The interviewees, because they are not all registered legislative lobbyists, do not fit a strict job classification. Their similarity in being lobbyists is that they are all recognized spokespersons for their organizations and communicate on behalf of their organizations to governmental institutions. They are also similar in that they operate at the "executive" level. Two-thirds of the subjects were directors of the Washington office, and even those that were not possessed a great deal of decision-making authority within the organizations. In general terms, the subjects fit the role description of director of legislation, director of litigation, or project director. If an organization had more than one person who conformed to these roles, the first person identified as such was selected to be interviewed.

In addition to the survey, there was time available to do two separate case studies of public interest groups. The two organizations chosen were the Fund for Animals, a group that promotes the humane treatment of animals and tries to protect endangered species, and the Women's International League for Peace and Freedom, a peace lobby whose origins go back to World War I.

The case studies were conducted from the perspective of a participant observer. I worked as an intern in both organizations, full time, for periods of five weeks each. This method was chosen over that of the researcher who keeps in touch with informants on a regular basis for two general reasons. First, it was felt that it would be best to use an approach as distinctly different from the structured interview as possible. The informant method was more of a middle ground between the two, and it would not permit the researcher to get away from conducting the inquiry on a question-and-answer basis. Second, participant observation seemed advantageous in that it would offer an opportunity to learn not only about the important aspects of the groups' work but also something of their day-to-day activities. As a learning tool, participant observation permits one to experience some of the frustrations, problems, and rewards that are associated with the work.

Although the survey was planned in great detail, with questions constructed to test specific hypotheses, the case studies were contemplated with a minimum of research design. It was hoped that the structure of the two studies would evolve freely out of the data, without being patterned by preconceived notions of what is, or is not, important.[23] By taking this course, it was hoped that the case studies of the two groups would most fully complement the survey research methodology.[24]

Overall, the survey and case studies provided a substantial body of data on the political and organizational behavior of public interest groups. The forthcoming material may be divided into three sections. The first section contains a broad overview of the public interest groups in the sample. Chapter II is a systematic treatment of the origins and maintenance of public interest groups. The third chapter deals with organizational resources such as finances and staffing. Also included in this chapter is a discussion of the way in which public interest groups are affected by

[23] In preparing for his field research on black street corner men, Elliot Liebow recalled that he was bothered by his project director's terse advice to "Go out there and make like an anthropologist" because he was unsure how one "makes like an anthropologist" on a ghetto street corner. This type of ignorance can have its advantages. Feeling unsure of oneself makes one more likely to "take in everything" without blinders or filters. What is significant can be determined at a later point in time. Liebow's book is an extraordinary example of the potential of participant observation. See *Talley's Corner* (Boston: Little, Brown, 1967), p. 235.

[24] A copy of the interview schedule can be found in Appendix A. The organizations in the sample are listed in Appendix B. Appendix C is an elaboration of the research methodology used in this study.

certain provisions of the Internal Revenue Code. Chapter IV takes a look at the Washington lobbyists of the groups and, more specifically, examines their personal background, job recruitment, and career orientation.

The second section is composed of the two case studies. Chapter V is a profile of the Fund for Animals, and Chapter VI is on the Women's International League for Peace and Freedom.

The third section focuses on the processes by which public interest groups choose their issues and tactics of advocacy. Chapter VII analyzes the dynamics of decision making within the organizations. Chapter VIII examines the individual techniques of influence used by the lobbies. Chapter IX covers coalition behavior, general organizational strategies, and the lobbyists' perceptions of their influence on governmental policy making. Finally, Chapter X presents some concluding observations on public interest groups.

CHAPTER II

The Origins and Maintenance of Public Interest Organizations

To inquire about the origins of interest groups is to ask a fundamental question about the American political process. Why is it that some groups of people become organized into interest groups whereas others remain unrepresented? A first step in trying to answer this complex question is to explore the genesis of interest group organizations. What is the process that leads to the establishment of an *organization* from a particular constituency? What are the factors that account for the rise of successfully organized groups?

A second step in this analysis is to look at the means by which interest group organizations sustain themselves over time. Once an organization has been started, how are new members attracted? Why do members remain loyal with continued financial support? What are the incentives associated with group membership?

It is the purpose of this chapter to examine the origins, development, and maintenance of public interest groups. It is especially important to study the manner in which public interest groups are organized because of the diffuse nature of the constituencies they try to represent. How is it that these organizations, which offer no exclusive, material rewards to their members, manage to exist and endure?

TWO THEORIES OF GROUP ORIGINS

The literature dealing with the origins of interest groups is not extensive, but two significant and intriguing theories on the subject can be found in the works of David Truman[1]

[1] David B. Truman, *The Governmental Process*, 2nd ed. (New York: Alfred A. Knopf, 1971). First published in 1951.

and Robert Salisbury.[2] Both theories seem to offer plausible explanations for the development of interest groups. Because Truman and Salisbury differ in their reasoning, an attempt was made to generate data from the survey of public interest groups that would facilitate a testing of the two theories. The evidence gathered does reveal a pattern, and it provides a measure of the adequacy of the Truman and Salisbury frameworks for explaining the origins of public interest groups.

The "disturbance" theory of David Truman was set forth in his seminal book, *The Governmental Process*. Truman observes that interest groups arise from two interrelated societal processes. To begin with, interest groups develop as society becomes more complex. In Truman's words, "it is obvious that the trend toward an increasing diversity of groups functionally attached to the institutions of government is a reflection of the characteristics and needs, to use a somewhat ambiguous term, of a complex society."[3] The increasing complexity of a society is best illustrated by the differentiation in the division of labor. As technology changes and the economy changes, new skills are required, and thus there develop new groupings of people according to these skills. Quite often, tangentially related groups will formally organize into associations that, in turn, almost always become *political* interest groups. Truman points out that all this is not just a response to the industrial revolution and past industrial technology, but is also a product of modern mass communications, which have facilitated the interaction of the units of potential associations.

The increasing complexity of society does not, by itself, explain "the proliferation of groups in our society."[4] Rather, one must look beyond this broad generalization to the specific catalytic factors that cause previously unorganized in-

[2] Robert H. Salisbury, "An Exchange Theory of Interest Groups," *Midwest Journal of Political Science*, vol. 13 (February 1969), pp. 1-32.

[3] *The Governmental Process*, p. 52.

[4] *Ibid.*, p. 56.

dividuals to organize into interest groups. The key to Truman's theory is that people are stimulated to organize because they undergo a disturbance that alters their relationship with other groups or institutions. A disturbance is some force that changes the "equilibrium" of the group with other elements in society. The purpose of forming an interest group or association is to overcome these disadvantageous forces and to stabilize relations so that a new equilibrium may be reached.[5] The effect of business cycles, wars, increased government activity, and the like are all identified as direct catalysts for the formation of various groups trying to restore equilibrium.[6]

Truman's disturbance theory stood relatively unchallenged for nearly 20 years. Robert Salisbury's article, "An Exchange Theory of Interest Groups," offered a critique of Truman as well as an alternative framework for understanding interest group formation. In his own research on the development of farm organizations, Salisbury found that the period 1867-1900 was one of "consistent market disadvantage" for the farmers.[7] He also found that although the economic disturbances may account for the rapid rise of farm groups during this period, there was an equally rapid decline of agrarian organizations *before* any semblance of an equilibrium had been reinstituted.[8] Salisbury concluded,

[5] V. O. Key, Jr., uses this framework on interest group development with some qualifications. See *Politics, Parties, & Pressure Groups*, 5th ed. (New York: Crowell, 1964), pp. 40-43.

[6] Salisbury treats the "proliferation" hypothesis and the "homeostatic mechanism" (disturbance) hypothesis as separate proto-theories. Truman seems to be using the disturbance conceptualization as a refinement to the proliferation thesis, rather than distinguishing them as distinct analytical approaches. Truman was trying to make the process of group origins more precise by clarifying the ambiguities of the proliferation interpretation.

[7] "An Exchange Theory of Interest Groups," p. 7.

[8] Salisbury states that Truman's disturbance theory predicts that membership in organizations will grow during times of adversity and drop off as equilibrium is approached. Salisbury uncovered membership figures for farm and labor organizations which show just the opposite, with a growth in members during prosperity and a decline during economic downturns. *Ibid.*, p. 8.

and rightly so, that any theory of how interest groups originate must also deal with organizational failure. In the case of the farm groups, why did some groups deteriorate and others cease to exist before the disturbances had ended? Salisbury feels that exchange theory is a more useful tool for studying interest group origins. Exchange theory postulates that individuals enter into interpersonal relationships because they derive some type of benefit from the relationship or "exchange."[9] Using this framework, Salisbury concentrates on the role of the political organizer or "entrepreneur." It is the entrepreneur who must make potential members aware of any benefits they may receive by joining his or her organization.[10]

For an understanding of what constitutes benefits that entrepreneurs and members may derive from organizations, Salisbury draws on Peter B. Clark and James Q. Wilson's theory of organizational incentive systems.[11] Clark and Wilson conclude that there are three kinds of incentives that may be secured from organizations. *Material* incentives are those related to tangible goods such as jobs, taxes, and market opportunities. *Solidary* incentives are the rewards obtained from the socializing and friendships involved in actual group interaction. *Purposive* incentives are those benefits one receives from the pursuit of nondivisible goods. In other words, a purposive incentive is the ideological satisfaction associated with the organization's efforts to achieve any collective goods "which do *not* benefit the members in any direct or tangible way."[12]

9 See, generally, Peter M. Blau, *Exchange and Power in Social Life* (New York: Wiley, 1964); and George Homans, *Social Behavior* (New York: Harcourt, Brace & World, 1961).
10 See Norman Frohlich, Joe A. Oppenheimer, and Oran R. Young, *Political Leadership and Collective Goods* (Princeton, N.J.: Princeton University Press, 1971).
11 Peter B. Clark and James Q. Wilson, "Incentive Systems: A Theory of Organizations," *Administrative Science Quarterly*, vol. 6 (September 1961), pp. 129-166.
12 *Ibid.*, p. 135. For an interesting application of this framework to the operation of the Massachusetts Welfare Rights Organization,

Salisbury's basic thesis is that the success of organizing potential groups is dependent on the quality of entrepreneurship. If the entrepreneur can gain a "profit" (e.g., a high salary, prestige, personal satisfaction) and can provide sufficient material, solidary, and purposive incentives, then the organization should succeed. In contrast to Truman, it is the organizer rather than the disturbing event that is the determining factor.

Although Salisbury claims that his is an alternative theory, it could be argued that the exchange and disturbance explanations are not truly discrete. Both stress the effect of external stimuli on groups of individuals with similar policy preferences. Salisbury's interpretation can be fit neatly into Truman's overall theory by considering entrepreneurial activity as a form of disturbance. Because Truman is attempting to isolate those catalytic factors that are responsible for interest group formation, it seems reasonable that initial leadership activities fall within the definition of disturbance. Because Salisbury does not make the case that leadership activity is completely unrelated to other external forces, it may be that these theories are complementary, with a matter of emphasis being the only difference between them.

The position implicit in Salisbury's work is that there is something more fundamental to be differentiated between the two theories than mere emphasis. Despite Truman's detailed commentary on the importance of leadership,[13] he never uses leadership as an example of a primary disturbance in all the cases he cites to illustrate interest group origins. One can make the assumption that Truman views the existence of a disturbance, independent of leadership activity, as a necessary precondition for interest group formation. The type of disturbances he describes precede

see Lawrence Neil Bailis, *Bread or Justice* (Lexington, Mass.: Lexington Books, 1974). For an alternative paradigm, see Amitai Etzioni, *A Comparative Analysis of Complex Organizations* (New York: The Free Press, 1961).

[13] *The Governmental Process*, pp. 156-210.

the leadership or entrepreneurial efforts that take place. For Salisbury, nonentrepreneurial disturbances are simply not necessary for the successful organization of an interest group. Rather, it is a certain level of skill and acumen on the part of leaders of incipient interest groups that is the essential ingredient. Both observers, therefore, are trying to make some distinction between catalytic factors and contributing factors, between primary stimuli and secondary stimuli.[14]

Before the data could be properly evaluated, Truman's ambiguous concept of "disturbance" had to be defined operationally. To clarify Truman's term so that it will have a more precise analytical utility, a disturbance is considered to be any event or series of events, other than leadership activity, which directly stimulates the formation of an interest group. Examples of disturbances are serious fluctuations in the economy; passage of laws by Congress; authoritative decisions by the President, administrative agencies, or the courts; international or domestic conflict; the formation of adversary interest groups; and rapid changes in technology.

During the interview sessions, each subject was asked about the origins of his or her organization. In coding the histories of each of these groups, those responses that tied the group's origins to an event or series of events were recorded as confirming Truman's thesis. If the role of the leader was of primary importance, in the *absence* of a significant disturbance, then Salisbury's entrepreneurial interpretation was supported.[15] The results lend support to

[14] The data analysis is not intended simply to prove one theory right and the other wrong, but rather the attempt here is to isolate the best foundation from which a more comprehensive theory of group origins can be built. For an overview of some of the problems involved in building such a theory, see James Q. Wilson, *Political Organizations* (New York: Basic Books, 1973), pp. 195-214.

[15] All groups, of course, have leaders or "entrepreneurs." Those responses that stressed the role of both leaders and events must be viewed as support for Truman, as he is contradicted only by organi-

the Salisbury exchange theory of interest groups. Roughly two-thirds of the sample organizations were begun by entrepreneurs working without significant disturbances as additional stimuli (see Table II-1). The origins of a much smaller number (29%) of organizations can be traced to a disturbance of some type.

TABLE II-1

Organizational Origins

	Environ-mental	General Politics	Con-sumer	Church	Civil Rights	Peace-Arms	Misc.	Total
Entrepreneur	17	7	13	4	3	5	6	66% (N = 5
Disturbance	4	4	—	1	2	11	2	29% (N = 2
NA	—	—	—	4ª	—	—	—	5% (N =
								100% (N = 8

ª The reason that it is not possible to categorize these church groups is that the Washingt offices evolved slowly out of long-standing denominational units.

Among those public interest groups that were disturbance initiated, close to half are concerned with the issues of national defense, world peace, or the nuclear arms race. These organizations fit quite nicely into the disturbance framework, with war and rapid changes in technology (e.g., the advent of nuclear weapons) being a direct causal link to their formation. The Vietnam War, for example, was the underlying stimulus for groups such as the National Peace Action Coalition and the Coalition to Stop Funding the War. Another major type of disturbance found in the sample was the introduction or passage of legislation. The Society for Animal Protective Legislation was started for the

zations that form without the stimulus of a disturbance. Another criterion for the coding that should be noted is that a group did not have to form immediately after an event had taken place to be evaluated as responding to a disturbance. Organizations did have to develop, however, within a reasonable period of time so that a cause-and-effect relationship could be confidently inferred.

purpose of lobbying for a humane treatment bill that had been introduced in the Congress in 1951. The Center for National Policy Review, begun in 1970, was a response to the need for an interest group to monitor implementation of all the civil rights laws passed during the 1960s.

The more common pattern is entrepreneurial dominance. The groups possessing this characteristic are products of their leaders and of changes in culture or values rather than of specific events. The Citizens Advocate Center is a case in point. Started by Edgar Cahn and others in 1967, its initial purpose was to fight hunger and malnutrition in the United States. Hunger had yet to become a highly salient national issue, but the work of activists like Cahn over the next few years made it a controversial subject. The development of the organization must be credited primarily to the skill and perseverance of the organizers.

Entrepreneurial origins are strongly associated with consumer and environmental groups. The Corporate Accountability Research Group was organized after Ralph Nader commissioned a study of antitrust matters. "We wanted an institutional follow-up. We wanted to effect institutional change." Consequently, a separate organization was set up by Nader to work on corporate responsibility issues. The Center for Science in the Public Interest is another example. Three young scientists decided that "A lot of citizens' groups need scientific help. We wanted to serve as an example to scientists." The Natural Resources Defense Council was started when some law students at Yale and some lawyers in New York thought that there was a need for an environmental law firm. Their applications to the Ford Foundation were joined together, and a subsequent grant made their idea a reality.

Overall, the results of the survey indicate that the entrepreneurial theory of group origins has greater explanatory power for public interest organizations. Most of Truman's analysis is based on examples he drew from the farm, labor, and business sectors, where material incentives and economic cycles are of critical importance. Had Truman given adequate consideration to public interest groups, the majority of which have origins that do not seem to be strongly related to economic conditions, his theory might have been constructed differently.

To say that specific events did not catalyze many of the groups does not mean that long-term structural changes in our society were of no consequence in aiding these groups' formation. Most certainly factors such as increases in education and leisure time in the past few decades contributed to the entrepreneurs' potential for starting their organizations. All incipient groups' chances for successful organization are affected by societal change; but "change" can be rather sudden and dramatic, and it can also be gradual to the point of being imperceptible.

The entrepreneurial theory is more applicable to public interest groups, but it is far from a complete explanation of how these organizations develop. It would push the theory too far to assume that organizations succeed or fail solely because of a leader's ability to provide substantial benefits.[16] Ideally, what is needed is a broader theory that would interrelate all significant correlates of interest group development, including nonentrepreneurial disturbances. Despite any shortcomings, however, the entrepreneurial theory is of considerable help in understanding the origins of public interest groups. Individual leaders, with great determination and zeal, are largely responsible for the formation of many of these groups. No one doubts that effective leadership is a necessary ingredient in any successful organization. For public interest groups, however, the quality of leadership may be more important than the quality of the cause or the strength of the disturbance. For those who believe that interest groups play an important role in representing

[16] A useful model of the stages of institutionalization of a developing interest group organization is outlined by Theodore J. Lowi in *The Politics of Disorder* (New York: Basic Books, 1971), pp. 32-61.

citizens before government, it might have been more com-
forting to learn that such organizations, were, as Truman's
theory predicts, products of disequilibrating events. For
public interest constituencies at least, Truman's stimulus-
response model of disadvantaged conditions and collective
action does not generally fit.[17]

PUBLIC INTEREST CONSTITUENTS

Not all public interest groups are, in fact, real membership organizations. Fully 30% of the sample are organizations that do not have individuals or other groups as members. Many of the groups that do not have memberships,
such as the Center for Law and Social Policy and the Citizens Communication Center, are supported by private charitable foundations. Part of the reason for studying public
interest groups is to learn more about the way in which
traditionally unrepresented interests become represented.
These foundation-backed groups are using the money given
to them to try to develop latent interests within society,
with the hope that their citizen constituencies will be able
to sustain them once they are activated.[18] A number of other
organizations are church-related social action groups that
have no membership distinct from the entire denominational affiliation. The United Methodist Church, for example, counts 11 million members. The Washington office of
the Methodists' Board of Church and Society–Division of
Human Relations acts as a public interest group. It has no
separate membership and it receives its funds from alloca-
tions granted by the national body. Although the 11 million
Methodists are represented by the Washington organiza-

[17] For a more extensive analysis of the formation of public interest
groups, see Jeffrey M. Berry, "On the Origins of Public Interest
Groups: A Test of Two Theories," *Polity* (forthcoming, 1977).

[18] A useful discussion of latent and manifest interests can be found
in J. David Greenstone and Paul E. Peterson, *Race and Authority
in Urban Politics* (New York: Russell Sage Foundation, 1973), pp.
51-68.

tion, they are members of a public interest group only in the most marginal sense. In the following discussion, the term "membership organization" will exclude such similar church groups. For the remaining groups, membership is defined as those people who make financial contributions or pay dues and whose support is recent enough to be carried on an organization's mailing list.

Group Size. There is a wide range of sizes of organizations, but the majority of groups have moderate to small numbers of members (see Table II-2). In addition to those groups whose members are individuals, there are seven groups that act as coalitions of other organizations.

TABLE II-2

Membership

None	30%	(25)
Less than 1,000	10%	(8)
1,000–24,999	17%	(14)
25,000–99,999	18%	(15)
100,000–199,999	5%	(4)
200,000+	7%	(6)
Membership is other organizations	8%	(7)
NA or DK	5%	(4)
	100%	(N = 83)

There are six groups in the sample that are notable because of their size: Common Cause, Consumers Union, the Liberty Lobby, the National Audubon Society, the National Wildlife Federation, and the Women's Christian Temperance Union. All have memberships of above 200,000 individuals. The largest of these organizations, in both financial resources and ostensible membership, is the National Wildlife Federation. The environmental group claims to represent 3 million people who, by a variety of means, contribute to the organization. There are 600,000 individuals who are direct or "associate" members by virtue of their subscription to the Federation's appealing magazine, *National Wildlife*. Another 800,000 further the activities of the group by purchasing the Federation's well-known wildlife stamps. The remainder are indirect members by their association with state wildlife federations, which have affiliated clubs within the states.

All but one of these large groups have had over 15 years to build up their membership. The exception is Common Cause, the self-proclaimed citizens' lobby, which was founded in the summer of 1970 by former Health, Education, and Welfare Secretary John Gardner.[19] Common Cause presents a fascinating contrast to the more normal pattern of public interest groups having considerable difficulty in gaining new members. Gardner was, simply, the right man at the right time. He tapped a responsive, underlying constituency, and in only six months Common Cause had 100,-000 members. In a little over a year, 230,000 individuals had signed up.[20] The initial membership solicitation for Common Cause was conducted through full-page advertisements in newspapers and direct mail appeals. The newspaper ads were, in the beginning, quite successful, and some attracted as many as 7000 new members. Their utility diminished, however, and after a $10,000 full-page ad in *The New York Times* received only 300 responses, the advertisements were curtailed.

In their first year alone, Common Cause sent out 6.5 million pieces of mail, and since then they have continued extensive use of direct mail circulars to entice new members. One Common Cause staffer remarked about the increased reliance on direct mail, "At the beginning we were able to

[19] For a brief history of Common Cause's first few years, see Paul Lutzker, *The Politics of Public Interest Groups: Common Cause in Action* (unpublished Ph.D. dissertation, The Johns Hopkins University, 1973).

[20] The membership drcpped as the 1972 election approached to about 200,000, but began to climb again after November and reached 300,000 in early 1974.

skim off the cream with the ads, but no longer. Now we've got to use the mail." Not only has Common Cause had success in enlisting new members, but it has also done a creditable job in retaining them. After an "average" 72% renewal rate in the first year, the group was running an unusually high 78% rate midway in the third year. But it takes money to raise money: Common Cause spent $1.5 million (a third of their budget) for membership solicitation during their second full year.[21]

Ralph Nader has also had remarkable success in raising funds from sympathetic Americans through his Public Citizen organization. Public Citizen was Nader's first effort to capitalize on his notoriety and raise money directly from the public. Public Citizen itself is really just an organization shell to collect money for a number of Nader satellites, including the Public Citizen Litigation Group.[22] Previously, money was raised through Nader's speaking engagement fees, book royalties, foundation grants, and a small number of private contributions.[23] Nader started Public Citizen not only to supplement his already overextended resources, but also to begin some new activities.[24]

Obviously influenced by the excellent return Common Cause was getting with its newspaper ads, Nader also used full-page appeals for members. Starting in June 1971, Public Citizen enlisted 62,000 contributors in its first year. Nader spent $314,000 to raise $1.1 million during the initial 12 months of Public Citizen's existence. Both the amount

[21] See Andrew J. Glass, "Common Cause Seeks to Have Broad Role on Issues in 1972 Campaign," *The Pressure Groups* (Washington, D.C.: National Journal, 1971), pp. 87-88. For Gardner's reflections on the first three years, see Elizabeth Drew's interview, "Conversation with a Citizen," *New Yorker*, July 23, 1973, pp. 35-55.

[22] When press stories mention actions taken by Public Citizen, they are almost always referring to the Litigation Group.

[23] See Charles McCarry, *Citizen Nader* (New York: Saturday Review Press, 1972), pp. 209-211.

[24] See Theodore Jacqueney, "Nader Network Switches Focus to Legal Action, Congressional Lobbying," *National Journal*, June 9, 1973, pp. 840-849.

expended for fund raising and the total contributions received have remained stable since that time. One of the most interesting aspects of the early Public Citizen fund raising was the disclaimer that appeared on the membership coupon one filled out to join the organization. It read, "Please don't send me a thank-you note or additional literature. I know what's wrong. What I want is to see something done about it." Unlike all the other mass-membership public interest groups, Public Citizen was trying to conserve the resources needed to publish a regular newsletter or magazine. Instead, members were mailed an annual report that contained summaries of the activities of the Nader organizations funded by Public Citizen. At the beginning of 1976, however, the organization started to publish a small newspaper, *The Public Citizen*.

Issues and Participants. Nader and Common Cause are very unusual, as few groups are able to straddle so many attractive issues. Not many other public interest groups are afforded the luxury of being able to (profitably) appeal to the public at large through full-page ads in major newspapers. Although Public Citizen and Common Cause do not really attract the public at large, but, rather, a more liberal, middle-class segment, they still have a broader basis of support than most public interest groups can ever hope to have. The average public interest group must work hard in seeking out their narrower "attentive public."[25]

Potential members are sought out in a number of ways, but direct mail is probably the most commonly used method among those groups that can afford membership drives. A drawback to direct mail is that it inevitably overlaps previously furrowed ground, because the lists of names come from the same sources and it is quite common for similar (liberal, conservative, environmental) public interest groups to trade their membership mailing lists. A direct

[25] See Francis E. Rourke, *Bureaucracy, Politics, and Public Policy* (Boston: Little, Brown, 1969), pp. 12-24.

mail campaign is always a financial risk, as there is no assurance that the return in new memberships will even reach the break-even point of postage, labor, and printing costs. Once a group is established, the maintenance of membership is not determined simply by the skills of the entrepreneur in providing benefits, selecting the right mailing lists for new membership solicitation, or obtaining favorable publicity for the group. The public's concern over the relevant issue is necessary, of course, to sustain the organization. Although an organization can, through its publications, try to nurture a continuing interest, issue attention cycles are unpredictable and uncontrollable.[26] Two examples of different public interest groups will illustrate the impact issue saliency can have on existing organizations.

Zero Population Growth, organized by population expert Paul Ehrlich and others, was started in 1969.[27] Public awareness of the problems of overpopulation was heightening, and by early 1972 the group had grown to a respectable 30,000 members. During the next year, numerous sets of statistics were released by the government that showed strong trends toward lower population growth. This year of good news about the nation's population culminated with a report released by the government in February 1973 which indicated that the birth rate had dropped to its lowest level ever, and that the fertility rate (the average number of children women have over their lifetime) had dropped below the replacement level of 2.10 children per family to 2.03.[28]

All this good news was, in one sense, bad news for Zero Population Growth. The membership in the organization

[26] See Anthony Downs, "Up and Down with Ecology—The 'Issue Attention Cycle,' " *Public Interest*, vol. 28 (Summer 1972), pp. 38-50.

[27] Ehrlich played a major role in arousing concern for the problem of overpopulation with his widely selling paperback, *The Population Bomb* (New York: Ballantine, 1968).

[28] This is not, in and of itself, zero population growth, but rather the rate that will make zero population growth possible if it is sustained for 70 years. See Jack Rosenthal, "Each Change Has Vast Impact," *The New York Times*, March 4, 1973, p. E9.

declined from 30,000 to 18,000 by April 1973. In that same month, the Executive Coordinator told a meeting of the Board of Directors that renewals were currently running at only 40% and that further decline in membership was likely to continue in the forseeable future. The extreme rate of membership drop-off leads to the inescapable conclusion that former members considered the problem to be on its way to being solved, and no longer of the critical importance it once had been.[29]

Issue saliency had an opposite effect on the Audubon Society. The organization, an old-line conservation group founded in 1905, began unexpectedly to increase their membership sharply during the late 1960s and early 1970s. Obviously this coincides with a time when Americans paid much more attention to environmental issues. Audubon's own survey of their membership showed that a smaller percentage of those who joined after 1968 listed an interest in bird watching as their primary reason for joining. They also found the median age of membership lower (51) and decreasing gradually.

Data taken from the survey seems to indicate that consumer issues have stimulated the greatest number of recently formed public interest groups (see Table II-3). Eleven of the 13 consumer groups in the sample were begun in the five-year period prior to the completion of the survey. Generalizing from the statistics in Table II-3 is difficult, as the field research could only include those organizations operating during the time of the interviewing. It is possible that consumer groups existed in equivalent numbers during earlier periods as well, but that they have been subject to shorter life spans than the other types of public interest organizations. To make valid comparisons between issue saliency and numbers of related organizations during specific time periods, information would be

[29] On the fate of some "successful" interest groups that challenged the status quo, see William Gamson, *The Strategy of Social Protest* (Homewood, Ill.: Dorsey Press, 1975).

needed on all groups that were active at one time, regardless of their mortality rate. Still, the evolutionary pattern of the consumer groups is dramatically different from that of the other kinds of organizations in the sample. As consumer issues gained prominence in the late 1960s and early 1970s, there were not a substantial number of established groups to take advantage of the growing concern in this area. This stands in contrast to the number of environmental groups that had been operating successfully long before the recent upsurge in interest in ecological problems.

TABLE II-3

Year of Origin

	Environmental	General Politics	Consumer	Church	Civil Rights	Peace-Arms	Misc.	Total	
1968–1972[a]	7	2	11	1	3	8	7	47%	(N = 3...)
1960–1967	4	2	—	—	2	5	—	16%	(N = 1...)
1940–1959	4	5	—	3	—	2	—	17%	(N = 1...)
1920–1939	4	2	1	1	—	—	—	10%	(N = ...)
Before 1920	2	—	1	—	—	1	1	6%	(N = ...)
NA or DK	—	—	—	4	—	—	—	5%	(N = ...)
								101%[b]	(N = 8...)

[a] Includes one group begun in January 1973.
[b] Rounding error.

The question of who belongs to public interest groups cannot yet be answered in full. National survey data on the characteristics of public interest members do not exist. Survey research has been conducted on membership in voluntary associations, interest groups, and organizations in general. The broad and consistent finding is that organizational membership is strongly correlated with measures of wealth and education.[30] One may suspect that public

[30] See Charles R. Wright and Herbert H. Hyman, "Voluntary Association Memberships of American Adults," *American Sociological Review*, vol. 23 (June 1958), pp. 284-294; and V. O. Key, Jr., *Pub-*

interest group members are also disproportionately high in socioeconomic characteristics. Relevant data from a Sierra Club survey of their membership shows that the majority of their members come from households where the main wage earner is in a high-status, white-collar position.[31] Public interest groups are, of course, a peculiar type of voluntary association.[32] Their benefits are primarily purposive, and many of their activities are carried out in Washington, remote from their membership. Some organizations, like the World Federalists and the American Civil Liberties Union, require a great deal of sophistication on the part of their members because of the nature of the abstract issues with which they tend to be involved. There is little doubt that most public interest group members are to be found in the more educated, more skilled, more wealthy, more politically aware segments of American society.

Membership in public interest groups can also be viewed from the perspective of political participation. It has often been assumed that the people who participate in different, active forms of participation (other than voting), such as party work, contacting government officials, or contributing money to candidates, are largely the same group of activists. The authors of *The American Voter* found that those groups of individuals who participated at various levels of campaign activity were "largely overlapping."[33]

---

lic Opinion and American Democracy (New York: Alfred A. Knopf, 1964), pp. 501-508.

[31] Managers and executives, 17%; lawyers, doctors, dentists, 12%; other, 12%; other professionals, 11%; other teachers, 10%; college teachers, 9%; clerical and blue-collar workers, 9%; engineers, 7%; technicians, 7%; students, 6%; homemakers, 1%. See Don Coombs, "The Club Looks at Itself," *Sierra Club Bulletin*, vol. 57 (July/August 1972), pp. 35-39.

[32] For a guide to voluntary associations, see C. Wayne Gordon and Nicholas Babchuk, "A Typology of Voluntary Associations," *American Sociological Review*, vol. 24 (February 1959), pp. 22-29.

[33] Angus Campbell, Philip E. Converse, Warren E. Miller, and Donald E. Stokes, *The American Voter* (New York: Wiley, 1964), p. 50.

36 Lobbying for the People

A major, recent study of participation by Sidney Verba and Norman Nie finds evidence to suggest that political activism is significantly more diffuse than has been thought. From their own survey data they conclude:

> The limited amount of political activity and the tendency of participation to be concentrated among some citizens are quite evident in our analysis. . . . What we have encountered, however, is a slightly different picture of participation—one in which the overall level of political activity seems somewhat higher, the distribution not quite so concentrated, and the cumulative structure not quite so pronounced as had been previously believed.[34]

The point that needs to be made here is that members in public interest groups should not necessarily be considered to be the same people who work in political campaigns or belong to other types of civic organizations. Public interest group membership should be thought of as an alternative form of participation, not restricted to those who are otherwise politically active.

MEMBERSHIP INCENTIVES AND ORGANIZATIONAL MAINTENANCE

The question of why people initially join public interest groups and then continue to maintain their membership has yet to be answered fully. It has been implied that people become members because of purposive incentives—individuals derive ideological satisfaction from the organization's pursuit of certain collective goods. This conclusion may be unfounded; alternative explanations of membership incentives have not been examined. Aside from public policy goods that selectively and materially reward members, which are excluded by definition, there are two other types of incentives that may stimulate public interest group

34 Sidney Verba and Norman H. Nie, *Participation in America* (New York: Harper & Row, 1972), p. 40.

membership. One possible reason why people join these groups is that although their organization lobbies only for collective goods, members may still receive selective benefits that have nothing to do with public policy objectives. A second explanation is that a great number of people receive solidary benefits from their membership. Through local chapters of the organizations, members can derive benefits from the act of socializing with their co-workers.

Lobbying as a "By-Product." An intriguing theory of why people become sustaining members of interest groups is offered by economist Mancur Olson.[35] Olson argues that it is irrational for an individual to maintain membership in a large interest group if persons are able to share in the goods sought without being dues-paying members. For example, why should a farmer join an agrarian organization that is lobbying for higher commodity price supports? Certainly he wants the higher price supports, but if the organization is already lobbying for these goods, why should the individual farmer waste his money by joining? He will share in the higher prices independent of whether or not he is a member.

Following this logic, it is only rational for an individual to join an interest group if he or she receives a "separate and selective incentive."[36] In other words, there must be some benefit that accrues to an individual only if he or she is an official member of the group. There are some qualifications that Olson makes. If a group is so small that a person's nonpresence will be noticed by other members, then it will not be irrational to maintain group membership in the absence of separate and selective incentive. Also, in some instances, individuals will have no choice but to join an interest group. A labor union with a closed-shop agreement

---

[35] Mancur Olson, Jr., *The Logic of Collective Action* (New York: Schocken, 1968). Unlike Truman and Salisbury, Olson does not deal so much with the germination of groups as he does with their ability to attract and maintain members once they have been organized.

[36] *Ibid.*, p. 51.

is one such case where the interest group is able to coerce potential recruits into becoming paying members.

What Olson is doing is attacking the conventional wisdom that people join an interest group because they want it to lobby the government on various policy questions. People really join large, noncoercive groups because of the separate and selective incentives. Olson states, "The common characteristic which distinguishes all of the large economic groups with significant lobbying organizations is that these groups are also organized for some *other* purpose."[37] Lobbies are really "by-products" of selective incentives that induce members to join. To cite one example, the Farm Bureau Federation attracted members not for its lobbying, but because of the technical assistance it offered members.

What can be said of noneconomic organizations such as public interest groups? Olson allows for what he calls philanthropic groups: those groups whose primary concern is not the welfare of their exclusive membership. He concedes that these groups are highly irrational and that their behavior is not explained as effectively by his theory. Public interest groups seem to fall into this philanthropic category, and it could easily be concluded that the by-product theory has little applicability for the organizations being studied here.

Olson, however, does not really test his theory for philanthropic groups, and it may be the case that the by-product theory has much more explanatory power for public interest groups than he has indicated.[38] It is entirely possible that public interest groups do offer their members some type of selective incentives. Under the definition of a public interest group, these incentives cannot, of course, be related in any way to the pursuit of material and selective

[37] *Ibid.*, p. 132.

[38] Olson does say that "logically, the theory can cover all types of lobbies" (p. 159), but clearly he treats noneconomic groups as anomalies and pays very little attention to them. *Ibid.*, pp. 159-165.

public policy goods. The type of incentives they may legitimately offer can be exclusive services to the members, or in-house publications. It may be that these services or publications are sufficiently lucrative to induce membership on their own.

To obtain evidence with regard to Olson's theory, pertinent questions regarding publications and membership services were asked of the public interest lobbyists. In addition, samples of newsletters and magazines were requested and were examined at a later time for format, style, and content. It is evident from Table II-4 that aside from providing publications, few public interest groups offer any tangible rewards or benefits to their members. Only six of the membership groups offer some type of service to those who contribute to the organization. These are mostly

TABLE II-4

Services

None	14%	(8)
Publication	76%	(44)
Publication and service	10%	(6)
	100%	$(N = 58)^a$

[a] Membership organizations only.

environmental groups such as the Audubon Society and the National Wildlife Federation, which have a small number of outdoor facilities for members. The Sierra Club has long offered outdoor activities to those who belong to the group. Interestingly, the Sierra Club survey of its membership showed that, as an incentive to join the Club, the outdoor activities are becoming increasingly unimportant. Of those members who joined 13 or more years ago, 61% said that their primary reason for joining was to participate in the outdoor activities. This is in contrast to only 30% of the more recent members (two years or less) who gave this reason. The newer members' primary motivation was to show support for the Club's conservation (lobbying) activities.[39]

Membership services do not, in sum, appear to be an important incentive for public interest groups. Even the handful of organizations that do offer some tangible services do not provide them to more than a minority of members.

Because most of the public interest organizations that have memberships give their contributors at least one publication, it is possible that these magazines and newsletters act as the primary membership incentive. A careful examination of samples of each of the group's publications suggests that this is not the case. Only one organization, Consumers Union, produces a publication that is clearly, by itself, a sufficient membership inducement. Their well-known *Consumer Reports* contains specialized and very useful information on a variety of over-the-counter products. By the ratings of brand names for each particular consumer commodity, its readers can confidently select the best buy when they go shopping at the store.

There are three other organizations—the National Wildlife Federation, Defenders of Wildlife, and the National Audubon Society—that publish magazines of such high quality that they may serve as the principal membership incentive. All three produce magazines that are unusually large in number of pages and filled with nature photographs. They are all beautifully packaged, are printed on good quality paper, and come out six times a year.

The remainder of the publications range widely in their quality and format.[40] The Society for Animal Protective Legislation mails single-spaced, mimeographed legislative alerts to its members when it wants them to write to their Congresspersons. The Young Americans for Freedom's *New Guard* has polished political analysis for its readers. The Humane Society's *News* is an easy-to-read newsletter with

[39] Coombs, "The Club Looks at Itself," p. 36.

[40] The organizations' publications are discussed in more detail in Chapter VII.

entertaining articles on the organization's social and political activities. What can be said in general terms is that these publications cannot be considered as sufficient incentives for membership, although they may act as an inducement of some measure. All publications constantly extol the efforts of their particular organization, and they surely help to make members feel that their money has been well spent.

As Olson suspected, his theory is not very useful in explaining the behavior of philanthropic organizations. In light of the evidence presented here, the Washington lobbies of public interest groups are not by-products of tangible organizational benefits. Few organizations have any real services to offer other than their magazine or newsletter, and some do not offer even that. The vast majority of these publications are not of a quality to be reason enough alone to explain group membership.

Solidary Incentives. For some public interest group members, the underlying motivation for joining may be solidary incentives. If an individual is given the opportunity actually to participate in group activities, the sense of group identity, the ties of friendship, and the overall satisfaction derived from associating with others may be the most important factor in explaining membership.[41] A survey of national public interest groups is, unfortunately, ill suited to measure the effect of solidary incentives. It is obvious that solidary incentives are of most consequence in the local community, where people can meet with other members of their organization.

One indication of the scope of opportunities available for this type of incentive to be operative is the number of chapters affiliated with the national groups (Table II-5). "Chapters" is not, however, a uniform distinction. Subordinate units are frequently an amalgam of local, intrastate, state, and regional groups that vary widely in size.

---

[41] See Clark and Wilson, "Incentive Systems: A Theory of Organizations"; and James Q. Wilson, *The Amateur Democrat* (Chicago: University of Chicago Press, 1962).

Only a third of the total sample of groups, and slightly less than half of the membership organizations, have chapters associated with the national organization. Even though it is evident that a majority of members in most of the groups do not have the opportunity to participate because there are no chapters, or none geographically close, the significance of these branches should not be underestimated. Those groups that do have chapters are able to take full advantage of zealots and potential activists. If the solidary incentives are strong enough, they may attract individuals

TABLE II-5

Chapters

None	67%	(56)
25 or less	12%	(10)
26-100	10%	(8)
Over 100	11%	(9)
	100%	$(N = 83)^a$

[a] Nonmembership groups are included because some have offices outside of Washington where volunteer and underpaid work is done.

who may not otherwise have become dues-paying members. Consequently, the role of solidary incentives should be evaluated on a case-by-case basis. For a group like the League of Women Voters, with 1300 local chapters and with great emphasis on local activities, social inducements are extremely important. But even within organizations, the attraction of solidary incentives can range considerably among the membership.

It must be concluded that purposive incentives are the most crucial type of inducement for public interest group membership. In Clark and Wilson's words, "the intrinsic worth or dignity of the ends themselves are regarded by members as justifying effort."[42] Although solidary incentives

[42] "Incentive Systems: A Theory of Organizations," p. 146.

cannot be ignored for some members of some groups, it is the more ideological, policy-oriented motivations of individuals that make it possible for most public interest groups to exist. For certain people, the knowledge that one has contributed money to an effort to change a governmental policy can be a very satisfying reward.

CONCLUSION

The natural constituency of any public interest entrepreneur lies in that narrow segment of population that is highly concerned about specific policy issues. They will not be easy to organize because there will be competition for their support by existing groups, and they are not usually attracted to organizations solely because of membership services or publications. Even if solidary incentives are operative within a group, they are still inextricably tied to the purposive goals of the organization.

The explanation here of why groups form is far from complete. To speak of the motivations of groups of individuals, without the proper survey data, is imprecise. Information on the social backgrounds, economic characteristics, political activity, and attitudes of public interest group members must be obtained before solid conclusions can be drawn on the nature of the supportive constituencies of these organizations. Although inferences can be drawn from a few questionnaire mailings of organizations in the sample and from the general literature on voluntary associations, more rigorous and comprehensive survey research is necessary for further inquiry into this subject. It would be particularly interesting to learn about individuals' perceptions of the organizations they join and their self-expressed reasoning for such political participation.

Future theory building in the area of interest group origins will need to take a broad perspective that includes all significant variables that affect the developing organization. The Salisbury exchange framework is a useful base for any such effort. The public interest group data has shown the importance of entrepreneurial activity, independent of disequilibrating disturbances, in the successful organization of an advocacy group. At the same time, other factors, such as the political culture of target populations, the interplay of laws and governmental attitudes, and issue attention cycles, must be integrated into new theories of group formation. The overriding question remains, why do some groups of people become organized whereas others do not?

CHAPTER III

Organizational Resources

PUBLIC interest organizations act as intermediaries between their constituents and government officials. How effectively they are able to communicate on behalf of their members is determined, in part, by the amount of resources they are able to utilize. To understand public interest lobbying it is essential to examine both the resources available to these groups and the manner in which the government regulates their resource capabilities and opportunities.

TAXATION AND REPRESENTATION

The behavior, and very existence, of public interest groups is strongly affected by the requirements of the Internal Revenue Code. Public interest groups are not big business, and they do not provide the government with any real, taxable income. Yet their ability to raise funds is subject to strict control by the Internal Revenue Service (IRS). Moreover, the existing laws and regulations influence the choices public interest groups make in deciding which institution of government they will approach.

Brother, Can You Spare a (Tax-Deductible) Dime? A major distinction that may be made among groups in the sample is between those groups that lobby the Congress and those that do not. In reality, the distinction is between those that lobby openly and those that are more circumspect in their legislative activities.

Traditionally, lobbying by "pressure" groups has been regarded as something potentially dangerous and, thus, deserving of constant vigilance. Congress has always felt some obligation to regulate it. Yet, with due regard to the constitutional right of petition, and for whatever other reasons, it has never enacted strong lobbying controls. Congress did pass the Federal Regulation of Lobbying Act of 1946, which requires any person who is seeking to influence legislation to register with the Congress and to file quarterly expenditure reports.[1] A subsequent Supreme Court decision, *U.S. v. Harriss*,[2] upheld the constitutionality of the statute but restricted its coverage to those whose principal purpose is the influencing of legislation.[3]

The sections of the Internal Revenue Code that contain the guidelines concerning tax exemptions for organizations make a similar distinction with regard to lobbying.[4] Most critically, if a group devotes a "substantial" amount of its activities to lobbying, it may not qualify under Section 501(c)(3) of the Internal Revenue Code. Not only are 501(c)(3) organizations exempt from income tax but, more important, individual contributions to these groups are tax deductible for the donors.[5]

Lobbying, or "legislative activity," is defined by the Internal Revenue Code as "attempts to influence legislation." Operationally this means that the 501(c)(3) group may not advocate the adoption or rejection of legislation, or urge its members to contact members of Congress with the purpose of suggesting that they support or oppose bills before them.[6]

[1] Public Law 79-601.   [2] 347 U.S. 612 (1954).

[3] For a concise history of lobbying laws, see *The Washington Lobby* (Washington, D.C.: Congressional Quarterly, 1971), pp. 13-28. There is an attempt under way in the Congress to strengthen the lobbying laws. Common Cause is a major proponent of legislation in this area. See Richard E. Cohen, "Ineffective Reporting Law Likely to Be Toughened, Extended," *National Journal*, April 19, 1975, pp. 571-578.

[4] Section 170 and Sections 501-521 of the Internal Revenue Code.

[5] Organizations that operate exclusively to promote the social welfare of the country, but engage in substantial lobbying, may still qualify for income tax exemption under Section 501(c)(4). Contributions to 501(c)(4) groups are not, however, tax deductible. See *Law and Taxation* (Washington, D.C.: The Conservation Foundation, 1970).

[6] They are also prohibited from intervening in any political campaigns. *Ibid.*, p. 20. See also "The Tax-Exempt Status of Public

Although 501(c)(3) groups are not permitted to lobby the Congress, they are able to advocate positions before administrative agencies and initiate litigation. This means that even though a 501(c)(3) group such as the Wilderness Society can file a monumental court suit leading to an injunction against the building of the trans-Alaska oil pipeline, the same organization is not legally allowed to lobby the Congress when the same issue is before the House and Senate.

Public interest groups that have 501(c)(3) status are not completely enjoined from communicating with the Congress. They are permitted to act in an "educational" capacity, which lets them provide the Congress with "technical" assistance. Consequently, although they may not take sides on specific bills, they can give the Congress information that is pertinent to current or proposed legislation. Although information sent to the Congress is supposed to be initiated by a congressional request, this is not always followed in practice.[7] Through their ostensibly educational role, most 501(c)(3) organizations do perform limited advocacy, but they try not to become too overt in their activities because the IRS can, at any time, rescind a group's tax deductibility if they deem the lobbying "substantial."

Not having 501(c)(3) tax deductibility for contributions severely limits the sources of income available to a public interest group. First, individual donors, particularly the large contributors who give $500, $1000, or more, may donate as much as they do only because their personal tax situation is such that they can use the deduction advantageously. Because an individual donor will often be able to

Interest Law Firms," *Southern California Law Review*, vol. 45 (Winter 1972), pp. 228-248.

[7] Because of the public nature of congressional hearings 501 (c) (3) public interest groups are careful not to appear unless they have a formal, written request as proof against any IRS charges. But even this is not always at the initiative of a Congressperson. In the words of a representative of a 501(c)(3) environmental group, "It's no trick to get an invitation."

choose from a number of groups working in the same issue area, the decision to give to one over another may be determined by the tax-deductibility status of the groups. Organizations that do not have the 501(c)(3) exemption are usually dependent on small, $10 or $15 contributions.

A second source of financial support that is affected by 501(c)(3) is private foundation money. Private foundations, such as Ford or Carnegie, because of their own tax-exemption requirements, cannot contribute to "political or propagandistic activity."[8] This stipulation thereby excludes non-501(c)(3) groups from receiving foundation grants. Because a number of public interest organizations are dependent on foundation donations, obtaining and keeping 501(c)(3) status can be a matter of life and death.

Political Repression. The proviso that 501(c)(3) groups cannot engage in substantial lobbying is enforced selectively by the Internal Revenue Service. Although it has not happened often, the IRS has, on occasion, taken tax-deductible status away from groups that were held to be in violation of the insubstantial rule. In addition, the IRS has been accused of political retribution in denying tax deductibility to newly forming groups by arbitrarily interpreting the 501(c)(3) requirement that organizations must have educational or charitable purposes.[9]

The IRS has never published any quantitative or qualitative guidelines to define explicitly what constitutes "substantial" legislative activity, so groups must run the risk of deciding this for themselves. One group whose interpretation ran afoul of the IRS is the Sierra Club, which was even-

[8] Previously, private foundations could not give any "substantial" part of their total grants to political activity. The Tax Reform Act of 1969 prohibited any funds at all for political purposes. See Waldemar A. Nielsen, *The Big Foundations* (New York: Columbia University Press, 1972), p. 19.

[9] For a discussion of the IRS's procedures in evaluating tax-exempt groups, see Steven S. Goldberg and Joel Cohen, "Does Higher Authority than IRS Guidelines Exist for Public Interest Law Firms?" *Journal of Taxation*, vol. 34 (February 1971), pp. 77-80.

tually stripped of its 501(c)(3) status. During the mid-1960s, the Sierra Club fought a government proposal to build two power dams on the Colorado River. A result of building the two dams (part of the Central Arizona Project) would have been the flooding of sections of the Grand Canyon. The Department of the Interior defended their proposal on the grounds that newly created artifical lakes would bring the canyon walls closer to the tourists.[10] Nevertheless, the Sierra Club, led by David Brower, was outraged at the plan, and they fought it with all their resources.

The Club took out full-page ads in the *San Francisco Chronicle*, the *Wall Street Journal*, *The New York Times*, and the *Washington Post* strongly condemning the Colorado River dams. Included in the ads was a coupon that readers could send to former House Interior Committee Chairman Wayne Aspinall (D., Colo.) to urge him to reject the proposal. Members of the Sierra Club were asked to write the President as well as their Representatives and Senators. In the face of public opposition, the dams proposal was dropped, but the Sierra Club lost for winning. In 1966, the IRS, possibly acting on complaints by pro-Central Arizona Project Congresspersons, ruled that the Sierra Club no longer qualified for a 501(c)(3) tax exemption.[11] The immediate consequence of this was that, as one Washington staffer noted, "People who were accustomed to giving five to ten thousand a year, well, they froze their contributions."

The Sierra Club was lucky in that it happened to have an affiliated Sierra Club Foundation which also had 501-(c)(3) status. Although the Foundation had been largely dormant, the Sierra Club resuscitated it and provided them-

[10] The Club ridiculed this assertion and sarcastically replied to it in their public relations pieces. Their advertisements read, in part, "Should we flood the Sistine Chapel, so tourists can float nearer the ceiling?"

[11] Accounts of this fight are interspersed in John McPhee's *Encounters with the Archdruid* (New York: Farrar, Straus & Giroux, 1971). See also "The Sierra Club, Political Activity, and Tax Exempt Charitable Status," *Georgetown Law Journal*, vol. 55 (May 1967), pp. 1128-1143.

selves with a means of still obtaining some large donations and private foundation grants.

Associated public foundations are a legitimate method that non-501(c)(3) organizations can use to get around the various restrictions of the Internal Revenue Code.[12] Organizations that can attract money for open lobbying activities may also have an affiliated public foundation to receive tax-deductible contributions, which can be used for permissible 501(c)(3) activities such as litigation or educational campaigns. A number of organizations have this arrangement: The League of Women Voters and the League of Women Voters Education Fund, Zero Population Growth and the Zero Population Growth Fund, and the American Civil Liberties Union and the ACLU Foundation are a few examples. Although the affiliate and the parent organization are free to act in coordinated efforts, they must observe strict regulations forbidding the commingling of funds.

It may appear that the affiliate foundation alternative would make the tax-deductible question moot, because groups could use non-tax-deductible money for their lobbying while large donations and foundation money could go to litigation. This arrangement does work for a dozen or so groups in the sample, but it is no more widespread than that (see Table III-1). There are many 501(c)(3) groups that are not capable of raising a sufficient number of small contributions to make it worth their while to start a lobbying arm. Although a notable, membership-based group like the Sierra Club was able to make the switch to a dependence on small, non-tax-deductible contributions, other less well-known organizations, without a substantial membership base, would have considerable difficulty in shifting the basis of their support. There are other groups that, because of the nature of their constituency, might not gain enough in the way of large donations to warrant setting up a tax-deductible 501(c)(3) unit.

[12] For the legal requirements of public foundations, see *Law and Taxation*, pp. 19-34.

TABLE III-1

Tax Status

No tax-deductible status	36%	(30)
501 (c) (3) organization	49%	(41)
Non-tax-deductible organization with affiliated 501(c)(3) unit	11%	(9)
501(c)(3) pending	4%	(3)
	100%	(N = 83)

The critical role of the IRS is further illustrated by decisions it has made that have worked against the formation of new public interest groups. The IRS is allowed a great deal of discretion in determining whether or not applicant groups fit the charitable or educational requirements of section 501(c)(3). During the Nixon years, unfavorable actions by the IRS concerning public interest groups were regarded by some as representing the political opposition of the administration to particular public interest groups.

One case that had grave implications for the future of tax-deductible public interest groups involved the IRS's review of the Natural Resources Defense Council (NRDC) request for a 501(c)(3) ruling. The NRDC, begun with Ford Foundation money, is an organization that uses legal advocacy as a means to preserve and protect the environment. The group applied for 501(c)(3) status in February 1970, and the IRS granted tax deductibility on the following March 16. In their ruling, the IRS attached an unexpected stipulation that the NRDC would have to gain prior clearance on any lawsuit it planned. The IRS would then be able to rule in each separate case whether the NRDC was doing anything to jeopardize its tax deductibility. Not unexpectedly, the NRDC found this to be an unreasonable infringement on their rights and hired a tax lawyer to fight the IRS's decision.

In October 1970, before the NRDC matter had finally

been settled, the IRS suspended all applications for tax exemptions for public interest groups. The IRS wanted to formulate some clear standards concerning who should be eligible for tax exemption. Officials in the IRS admittedly were worried about the consequences of awarding tax deductibility to every group that wanted to litigate on behalf of the public interest. Protest over the IRS's actions came from environmentalists, members of Congress, and, significantly, from sympathetic members of the administration, such as Russell Train, Chairman of the Council on Environmental Quality, and William Ruckelshaus, then a nominee to be head of the Environmental Protection Agency.[13] Finally, on November 12, 1970, the IRS backed away from its threats against the environmental law movement with the publication of guidelines that do not require prior clearance for litigation and seemingly allow for a wide range of permissible public interest advocacy.[14]

The final NRDC ruling may have appeared to signal a relaxation of IRS hostility against public interest groups, but the subsequent case of the Center for Corporate Responsibility suggests that this was not so. The Center for Corporate Responsibility is an affiliate of the Project on Corporate Responsibility, which does not have 501(c)(3) status. The Project, which owns a few shares of common stock in a number of large business corporations, is trying to influence those corporations to be more socially responsible. On occasion, the organization has tried to get company shareholders to vote their proxies for Project-sponsored floor resolutions at annual corporate business meetings.

13 Richard Corrigan, "Public Interest Law Firms Win Battle with IRS over Exemptions, Deductions," *National Journal*, November 21, 1970, pp. 2541-2549.
14 "Guidelines Under Which the IRS Will Issue Advance Rulings of Exemption to Public Interest Law Firms," Internal Revenue Service, November 12, 1970. See also Richard N. Goldsmith, "The IRS Man Cometh: Public Interest Law Firms Meet the Tax Collector," *Arizona Law Review*, vol. 13 (1971), pp. 857-885.

The people in the Project on Corporate Responsibility knew soon after they started that they would be unable to raise the necessary funds from small, individual donations, and they decided to start a tax-deductible arm of the organization. They applied to the IRS, under the name Center for Corporate Responsibility, for a 501(c)(3) exemption in February 1970. Meanwhile, their attacks on the business community mounted. Particularly notable was "Campaign GM," which was an effort by the Project to get shareholders of General Motors stock to vote for resolutions that would have weakened management's control over the selection of directors and forced GM to make more detailed reports on its work on antipollution devices, minority hiring, and similar issues. Although Campaign GM and other shareholder actions were, by the Project's own admission, largely a failure, they did arouse a great deal of resentment and suspicion among corporate executives.[15]

As the staff and directors of the Project realized that it would be necessary to shift from shareholders' actions to litigation if they were really going to influence corporations, the need for the tax-deductible Center became even more apparent. The Project, however, did not receive a ruling from the IRS for two and one-half years. There is little doubt that this extraordinary delay was political in nature. Finally, the Project was able to get the consumer-minded correspondent of the *Washington Post*, Morton Mintz, to write a story concerning the Center's plight. Mintz's sympathetic article gave credence to the Center's charge that it was being "strangled" by the IRS's purposeful indecision.[16]

Two weeks after Mintz's article, the IRS officially refused

[15] See Norman Pearlstine, "GM Management Wins Smashing Victories over Social Critics at Its Annual Meeting," *Wall Street Journal*, May 24, 1971, p. 1. See also Donald E. Schwartz, "The Public-Interest Proxy Context: Reflections on Campaign GM," *Michigan Law Review*, vol. 69 (January 1971), pp. 421-538.

[16] Morton Mintz, "Strangled by IRS, Group Says," *Washington Post*, May 4, 1973, p. D13.

the Center's 501(c)(3) application because it said that the exemption would serve no charitable or educational purpose.[17] A spokesman for the Center accused the Nixon administration and its man at the IRS, Roger V. Barth,[18] of crushing the Center—which had already lost its professional staff for lack of funds—for political reasons. The Center also responded with litigation charging the IRS with retribution against White House "enemies."[19] A federal district court judge ruled in favor of the Center and ordered the IRS to grant the organization its requested tax status. Judge Charles R. Richie said that the White House's refusal to give the court some documents in the case constituted an admission that the White House had tried to exercise improper political pressure on the IRS.[20]

Although the IRS has denied or removed 501(c)(3) status from only a small number of groups, their actions have had repercussions far beyond these few organizations. The existing 501(c)(3) public interest groups are all too

[17] "Tax Exemption Denied to Research Group," *Washington Post*, May 18, 1973, p. D15.

[18] For similar suspicions concerning Barth, see Jack Anderson and Les Whitten, "The President and His Friends at the IRS," *Washington Post*, November 24, 1973, p. B11.

[19] "Privilege Use Seen Relaxing," *Washington Post*, August 11, 1973, p. A10.

[20] Eileen Shanahan, "Tax Ruling Scores White House Role," *The New York Times*, December 12, 1973, p. 1. The IRS moved to appeal the decision, but later dropped its suit, "IRS Drops Legal Battle on Gadfly Group's Status," *Wall Street Journal*, February 22, 1974, p. 19. The effort of the Nixon White House to misuse the Internal Revenue Service was exposed in great detail during the series of revelations surrounding the Watergate scandal. The withholding of favorable tax exemptions was just one of the unsavory or illegal political tactics used by the White House. As early as March 1969, Patrick Buchanan wrote in a memo to the President that the administration needed "a strong fellow in the Internal Revenue Division; and an especially friendly fellow with a friendly staff in the Tax-Exempt Office." In July 1969, the administration set up a secret Special Service Group within the IRS. Jonathan Schell writes, "The service this organization would render would be to lay the groundwork for taking away a group's tax-exempt status if someone decided that the group was 'extremist.' " Schell, "The Time of Illusion-II," *New Yorker*, June 9, 1975, p. 77 and p. 95.

aware of what the IRS has done in such cases as those involving the Sierra Club, the Natural Resources Defense Council, and the Center for Corporate Responsibility.[21] The power of the IRS over tax-deductible groups is even greater today with recent Supreme Court decisions that have ruled that organizations that have had their tax exemptions revoked may not enjoy 501(c)(3) privileges while they are appealing the IRS decisions.[22] The importance of 501(c)(3) status as a constraint upon the political behavior of public interest groups should not be underestimated. For 501(c)(3) organizations, the potential response of the IRS is something that must be considered in deciding on certain types of political activities.[23]

Target of Influence. The tax exemption question is only one factor that influences an organization's choice in determining which institutions of government it will lobby. Surely, the strongest lobbies are those with the skill and knowledge that enable them to approach any branch of government as the occasion dictates.[24] Nevertheless, because

[21] An example of how public interest groups are aware of their common lot involves the Christian Echoes National Ministry, headed by the politically conservative evangelist, Rev. Billy James Hargis. Christian Echoes lost its tax exemption in 1964 when the IRS ruled that it was too politically active. Hargis took the case to court and won a favorable decision against the IRS in 1971, but lost to the government on appeal a year later. Prior to adjudication by the Supreme Court, an *amicus curiae* brief was filed on Hargis' behalf by the liberal National Council of Churches. Not only is the NCC diametrically opposed to Hargis' politics, but Hargis has continuously and vitriolically denounced the NCC. Church groups like the NCC, which speak out on public issues, are afraid that what is happening to Hargis will happen to them next. See William Willoughby, "Church Ask: To Speak or Not to Speak?" *Washington Star-News*, May 5, 1973, p. A-9.
[22] *Alexander v. "Americans United" Inc.*, 416 U.S. 752 (1974); and *Bob Jones University v. Simon et al.*, 416 U.S. 725 (1974).
[23] See, generally, Robert L. Holbert, *Tax Law and Political Access*, Sage Professional Papers in American Politics (Beverly Hills, Calif.: Sage, 1975).
[24] See Lewis Anthony Dexter, *How Organizations are Represented in Washington* (Indianapolis, Ind.: Bobbs-Merrill, 1969), pp. 1-17.

56 Lobbying for the People

of limited resources, initial organizational purpose, the 501(c)(3) problem, specialization among staff, and many other reasons, most public interest groups tend to particularize their efforts. In an attempt to find out how public interest groups are distributed in terms of their areas of concentration, respondents were asked, "When this organization has made efforts to influence public policy, who or what has usually been the target of your activity?" Fully 73% of the sample listed the Congress as either the primary or secondary target of their advocacy efforts (see Table III-2).[25]

TABLE III-2

Institutional Target

	Major Target		Major or Secondary Target	
Congress	60%	(50)	73%	(61)
Administrative agency or department	25%	(21)	47%	(39)
White House (President)	2%	(2)	11%	(9)
Public opinion	5%	(4)	11%	(9)
Corporations	4%	(3)	7%	(6)
Other	4%	(3)	12%	(10)
No second target mentioned	X	X	39%	(32)
	100%	(N = 83)	X	X

It is not unexpected that Congress is the primary target of most non-501(c)(3) groups (73%) and of *all* the organizations that have affiliated public foundations (see Table III-3). What may seem surprising is that 44% (18) of the groups that are 501(c)(3) organizations are interested primarily in influencing the Congress. These are groups that,

[25] Although many organizations' primary lobbying tool is litigation, respondents did not see the court system as an institutional target. Rather, the courts were viewed as a means to influence another component of government.

TABLE III-3

Target and Tax Status[a]

(primary target only)

	No 501(c)(3)		501(c)(3)		Affiliated 501(c)(3)	
Congress	73%	(22)	44%	(18)	100%	(9)
Administrative agency or department	10%	(3)	42%	(17)	—	
White House (President)	3%	(1)	2%	(1)	—	
Public opinion	3%	(1)	7%	(3)	—	
Corporations	7%	(2)	2%	(1)	—	
Other	3%	(1)	2%	(1)	—	
	99%[b]	(N = 30)	99%[b]	(N = 41)	100%	(N = 9)

[a] Excludes the three groups with pending 501(c)(3) status.
[b] Rounding error.

by law, should not be doing more than "insubstantial" legislative activity.

In light of the previous discussion of the problems associated with losing 501(c)(3) status, it may appear that there is a great deal of risk taking on the part of these legislatively oriented 501(c)(3) groups. To a certain extent this is true; some of the interviewees from this subsample of groups acknowledged that they were treading on thin ice, and admitted that they were very much in fear of the IRS. A few mentioned that their group had had their records audited by a suspicious IRS. One director of an environmental group noted the fine line they tried to follow to escape IRS sanctions, "We can't lobby. We can't say [to our members], 'Write to your Congressman,' but we can say, 'People are writing their Congressmen.'"

All 501(c)(3) legislative lobbies are much more restrained in their behavior than are the groups that may lobby the Congress legally. They strongly tend to communicate only with their "friends" on Capitol Hill, so as not

to offend anyone who might complain to the IRS.[26] Because
the IRS has not defined what constitutes substantial legislative activity, each group must determine on its own how
far they can go in their lobbying. Most of the lobbyists for
these organizations realize that they may be breaking the
law, but they feel that it is necessary to take the chance if
they are to accomplish their goals. There were, however, a
half dozen or so respondents who believe that they are acting in a legitimate educational capacity and are not violating the letter and spirit of the law. One conservationist, who
works in the area of endangered species, gave the following
account of his "nonlobbying":

> We called up Julia Butler Hansen's[27] administrative as-
> sistant and told him that the Office of Endangered Species
> wasn't doing their job. Our demand was to hold up their
> appropriation. Well, two days later they put the spotted
> cats on the Endangered Species List. Now this goes to
> show you, how, without lobbying, we can influence the
> Congress.
> Q: Wasn't your activity with the appropriations matter
> "lobbying"?
> A: No, it didn't involve a bill.
> Q: Isn't an appropriation a bill?
> A: No, it's an everyday function of the Congress.

In terms of structuring their behavior around the requirements of the Internal Revenue Code, there are four alternatives open to public interest groups. First, they may be committed to lobbying or participating in political campaigns
and eschew tax-deductible dollars. The second, and most
advantageous alternative, is to have a lobbying unit and a

---

[26] Lewis Anthony Dexter, in "The Representative and His District,"
Human Organization, vol. 16 (Spring 1957), pp. 2-13, states that it
is generally true that lobbyists communicate with their friends. In
the case of public interest groups, Dexter's observation needs some
qualifications. See Chapter VIII.

[27] At the time Congresswoman Hansen chaired the Interior Subcommittee of the House Appropriations Committee.

501(c)(3) affiliated public foundation. Third, organizations may take their 501(c)(3) exemption seriously and restrict their advocacy to administrative agencies or the courts. Fourth, 501(c)(3) groups may try to influence the Congress, consciously or unconsciously violate the law, and run the serious risk of getting into trouble with the IRS.

WASHINGTON RESOURCES

It has long been a popular myth that interest groups are well-endowed organizations whose Washington representatives have large sums of money at their disposal. In their study of foreign trade policy, Raymond Bauer, Ithiel de Sola Pool, and Lewis Anthony Dexter found that the free-spending lobbyist was more fancy than fact. Although time and again they heard people on one side of the issue accuse their opponents of spending vast sums of money, they found most claims to be highly exaggerated. "Yet, whenever one looked at the persons actually spending that money, one saw only harassed men with tight budgets and limited campaign funds, once their essential overheads had been met."[28]

It is possible that Bauer, Pool, and Dexter underestimated the resources of private interest groups. Foreign trade legislation may be an atypically low-spending issue for interest groups. It is unusual in that an omnibus foreign trade bill can affect a single corporation in many different ways. Still, they did look at a variety of different types of interest group organizations, which makes their argument a persuasive one.

If private interest lobbies are generally restricted to low funding, then one might suspect that public interest lobbies, which have no economic self-interest to defend, may have budgets that are even more austere. It might be suspected that public interest groups are similar to the minority and

[28] Raymond A. Bauer, Ithiel de Sola Pool, and Lewis Anthony Dexter, *American Business and Public Policy* (New York: Atherton, 1963), p. 345.

low-income groups that Michael Lipsky has studied. Lipsky concluded that the local, urban groups he observed were "relatively powerless" because of their lack of resources. This lack of resources, financial and otherwise, forced them to rely on protest demonstrations as a means of compelling governmental officials to bargain with them.[29]

The results of questions concerning the finances and personnel of public interest groups suggest that they are far from resourceless. An examination of their annual budgets reveals that the sample of public interest groups shows a wide range of financial resources (see Table III-4). The amount of money available to groups runs from organizations like the Washington Peace Center, with an annual budget of $12,000, on the one hand, to those like the $10-million-a-year National Wildlife Federation on the other.

TABLE III-4

Financial Assets

	Total Assets		Washington Office Assets	
Less than $50,000	13%	(11)	25%	(21)
$50,000–$99,999	12%	(10)	18%	(15)
$100,000–$199,999	14%	(12)	18%	(15)
$200,000–$499,999	24%	(20)	18%	(15)
$500,000–$999,999	6%	(5)	6%	(5)
$1,000,000+	19%	(16)	7%	(6)
NA or DK	11%	(9)	7%	(6)
	99%[a]	(N = 83)	99%[a]	(N = 83)

[a] Rounding error.

One interesting aspect of the groups' finances is the disparity between the total organizational assets and the assets available to the Washington offices for some of these groups. It should be noted that for over half of the sample

[29] Michael Lipsky, "Protest as a Political Resource," *American Political Science Review*, vol. 62 (December 1968), pp. 1144-1158.

the total organizational budget is the same as the Washington budget, because these groups have no branch office expenses.[30] Even so, although 49% of the organizations have $200,000 or more to spend, only 31% of the Washington offices reach this level of affluence. Sometimes the difference between what an organization has at hand and how much it is willing to spend on Washington-based activities is rather dramatic. The National Council of Churches has an annual income of $14 million; their Washington office has a yearly budget of about $100,000. For the fiscal year ending in 1972, the National Audubon Society recorded an income of over $7 million; the Washington office had $20,000 budgeted for fiscal year 1973.

It must be said in all fairness that much of the money that is spent outside of Washington by these groups may be very useful for the purposes of influencing public policy. The Audubon Society, for example, sponsors some original scientific research and field studies. Surely the data derived from these studies provide them with supporting evidence for their advocacy and "educational" efforts before governmental bodies. Groups that conduct a great deal of litigation, such as the ACLU or the Natural Resources Defense Council, are able to file many of their lawsuits in federal court in New York, or in other areas of the country where they have major offices.

The number of total workers and professional employees for the organizations reflects the same general distribution as that of financial resources (see Table III-5). Approximately a quarter (24%) of the groups had seven or more full-time professionals, which seemingly indicates a very high potential capability for advocacy efforts on their part.[31] On the other side of the spectrum, a roughly equal number

[30] This figure includes some groups that have chapters, but where the chapters are completely self-sufficient.

[31] Respondents were not given criteria to distinguish "professional" from nonprofessional employees when they were asked this question (see question #4, Appendix A). If they asked me what I meant by professional, I replied, "Professional, as opposed to clerical or purely support staff."

of groups (25%) did not have more than one full-time, paid professional. Yet one-person offices are common among private interest groups as well, and this figure should not be taken as being peculiarly indicative of public interest lobbies.[32]

TABLE III-5

Employees

	Total Number of Workers		Full-Time, Paid Professionals	
0	X	X	5%	(4)[a]
1	6%	(5)	20%	(17)
2–3	28%	(23)	29%	(24)
4–6	23%	(19)	19%	(16)
7–10	19%	(16)	16%	(13)
11–20	12%	(10)	5%	(4)
21–40	6%	(5)	1%	(1)
41+	5%	(4)	2%	(2)
NA	1%	(1)	2%	(2)
	100%	(N = 83)	99%[b]	(N = 83)

[a] Cases where the professional employees did not work full time, or worked without remuneration.
[b] Rounding error.

To talk about the total budgets of private or public interest groups may be a misleading focus. In terms of organizations influencing public policy, budgets represent *potential* resources. In studying a particular public policy matter, the more pertinent information is the amount of organizational resources committed to advocacy work on that one issue. It is also important to ascertain how well groups maximize the resources at their disposal. Simply put, do interest groups get the most for their money? A precise cost-effectiveness evaluation of public interest groups would necessitate far more data than are presently available. A few

[32] See Dexter, *How Organizations Are Represented in Washington.*

preliminary statements can be made, however, on the expenditure of resources on certain overhead items.

One general observation is that public interest groups do an excellent job of keeping some basic overhead costs to a minimum. The offices used by the organizations were rarely impressive. Many groups inhabit a floor in an old townhouse on Capitol Hill or in Washington's Dupont Circle area. Those offices that are in downtown office buildings tend to be in the older structures where the rents are low, rather than in the modern concrete-slab and glass edifices along K Street and M Street. Even the larger organizations, such as Common Cause and the League of Women Voters, which occupy whole floors of office buildings, pack their employees close together to make maximum usage of the space available. The furnishings of the offices range from dilapidated to utilitarian, although there are a few groups that provide their top employees with a bit of luxury in their personal offices.[33]

Most of the larger organizations, such as the Americans for Democratic Action, the Wilderness Society, and the Lawyers' Committee for Civil Rights Under Law, provide their staffs with adequate secretarial help. The smaller groups, and many of the middle-size ones as well, consider clerical help as something for which little money should be spent. In the less endowed organizations, ratios of four or five professionals or more to one secretary are common. It is not only a matter of rational resource allocation that has brought about this low priority in clerical help. The women's movement and changing occupational patterns are important factors in the way that many offices, particularly the

[33] Overly comfortable office surroundings may appear to be inconsistent with the *raison d'être* of public interest groups. After some press stories described the wall-to-wall carpeting and other nice office furnishings, Common Cause became worried about its public image. They proceeded to "deposh the place." Andrew J. Glass, "Common Cause Seeks to Have Broad Role on Issues in 1972 Campaign," *The Pressure Groups* (Washington, D.C.: National Journal, 1971), p. 88.

more recently formed ones, are set up. There seems to be a growing sensitivity to coequality for workers among the smaller, liberal groups, resulting in a modification of traditional office roles.[34] At Environmental Action, all the blue-jeaned workers are "professionals"—with no secretary, they all share the clerical work. The seven professionals at the Center for Defense Information must do much of their own typing, because they have only one bona fide secretary.[35]

"Professionalizing" an entire staff does, of course, have its drawbacks. Having everyone do typing is not necessarily the most efficient way to run an office. As one Nader lieutenant, who was about to hire a secretary for his eight-person staff for the first time, admitted, "You know, you can only carry this thing so far." He added in a lower voice, "The one who gives me the most crap about not having a typist is my woman lawyer."

VOLUNTEER LABOR

A major resource of public interest groups is the deep commitment of their employees, who are willing to work long hours for modest or low salaries. A profile of the Washington representatives of the organizations in the sample will be presented in the next chapter. In addition to their permanent staff, most public interest groups utilize volunteer labor. This adds an invaluable dimension to the capabilities of many of the individual organizations (see Table III-6).

[34] Orion White has described a somewhat similar situation in a social welfare agency where traditional hierarchical roles have been largely abolished. See "The Dialectical Organization: An Alternative to Bureaucracy," *Public Administration Review*, vol. 29 (January/February 1969), pp. 32-42.

[35] Again, this upgrading of clerical roles is not so much in evidence in the larger organizations. One reason is, of course, that the sheer volume of paperwork is so high that secretaries and other clerical workers are much more of a necessity. In addition, these larger groups have consistently high percentages of female professionals, and this may reduce internal pressures to turn women hired as secretaries into professionals.

Nearly two-thirds of the groups use volunteer labor in some capacity. There is no single reason to explain why the other third of the sample had not taken advantage of this potential resource. A few interviewees said that their organization had had unsatisfactory experiences with volunteers or interns and that there had been a decision not to use them again. Others said simply that they had yet to find a use for them. The remainder professed that it was something that the people in the organization had never really considered.[36]

TABLE III-6

Volunteers

None, negligible	35%	(29)
Irregular usage	33%	(27)
A few volunteers on a regular basis	14%	(12)
Extensive utilization	17%	(14)
NA	1%	(1)
	100%	(N = 83)

The extent of volunteer and intern usage falls roughly into three different levels. Most frequently, volunteers will work for the organization on an irregular or special-project basis. For example, many groups, such as the Society for Animal Protective Legislation, will call upon members from the metropolitan Washington area to lobby on Capitol Hill when a critically important bill is before the Congress.

[36] For an overview of the extent and scope of voluntary participation across the country, see David Horton Smith and Burt R. Baldwin, "Voluntary Associations and Volunteering in the United States," in David Horton Smith, ed., *Voluntary Action Research: 1974* (Lexington, Mass.: D. C. Heath, 1974), pp. 277-305. On the environmental movement, see Clem L. Zinger, Richard Dalsemer, and Helen Margargle, *Environmental Volunteers in America*, National Center for Voluntary Action's Environmental Project (Washington, D.C.: Environmental Protection Agency, 1973).

Another case is the Americans for Constitutional Action. When they hold a reception for a Congressperson, they will get as many as 10 volunteers to make phone calls to potential guests. Some organizations will not make use of volunteers during the school year, but will have large summer intern programs. The American Conservative Union and the Center for Science in the Public Interest have brought in as many as 15 or so interns for the summer months.

A smaller number of organizations never have more than one or two volunteers at a time, but they do have them regularly throughout the year. Often this volunteer will be a college intern who is on a semester-in-Washington program, or is from a Washington area school, and receives course credit for full-time, or nearly full-time work in the organization.

Finally, there are those organizations that make consistent and extensive utilization of numerous volunteers or interns. A group such as the National Peace Action Coalition, which always has a protest demonstration in the works, could not carry out its work without the help of many volunteers. The League of Women Voters has a League Lobbying Corps made up of women from the Washington area who donate up to two days a week of time for work on Capitol Hill. The women are trained in the techniques of lobbying and they are briefed on substantive issues before a coordinated effort begins.

Common Cause is another group that has made substantial use of volunteers in its Washington operations. During 1972 Common Cause made campaign finance reform one of its issue priorities. After the passage of the Federal Election Campaign Act, the organization moved to monitor the law by training volunteers, both in Washington and around the country, in the mechanics of reading candidate expenditure and contribution reports. These reports, which are filed with the Congress and with secretaries of state around the country, list the names, occupations, and addresses of all contributors of more than $100.

Common Cause distributed a detailed manual that explained the provisions of the law as well as instructing the reader in how to spot violations and conflicts of interest when inspecting the candidate reports.[37] Common Cause had 300 volunteers working out of their Washington office, and as many as 1000 members around the country, checking reports of congressional candidates. The extent of the Common Cause effort just about ensured that any candidate who did not comply fully with the law would have his or her negligence reported to the press in the district.[38]

The campaign finance monitoring project was only the beginning of Common Cause's volunteer programs. Their OUTS (Open Up The System) effort has activated hundreds of volunteers around the country and in Washington. The OUTS program first utilized volunteers for grass roots lobbying of congressional candidates with regard to proposed reforms concerning the seniority system and committee secrecy. Deeming their first OUTS endeavor a success—congressional reforms were enacted at the beginning of the 93rd Congress—Common Cause decided on a continuation of the program to push for further reform in the areas of conflict of interest, full lobbying disclosure, and the public financing of elections.[39]

By the spring of 1973, Common Cause had 525 volunteers putting in time at the national headquarters in Washington. On Tuesday through Thursday, the office is open from 8:30 a.m. to 10:30 p.m. to accommodate all the work that is being done. The Common Cause staffers who direct the volunteer labor are proud of the fact that the work assigned

[37] Fred Wertheimer, *The Common Cause Manual on Money and Politics*, March 1972.

[38] See Jeffrey M. Berry and Jerry Goldman, "Congress and Public Policy: A Study of the Federal Election Campaign Act of 1971," *Harvard Journal on Legislation*, vol. 10 (February 1973), pp. 331-365.

[39] See Theodore Jacqueney, "Common Cause Lobbyists Focus on the Structure and Process of Government," *National Journal*, September 1, 1973, pp. 1294-1304.

is substantive rather than purely clerical. One staffer noted jokingly, "We have so many interesting things for volunteers to do, we can't get them to lick envelopes anymore."

Another ambitious program for bringing large numbers of people into public interest advocacy work is Ralph Nader's effort to set up local, regional, or statewide Public Interest Research Groups (PIRGs) to carry on the work that must be done outside of Washington. The nucleus of these groups are college students, but full-time activists are also hired to give the organizations professionalism and continuity. Although they are autonomous from Nader, they have been initially organized by Nader and his associate, Donald Ross, and they pattern their lobbying on the style of the national Nader groups. Typical efforts of PIRGs, now operating in 20 states, have been conducted in the areas of utility rate setting, toy safety, meat inspection practices, and advertising fraud.[40]

Although the Common Cause and Nader projects are impressive in their scope and intentions, they do not represent anything new to the public interest movement. For years and years, older organizations such as the League of Women Voters, the Americans for Democratic Action, and the American Civil Liberties Union have had extensive participation by members of their state and local affiliates. Moreover, public interest groups have long emphasized procedural reforms in government that would facilitate greater public participation. The underlying rationale for this type of endeavor by public interest groups is that extensive citizen participation is beneficial to the governing of the "good society." Although political theorists and other social scientists have struggled with the question of "How much participation is truly good?" public interest practitioners seem to be of one mind.[41] If a guiding manifesto

[40] See Ralph Nader and Donald Ross, *Action for a Change: A Student's Guide for Public Interest Organizing*, 2nd ed. (New York: Grossman, 1972).

[41] Two useful books that synthesize the debate concerning democracy and the desirable degree of participation are Carole Pate-

to the public interest movement existed, it might very well state that "Increased citizen participation is a critically important factor in bringing about governmental decisions that are in the public interest."[42]

Some of the most important work with volunteers is being done by a few organizations that are training future public interest lawyers.[43] One such place is the Institute for Public Interest Representation, which is supported by the Ford Foundation and is affiliated with Washington's Georgetown University Law Center. A director and a deputy director supervise five recently graduated law students and 30 Georgetown law students per year. The students take a seminar from the director, but most of their work is research to be used for formal petitions before administrative agencies and, on occasion, litigation.

By training young lawyers for public interest work, the law school and the sponsoring Ford Foundation hope to

man, *Participation and Democratic Theory* (Cambridge: Cambridge University Press, 1970); and Dennis F. Thompson, *The Democratic Citizen* (Cambridge: Cambridge University Press, 1970).

[42] One effort to capture and analyze the ideology of the public interest movement is Simon Lazarus, *The Genteel Populists* (New York: Holt, Rinehart and Winston, 1973). For some views that strongly attest to the value of public interest citizen participation, see Nader and Ross, *Action for a Change*; Donald Ross, *A Public Citizen's Action Manual* (New York: Grossman, 1973); and Odom Fanning, *Man and His Environment: Citizen Action* (New York: Harper & Row, 1975).

[43] On public interest law generally, see Edward Berlin, Anthony Roisman, and Gladys Kessler, "Public Interest Law," *George Washington Law Review*, vol. 38 (May 1970), pp. 675-693; Edgar Cahn and Jean Camper Cahn, "Power to the People or the Profession?— The Public Interest in Public Interest Law," *Yale Law Journal*, vol. 79 (May 1970), pp. 1005-1048; Note, "The New Public Interest Law," *ibid.*, pp. 1069-1162; Marlisle James, *The People's Lawyers* (New York: Holt, Rinehart and Winston, 1973); Lazarus, *The Genteel Populists*; Robert L. Rabin, "Lawyers for Social Change: Perspectives on Public Interest Law," *Stanford Law Review*, vol. 28 (January 1976), pp. 207-261; and "Symposium: The Practice of Law in the Public Interest," *Arizona Law Review*, vol. 13 (1971), pp. 797-973. All these works use a much broader definition of public interest work than is used here.

bring well-qualified, skilled practitioners into the field.[44] The students and graduate fellows have been involved in such actions as petitioning the FTC to force the manufacturers of little cigars to carry a health warning during television commercials; asking the National Park Service to publish rules concerning the awarding of concessions and the accountability of concessionaires to the public; and a series of interventions before the Bureau of Land Management trying to get them to deny grazing rights to ranchers who are responsible for the killing of eagles. The potential resources of this organization are illustrated by their January 1973 report, which showed that they had just completed, or were currently involved in, 10 lawsuits, 17 administrative actions, and three major research reports.[45]

One additional source of volunteer labor that has been available to some of the public interest groups is *pro bono publico* work by Washington law firms. Out of a sense of duty to the community and to the public interest, the firms donate time to do work on behalf of those that cannot pay. A great deal of *pro bono* work is done for the indigent through existing legal aid programs. In Washington, private law firms have also become involved in a number of consumer and environmental areas.

One firm, Arnold and Porter, has been particularly generous with its time; at least three different public interest groups have received considerable assistance from them. Arnold and Porter is one of the most prestigious law firms in Washington, and it is identified as Democratic in its politics, although critics contend that it is not nearly as

[44] See Gordon Harrison and Sanford M. Jaffe, *The Public Interest Law Firm* (New York: Ford Foundation, 1973).

[45] Other organizations in the sample that train law students are the National Center for Policy Review and the Center for Law and Social Policy. On the latter, see Charles R. Halpern and John M. Cunningham, "Reflections on the New Public Interest Law: Theory and Practice at the Center for Law and Social Policy," *Georgetown Law Journal*, vol. 59 (May 1971), pp. 1095-1136.

liberal as it once was.[46] Other firms that have contributed *pro bono* work to public interest groups are Covington and Burling, Caplin and Drysdale, Hogan and Hartson, and Wilmer, Cutler, and Pickering. These firms have in common that they are all well known, prestigious, and, undoubtedly, highly profitable. For all the good intentions, *pro bono* work is still a luxury that not all law firms think they can afford.[47]

The public interest groups that have made the most use of *pro bono* work are the public interest law firms. There appear to be two reasons for this. First, the people in these groups conceptualize problem solving in legal terms, and they are more likely to approach private law firms for assistance. Second, many of the lawyers for public interest law firms previously worked for these private firms or otherwise know firm members, and this familiarity or "connection" surely helps when the private firm decides among competing demands for *pro bono* aid.[48]

FOUNDATION SUPPORT

One factor that explains the apparent increase in the number of consumer and environmental groups is the willingness of private foundations to donate large sums of money that might not otherwise be available.[49] Roughly a third (14) of all the groups that have begun in the past five years were obtaining at least half of their total income

[46] See Joseph C. Goulden, *The Superlawyers* (New York: Dell, 1973), pp. 116-149 and 353-392.

[47] For an overview, see Marna Tucker, *The Private Law Firm and Pro Bono Publico Programs: A Responsive Merger* (Washington, D.C.: American Bar Association, 1972). For a critical assessment of the Washington legal establishment by a veteran of the public interest movement, see Mark J. Green, *The Other Government* (New York: Grossman, 1975).

[48] The discussion here has been limited to the contributions by private interest law firms. A few groups, like the American Civil Liberties Union, make extensive use of individual volunteer lawyers.

[49] For a critical analysis of the role of foundations in fostering social change, see Nielsen, *The Big Foundations.*

from foundations at the time of the interviews. In total, a little over half of the organizations in the sample receive no foundation money (see Table III-7). Most of the organizations not receiving any foundation assistance are non-501(c)(3) groups.

TABLE III-7

Foundation Support[a]

None	53%	(44)
Less than 10%	10%	(8)
10–49%	13%	(11)
50–89%	8%	(7)
90%+	11%	(9)
NA	5%	(4)
	100%	(N = 83)

[a] Percentage of total annual income (current budget).

No other private foundation has played a bigger role in aiding the public interest movement than the Ford Foundation. Between 1970 and 1974, under a special public interest law program, the Ford Foundation has made grants totaling close to $10 million to over a dozen public interest groups oriented toward litigation or having an affiliated public foundation that uses litigation. Those of the groups that have an office in Washington are the Center for Law and Social Policy, the Citizens Communication Center, the Environmental Defense Fund, the Institute for Public Interest Representation, the Natural Resources Defense Council, and the Sierra Club.[50] Of these six groups, all but the Sierra Club were given Ford money during their initial years.

Under different Ford Foundation programs, large grants have also been awarded to three civil rights-poverty groups in the sample: the Lawyers' Committee for Civil Rights

[50] See Harrison and Jaffe, *The Public Interest Law Firm*; and Sanford Jaffe, *Public Interest Law: Five Years Later* (New York: Ford Foundation/American Bar Association, 1976).

Under Law, the Citizens Advocate Center, and the Center for National Policy Review. In addition, the League of Women Voters has received over $650,000 for the purpose of working on voting rights and developing a litigation capability.

The Ford Foundation's generosity reflects a phase in its larger philanthropic effort to encourage social change. In a description of its public interest law program, Gordon Harrison and Sanford Jaffe set forth the Foundation's purpose:

> The Ford Foundation's main interest in assisting the development of public interest law is to advance necessary social change constructively. It seeks to demonstrate that representation of the underrepresented in legal actions affecting class or general public interests is both feasible and socially useful, that public interest advocacy will improve the performance of administrative agencies, and that public confidence in the process of law will be strengthened by opening up traditional procedures to deal with new, legitimate grievances.[51]

Through its financial contributions, the Ford Foundation has not only directed political activism into meaningful channels "within the system," but has also helped to legitimize public interest groups as beneficial components of the governmental process.[52]

Ford is not, of course, the only foundation that has supported public interest groups. Carnegie, Field, Stern, and Rockefeller—all familiar names in philanthropy—have made major contributions to two or more of the groups.[53] Quite

---

[51] Harrison and Jaffe, *The Public Interest Law Firm*, p. 39.

[52] Waldemar Nielsen considers Ford to be one of the more progressive foundations because of its willingness to fund new and potentially controversial types of activity. In his words, "the foundation has not chosen to seek maximum safety and minimum controversy" (p. 98). See Nielsen, *The Big Foundations*, pp. 78-98.

[53] Other foundations that were mentioned by respondents: Bernstein, Cummins, D.J.B., Eldridge, Irving, Krim, Lasker, McIntosh,

often foundations have particular interests in certain, substantive areas, and they will only fund organizations working on those issues. The Carnegie Endowment for Peace,
for example, provides primary support for the Arms Control
Association and the Student Advisory Committee on International Affairs.

Although recent foundation money has enabled a number
of groups to come into existence, there is no assurance that
all these groups will be able to continue in operation.
Foundation money is usually "seed" money; that is, it is
given to initiate a new organization or a new project. It is
not the intention of the foundations to offer the public
interest lobbies permanent sources of funding.[54] The down-
turn in the economy during the early 1970s reduced the
available foundation funds and made fund raising even
more difficult for public interest groups.[55]

Organizations that were started with foundation money
have been searching for other means of support. This can
be a considerable problem, because not all groups are capable of shifting to a mass membership basis or attracting
large, private donations. Some of the newer groups, such
as the Environmental Defense Fund, have already been
able to shift from foundation to membership support. The
organization has been able to attract 35,000 dues-paying
members at a minimum of $15 apiece. A number of suc-

Midas International, New York (Fund), New World, Norman, Ot-
tinger, and Sunnen.

[54] The Ford Foundation announced in 1973 that it would be reducing its support of environmental groups. Cathe Wolhowe, "Environmental Groups Face Fund Cut," *Washington Post*, September
28, 1973, p. A6. The funding for public interest law firms including
many with environmental concerns, has nevertheless remained high.
See, Jaffe, *Public Interest Law: Five Years Later*.

[55] Consumers Union has also had to curtail its financial support
of other consumer groups, including the Center for Auto Safety and
the Consumer Federation of America. Frances Cerra, "Consumer
Organizations over Nation Hurt by a Loss of Grants," *The New
York Times*, July 8, 1975, p. 16. See also Roger Ricklefs, "Consumers
Union Is in Consumer Trouble; Budget Is Unbalanced," *Wall Street
Journal*, May 5, 1975, p. 1.

cessful efforts, most notably their leadership in the fight to ban DDT, has helped the Environmental Defense Fund to "sell" itself to the public.

Others of the foundation-supported groups may not be so fortunate. The Children's Foundation is one lobby that has been struggling to find a new source of funding. After the initial round of foundation grants ran out, the organization began existing on a hand-to-mouth basis on small, emergency grants from foundations to carry them for a few more months. Activities and staff have been cut back, and their future is uncertain. Other groups, such as the Citizens Communication Center or the Agribusiness Accountability Project, may have an equally difficult time finding a natural constituency to sustain their endeavors if their foundation money dries up.[56]

Many public interest law firms were hopeful that they would be able to replace much of the foundation money with court-awarded fees given to them as the winning side in costly litigation efforts. Under the "American rule," lawyers' fees are not usually charged to the losing side. In recent years, however, a number of federal court decisions ruled that victorious public interest plaintiffs deserved remuneration because they were acting as "private attorneys general" by their actions that helped to ensure the proper enforcement of the laws.[57]

[56] A new organization, the Council for Public Interest Law, was begun in March 1975 for the purpose of finding new, long-term sources of funding for public interest law firms. The Council has an expected life span of three years, and is supported by grants from the American Bar Association, the Ford Foundation, the Rockefeller Brothers Fund, and the Edna McConnell Clark Foundation. It is headed by Charles Halpern, one of the founders of the Center for Law and Social Policy. See Kathleen Hendrix, "Holding a Brief for Public Interest Law," Los Angeles Times, May 15, 1975, part IV, p. 1; and Richard E. Cohen, "Public Interest Lawyers Start Looking Out for Their Own Interests," National Journal, June 19, 1976, pp. 860-864.

[57] On the development of fee awards through the private attorneys general doctrine, see John P. Dawson, "Lawyers and Involuntary Clients in Public Interest Litigation," Harvard Law Re-

The first restriction on this source of funding came when the Internal Revenue Service ruled that while 501(c)(3) public interest groups could receive court-awarded fees and maintain their tax status, no group would be allowed to obtain more than 50% of its litigation budget from such fees.[58] This decision by the IRS in October 1974 would seem almost insignificant in light of what was to come. In *Alyeska Pipeline Service Co. v. Wilderness Society et al.*, the Supreme Court ruled that federal courts could not award fees to "private attorneys general" acting in the public interest except in those areas of the law where the practice is specifically authorized by an act of Congress.[59] The immediate effect of the decision was to deny estimated court-awarded fees of $100,000 to the Wilderness Society, Friends of the Earth, and the Environmental Defense Fund, even though their litigation had forced the consortium of oil companies (Alyeska) to build more environmental safeguards into their pipeline. The more important, long-term implication of the Court's decision is that a major source of funding for public interest groups that utilize litigation has been severely diminished in its potential. With foundation grants dwindling, the impact of *Alyeska* will not only hurt existing groups, but it will make it that much more difficult for new public interest law firms to arise. It is now up to the Congress to decide if the "private attorneys general" concept should be expanded through new legislation.

view, vol. 88 (March 1975), pp. 849-930; Note, "Awarding Attorney and Expert Witness Fees in Environmental Litigation," *Cornell Law Review*, vol. 58 (July 1973), pp. 1222-1254; Note, "Private Attorney General Fees Emerge from the *Wilderness*," *Fordham Law Review*, vol. 43 (November 1974), pp. 258-272; Note, "Awarding Attorneys' Fees to the 'Private Attorney General': Judicial Green Light to Private Litigation in the Public Interest," *Hastings Law Journal*, vol. 24 (March 1973), pp. 733-770; and Comment, "Court Awarded Attorney's Fees and Equal Access to the Courts," *University of Pennsylvania Law Review*, vol. 122 (January 1974), pp. 636-713.
[58] *Wall Street Journal*, October 23, 1974, p. 1.
[59] 421 U.S. 240 (1975).

CONCLUSION

It is evident from the analysis here that it is fallacious to conceive of fund raising as a simple relationship between the skills of an entrepreneur and the sympathy of potential supporters. What is most striking is the importance of governmental regulations and law in structuring the flow of money from various funding sources to the treasuries of public interest groups. The U.S. government may not "control" the funding of these private organizations, but it certainly has a strong hand in regulating it.

The ultimate significance of the government's making it easier or harder for these groups to raise money is that the amount of money available affects the extent to which public interest groups can represent their constituencies. If one accepts the idea that public interest groups play a valuable role in acting on behalf of the unrepresented or underrepresented segments of society, then it is all too obvious that recent governmental decisions have endangered the quality of representation these "interests" may receive.[60] What is at question now is whether or not it should be the policy of the federal government to take remedial action to facilitate the funding of public interest groups. Such steps might include an end to the 50% rule for court-awarded fees, legislation to expand the application of the private attorneys general doctrine beyond the confines of *Alyeska*, a clear and rational redefinition of the 501(c)(3) requirements, and positive movement by administrative agencies to make it easier, and thus cheaper, for public in-

---

[60] This discussion certainly provides much grist for the mill of pluralist critics. William Gamson's observation concerning the ability of interest groups to arise and represent all those needing representation is relevant here: "My central argument is that the American political system normally operates to prevent incipient competitors from achieving full entry into the political arena." See "Stable Unrepresentation in American Society," *American Behavioral Scientist*, vol. 12 (November/December 1968), p. 18. On the IRS and "equal access," see Holbert, *Tax Law and Political Access*.

terest groups to intervene in administrative proceedings.[61] A bill now before the 94th Congress to reform 501(c)(3) requirements and a new Federal Trade Commission program to provide financial aid to public participants in rulemaking proceedings are two encouraging signs for the public interest movement.

Despite these problems, however, substantial sums of money are raised by both 501(c)(3) and non-501(c)(3) groups. The amount of resources available varies widely among the individual organizations, but, as a whole, the combined assets of the public interest groups are impressive. How efficiently public interest lobbies exploit their resources is a question that remains to be answered in full. What may be concluded at this time is that however fragile the future of public interest group funding, the organizations that existed in the early 1970s had tapped a substantial reservoir of support from private citizens and philanthropic foundations.

[61] See, generally, Roger Crampton, "The Why, Where and How of Broadened Public Participation in the Administrative Process," *Georgetown Law Journal*, vol. 60 (February 1972), pp. 525-550; Ernest Gellhorn, "Public Participation in Administrative Proceedings," *Yale Law Journal*, vol. 81 (January 1972), pp. 359-404; Comment, "Public Participation in Federal Administrative Proceedings," *University of Pennsylvania Law Review*, vol. 120 (April 1972), pp. 702-845; and Edgar Shor, "Administrative Representation for the Under-Represented," paper delivered at the annual meeting of the American Political Science Association, Washington, D.C., September 1972.

CHAPTER IV

Public Interest Representatives

THE primary unit of analysis thus far has been the public interest organizations. No study of political organizations can afford to overlook the role of the individual activists. This is particularly true of lobbies, where the "organization" is often just one or two people. Because there exists a good deal of data on the backgrounds of private interest group lobbyists, some interesting and direct comparisons can be made. Beyond contrasting public interest activists with their private interest counterparts, this chapter has two further objectives. The first is to ascertain how the personal background and nature of the activists contribute to the capabilities of the public interest groups. The second is to find out in what way the organizational characteristics of the lobbies affect the career patterns of the activists.

RECRUITMENT

Much can be learned about the vocation of public interest lobbying by examining the manner in which activists are initially brought into the organizations.[1] There appear to

---

[1] The literature on political recruitment has focused primarily on elected officials. There has been relatively little done on the recruitment of lobbyists. The literature is too voluminous to list here, but see, generally, James D. Barber, *The Lawmakers* (New Haven, Conn.: Yale University Press, 1965); Herbert Jacob, "Initial Recruitment of Elected Officials in the U.S.—A Model," *Journal of Politics*, vol. 24 (November 1962), pp. 703-716; Michael L. Mezey, "Ambition Theory and the Office of Congressman," *Journal of Politics*, vol. 32 (August 1970), pp. 563-579; Kenneth Prewitt, *The Recruitment of Political Leaders* (Indianapolis, Ind.: Bobbs-Merrill, 1970); Joseph A. Schlesinger, *Ambition and Politics* (Chicago: Rand McNally, 1966); and Lester G. Seligman, "Political Parties and the Recruitment of Political Leaders," in Lewis Edinger (ed.), *Political Leadership in Industrial Societies* (New York: Wiley, 1967), pp. 294-315.

be three different paths of entry. The activists may seek out a job in an organization, may be personally recruited to fill a position, or may, for one reason or another, "drift" into their work.

Those public interest lobbyists who made initial inquiries concerning a job, or outright applied for one, may be termed "self-recruited." These people are similar in that they not only wanted a job in a public interest group, but they were motivated enough actually to try to seek a position. A 26-year-old antiwar activist recalls both his past and his recruitment into his public interest group:

> I was in the Peace Corps for 11 months, but I was "terminated" because of my protesting the Cambodian invasion. I was involved in Referendum '70 and I worked doing research on peace candidates. I worked for three months on the April 24th march. Then I worked for Senator Gravel for awhile on a project; after that, Project Air War. I then organized Vietnam Vets for the McGovern campaign. When you work with these types of projects, you make contacts. I heard about this project while I was playing football. Someone said, "Hey, there's a new project starting up." I said, "I might be interested in that." So, I got in contact with them.

A public interest lawyer with a consumer group tells of his progression to his present job from the time he graduated from law school:

> I went to work for a big law firm here in town, Covington and Burling, and I worked in the broadcast area there. Then I was a legal assistant to Nicholas Johnson at the FCC. I heard that they were setting up a law firm here and I inquired about it. They interviewed me and I came to work.

A second pattern of job placement is recruitment of the individual by the organization. In these cases, some person or persons within the group sought out an individual and asked him or her to join the staff. A 57-year-old environmental lobbyist describes his varied career:

I went to work for UPI after college in the western states: Utah, Idaho, Oregon, Washington, California. I became a war correspondent during the war. After the war I went to work in Boise, Idaho, where I published a paper for eight years. [During that time] I got involved in the Hells Canyon issue. I worked with Dick Neuberger when he ran for the Senate. I came here as his press secretary for a year and a half, then I became his Administrative Assistant, then AA for his wife [after he died]. When she decided not to run, I didn't have any plans, so I sailed for a year. Then I got a call from the _____ and they asked me if I'd like to become their Washington representative.

A younger man's life was also changed by a phone call:

I got out of college in 1962. I was in the Peace Corps for two years between 1962 and 1964. I then went to law school, and when I graduated I went to work for the Treasury Department between 1967 and 1972. There was a fellow who went to get the money [that started the group] who used to work at Treasury, and he called me up and asked if I'd like to do this.

Finally, there are those who "drift" into a job. In the sample of public interest representatives, the drifters fall into two categories. Some of these activisits evolved into their present position from previous work as a volunteer, intern, temporary, or part-time worker in the organization. Others came to their jobs by chance or accidental circumstances. A middle-aged lobbyist for a general politics group exemplifies the latter type of entry:

I had organized a political science league [for my corporation] and we held seminars with a professor of political science from Temple [University] who came to speak to these banking and industrial leaders. We started to endorse candidates and this got us into trouble with some candidates who tried to get me fired. They went to my boss who told them "nothing doing." Then they went over his head to his boss and that worked—they were going to transfer me. My boss said he'd try to get me a job in Washington. At his urging _____ hired me in 1959.

One of Ralph Nader's men recounts his ascension from a summer internship:

I was looking for a job for my second summer in law school. Nader was looking for people at Harvard. Someone he knew, knew me, mostly by reference. I went to work for the summer and got hooked. While at Harvard my senior year I did some volunteer work. I then came here in 1970.

The data in Table IV-I reveal that there is no dominant pattern of recruitment.[2] Self-recruitment and organizational recruitment show a moderately stronger response rate than does the drift category. These findings do, however, contrast sharply with those of Harmon Zeigler and Michael Baer. In their four-state survey of primarily private interest lobbyists, they found that the drifters were roughly twice as prevalent as the recruited, and three times as prevalent as the self-recruited.[3]

[2] To make the sample of public interest lobbyists more representative, supplementary interviews were conducted at the larger organizations. If a group had more than 10 professional staff members, one additional interview was conducted. If there were more than 20 professional staffers, two supplementary interviews were done. See Appendix C. The battery of standardized interview questions that dealt with personal background and career orientation was asked of these additional respondents. See Appendix A.

[3] Strict numerical comparisons are not possible because Zeigler and Baer permitted multiple responses. The four states they studied were Massachusetts, Oregon, Utah, and North Carolina. The mean scores for the four subsamples were self-recruited, 28%; recruited, 43%; and drifted, 85% ($N = 644$). Harmon Zeigler and Michael Baer, Lobbying (Belmont, Calif.: Wadsworth, 1969), pp. 46-48.

TABLE IV-1

Recruitment

Self-recruited	38%	(35)
Recruited ("co-opted")	36%	(33)
Drifted	23%	(21)
NA	2%	(2)
	99%[a]	(N = 91)

[a] Rounding error.

One possible explanation for this rather large disparity may lie in the different nature of the organizations served by public and private interest representatives. For the business or labor lobbyist, the job of becoming a legislative representative may be a career opportunity, a promotion, or a gradual extension of specialized work they began when they entered the organization. For the in-house lawyer, or the lawyer on retainer, lobbying may be a part of their larger obligations to their employer. Most public interest groups do not offer a great deal of intraorganizational career mobility. For many groups, the Washington lobby is the functioning organization and, therefore, there are not other organizational positions to drift out of. Although a couple of representatives for church groups said that they had come to Washington at the request of their national headquarters, the sample included few other examples of personnel being transferred to lobbying work. In addition, only a small number of public interest groups hire lawyers on retainer, so there is less chance of attorneys in private firms drifting into public interest lobbying.

Most critically, there is a basic difference in the way in which potential job holders conceive of the two types of jobs that are being discussed here. The job of legislative lobbyist for a group like a labor union or a trade association is probably not an occupation people seek out. Becoming a (private interest) lobbyist requires that one rationalize or accept the pejorative connotations of the title and the accompanying stereotypes.[4] Surely this superficially unflattering occupational image does not keep many people from becoming lobbyists; it may, however, act as an inhibiting factor that reduces the chances that an individual will actually aspire to the vocation.

The prospective public interest worker is not likely to approach lobbying with the same initial attitude. Public interest work may easily be thought of as a "higher calling" where one's motives and intentions are beyond question. The popular image of a Nader Raider or defender of the unrepresented gives public interest activism a bit of glamor and status, particularly to the young. In sum, it is much easier to understand why people are more likely to seek out public interest work than private interest work.[5]

PERSONAL BACKGROUND

As is the case with private interest lobbying, and with almost all other careers in politics, public interest lobbying

[4] Milbrath found that a high percentage (17% of those who responded) rejected the idea that they were lobbyists; they registered "only to be safe." Because his and Zeigler and Baer's samples were drawn from the filing lists of lobbyists, their respondents reflect a bias toward admitting to being a lobbyist. A sample of more general interest group representatives, where not all are registered, such as the public interest activists, would show a higher percentage of those that disclaim the lobbyist title. Despite the political sophistication of Washington representatives, there is still some unwillingness to accept the notion that one is, in fact, a "lobbyist." Lester W. Milbrath, *The Washington Lobbyist* (Chicago: Rand McNally, 1963), pp. 57-88.

[5] One of the ways that private interest lobbyists rationalize their work is to consider themselves as public interest representatives. Zeigler and Peak recount the following: "A few years ago a state university . . . invited several people registered as lobbyists at the state capital to explain their work. Without exception, each began his remarks by explaining that his organization was not a pressure group since its goals were in the public interest." L. Harmon Zeigler and G. Wayne Peak, *Interest Groups in American Politics*, 2nd ed. (Englewood Cliffs, N.J.: Prentice-Hall, 1972), p. 38.

is largely "man's work." Three-quarters (76%) of the sample is male. This figure for women does compare favorably with Milbrath's sample of Washington lobbyists (conducted during 1956-1957), which was 94% male. Although 24% may be a disappointing percentage of female public interest activists, it is quite possible that the number of women in the field is growing. This nation's changing attitudes toward women and their work roles indicate that women will become increasingly active in all facets of politics.

One of the most striking differences between public interest and private interest lobbyists is their respective ages. Younger people seemingly find more opportunity or attraction in public interest work. The Milbrath sample showed that only 9% of the private interest activists were below the age of 40, and there was only one lobbyist below 30. This contrasts with close to two-thirds of the public interest activists who are less than 40 years of age (see Table IV-2).

TABLE IV-2

Age

	Public Interest Lobbyists	Milbrath's Washington Lobbyists
20–29	26%	1%
30–39	36%	8%
40–49	19%	37%
50–59	12%	34%
60+	7%	20%
	100% (N = 91)	100% (N = 102)

There appear to be three reasons for the comparatively younger ages of public interest activists. First, public interest work is probably most attractive to the idealistic, and this characteristic is often thought to be associated with those younger in years. Second, as noted above, public interest activists are not likely to be people who have worked their way up through an organization, or drifted slowly into lobbying.[6] Third, public interest jobs are often low in salary potential. Consequently, public interest work may become less economically feasible as individuals grow older and assume greater financial responsibilities. In comparison, skilled private interest lobbyists, especially lawyers on retainer, may find their income rising rapidly as they gain experience.

Coupled with the relative youth of the public interest activisits is their inexperience in their present work. Fully one-fifth (22%) of the sample had been on the job less than a year. Nearly two-thirds (65%) of them had less than three years experience (see Table IV-3). Comparative data from Zeigler and Baer's study might suggest that public interest organizations have a much higher rate of professional staff turnover.[7] It must be remembered, however, that close to half of the sample of public interest groups are less than five years old. What appears to be staff turnover may really represent the newness of the organizations. Regardless of the reason, years of professional staff experience should be considered as part of a lobby's resources. Zeigler and Baer point out the significance of experience: "those lobbyists who hold their job the longest are those most likely to find themselves in demand as a source of information. In other words, simply 'being around' helps quite a bit."[8] Public interest lobbies are obviously low in this resource.

It is no surprise that, as a group, the public interest activists are a highly educated lot. Their educational backgrounds do not show much difference from Milbrath's sample of Washington lobbyists: 65% of both samples have done

[6] Age is thus associated with the tendency for "drifting" as an entry mechanism for private interest lobbyists. Older men will have more of a chance for their work to lead them gradually into lobbying.

[7] Zeigler and Baer, *Lobbying*, pp. 60-62.

[8] *Ibid.*, p. 136.

TABLE IV-3

Years of Experience

	Public Interest Lobbyists		Zeigler and Baer's State Lobbyists	
Less than 1 year	22%)	65%	21%	"low"
1–2 years	43%)			
3–5 years	24%)	25%	41%	"medium"
6–10 years	1%)			
11–20 years	9%)	10%	38%	"high"
21+ years	1%)			
	100%	(N = 91)	100%	(N = 638)

work beyond a college degree, and a law degree is frequent in both groups of lobbyists (see Table IV-4).[9]

Career Training. The vocation of public interest lobbying is not a well-defined one. Much like legislative offices, there are no special programs or courses of study that really prepare one for the actual work involved. But unlike members of Congress, who are likely to serve in a state or local office before coming to Washington,[10] public interest activists do not usually have any prior, relevant experience as lobbyists.

The data show that a law degree is common for both private and public interest lobbyists. Yet it is far from an adequate preparation for what lobbyists do on a day-to-day basis. In terms of litigation and formal administrative proceedings, law schools are, however, becoming more useful in the training of certain types of public interest representa-

[9] All comparisons with Milbrath's sample must be tempered with the fact that he did his interviewing roughly 15 years earlier. For example, because many of his respondents were of college age during the depression, it is possible that an updated survey of private interest lobbyists might show an overall greater degree of education.

[10] See Mezey, "Ambition Theory and the Office of Congressman."

TABLE IV-4

Education

	Public Interest Lobbyists	Milbrath's Washington Lobbyists
High school	2%	11%[a]
Some college	9%	13%
College degree	23%	11%
Some graduate work 9% Master's degree 11% Uncompleted or in- progress Ph.D. 5%	25%	15%
Ph.D.	5%	7%
Law or other pro- fessional degree	35%	43%
	99%[b] (N = 91)	100% (N = 105)

[a] Includes five who did not graduate.
[b] Rounding error.

tives. As noted earlier, three organizations in the sample, the Institute for Public Interest Representation (Georgetown Law Center), the Center for National Policy Review (Catholic University Law School), and the Center for Law and Social Policy (five affiliated law schools) directly train law students for public interest work.[11] In addition, law schools around the country offer related training with classes and field work in the areas of poverty, consumer, and en-

[11] Students at Washington's George Washington University also receive training under the supervision of Professor John Banzhaf. Students have been informally organized and have filed suits and complaints under acronyms, such as SOUP (Students Opposing Unfair Practices) and SCRAP (Students Challenging Regulatory Agency Proceedings). Banzhaf is the crusader who is responsible for the banning of cigarette commercials on television. See Thomas Whiteside, "Annals of Advertising," *New Yorker*, December 19, 1970, pp. 42-95; and Joseph A. Page, "The Law Professor Behind ASH, SOUP, PUMP, and CRASH," *The New York Times Magazine*, August 23, 1970, p. 32ff.

vironmental law. It can be concluded that a law background does provide both public and private interest lobbyists tools that are necessary or helpful for some lobbying jobs.[12] It is not, of course, a requisite for entering the general field; most lobbyists do not have law degrees.[13]

In a further effort to examine the backgrounds and training of public interest lobbyists, the interviewees were each asked to summarize their occupational histories. Their responses reveal that there is no real common vocational background for public interest activists (see Table IV-5). Approximately a quarter (26%) of the public interest activists came from jobs in government, but beyond that, there is a wide variety of previous occupations. In addition to the more mundane backgrounds, such as law practice or business, the sample included a retired admiral, a bank clerk, two CIA agents, a director of H. L. Hunt's youth program, a radio newsman, a middle-level executive in the phone company, a partner in Merrill, Lynch, Pierce, Fenner and Smith, a society matron, numerous housewives who decided they wanted a career, a musician, and a taxicab driver.[14]

An interesting comparison of the job backgrounds of private and public interest lobbyists can be made by using the data collected by Lester Milbrath. In contrast to the 26% of the public interest lobbyists who came from positions in the government, Milbrath found that over half his sample (57%)

[12] On law as preparation for legislative work, see Heinz Eulau and John D. Sprague, *Lawyers in Politics* (Indianapolis, Ind.: Bobbs-Merrill, 1964), pp. 111-117.

[13] Both DeVries, and Zeigler and Baer find that lawyers are not more effective lobbyists than are nonlawyers. Walter D. DeVries, *The Michigan Lobbyist* (unpublished Ph.D. dissertation, Michigan State University, 1960), pp. 210-246; and Zeigler and Baer, *Lobbying*, pp. 135-141.

[14] For some profiles of private interest lobbyists, see James Deakin, *The Lobbyists* (Washington, D.C.: Public Affairs Press, 1966), pp. 153-181; and Robert W. Miller and Jimmy D. Johnson, *Corporate Ambassadors to Washington* (Washington, D.C.: The American University, 1970).

90   Lobbying for the People

TABLE IV-5

Prior Career Experience

| | Public Interest Lobbyists | | Milbrath's Washington Lobbyists |
	Career Pattern	Most Recent Job	Most Recent Job
Law (private practice)	16%	11%	8%
Business	9%	11%	17%
Government	26%	26%	57%[c]
Journalism	10%	2%	1%
Teaching	6%	4%	X
Religion	5%	4%	X
Interest group work	7%	14%[a]	2%[d]
Liberal arts (college background only)	9%	14%[b]	X
Other	11%	12%	15%[e]
	99%[f]	98%[f]	100%
		(N = 91)	(N = 106)

[a] Indicates another separate interest group.
[b] Came directly from an educational institution.
[c] Includes three former U.S. Representatives.
[d] Coded, "Never did anything else" (but lobbying in this position); not directly comparable.
[e] Includes "labor union employee" (5%) and "other professional" (4%).
[f] Rounding error.
X = not coded, presumably negligible or zero percent.

came directly from the administrative or legislative branches of government.[15] The transfer of governmental officials straight into private interest lobbying is considered by some, if not unethical, at least unsavory. Going "in and out" of government, particularly for an attorney, practically guarantees an increase in earning capacity. The pattern is a familiar one: the antitrust expert in the Justice Department who goes to work for a corporate law firm; the staff lawyer in the FAA

15 Milbrath, *The Washington Lobbyists*, p. 68.

or CAB who accepts a position as an attorney for a commercial airline; or the high-level bureaucrat in the Internal Revenue Service who quickly becomes a leading Washington tax lawyer.

Gaining expertise in government and then using that knowledge on behalf of private interest groups may or may not be a desirable by-product of governmental service, but it is, in fact, a widespread practice in Washington. In addition to expertise, it is often thought that government experience is valuable for lobbyists because of the contacts that are made. Milbrath found, however, that expertise in a substantive area, or knowledge of a particular institutional process, is a much more desirable quality than having a circle of contacts. Milbrath concluded from his sample "that almost half of them believe that contacts are of no importance at all and that only fifteen think that they are of considerable or major importance."[16]

Although expertise seems to be a highly valued quality, governmental service is far from being an exclusive source of process or substantive knowledge. One journalistic study of Washington lawyers suggests that governmental service may be an overrated attribute for lobbyists. In doing research on Washington's largest, and one of its most prestigious, national corporate law firms, Covington and Burling, Joseph Goulden discovered that the firm did not, as a rule, recruit people from government. Rather, they hired only the top graduates of the best law schools, such as Harvard and Yale, and let them develop expertise in certain areas as they worked their way up through the firm.[17]

Although no one doubts that expertise is very desirable in a lobbyist, Bauer, Pool, and Dexter found that lobbyists, generally, are not very expert. More precisely, the lobbyists they observed in their study of foreign trade legislation were

[16] *Ibid.*, p. 63.
[17] Joseph Goulden, *Superlawyers* (New York: Dell, 1973), pp. 25-71. A "national" Washington firm is one that is recognized for being able to deal with the federal government for clients from around the country. See also Mark J. Green, *The Other Government* (New York: Grossman, 1975).

not very skilled in their work, despite any substantive knowledge they might possess. In their own words:

> Most mothers would say, "I didn't raise my boy to be a lobbyist." As long as that situation prevails, the best talent will not be found in pressure politics. . . . This is a difficult point to document. We have no evidence on intrinsic ability; yet it is our distinct impression that, except for a few highly capable men at the top of the heap, the best men leave the field.[18]

The evidence concerning what makes for good training for a lobbyist appears to be thoroughly confusing. Moreover, a primary source of information has been ignored. No one has interviewed the people who actually hire staff lobbyists or lobbyist entrepreneurs to ask them about what qualities they look for. It is entirely possible that employers have no clear idea either of what qualifies a person to be a lobbyist.[19]

A synthesis of the previous research on lobbyist backgrounds suggests that expertise, regardless of how it is acquired, is desirable, but that many lobbyists are not highly knowledgeable.[20] Not surprisingly, the data on the sample of public interest activists display the same vagueness in regard to what constitutes a valuable background. It is very difficult to generalize about the sample because there is such a wide variety of previous career patterns.

[18] Raymond A. Bauer, Ithiel de Sola Pool, and Lewis Anthony Dexter, *American Business and Public Policy* (New York: Atherton Press, 1963), p. 345.

[19] This type of ambiguity of personnel qualifications is not limited to lobbyists. Zurcher and Dustan found a somewhat similar situation in the staffing of private foundations: "foundations have indulged in little or no systematic thinking about staffing and . . . formal discussions on the subject are virtually nonexistent." Arnold J. Zurcher and Jane Dustan, *The Foundation Administrator* (New York: Russell Sage Foundation, 1972), p. 35.

[20] Dexter suggests that one of the most important characteristics of a competent lobbyist is knowing the limits of his knowledge. Lewis Anthony Dexter, *How Organizations Are Represented in Washington* (Indianapolis, Ind.: Bobbs-Merrill, 1969), p. 44.

Expertise, again, is the most common and clearly identifiable qualification. But also again, it is not a necessity. One environmental lobbyist exaggerated only a little in his interview when he recalled, "I didn't even know what the word 'environment' meant until I got here." At the other extreme, however, are individuals with a deep, specialized knowledge, such as the graduate student who wrote his dissertation on international air fares and then went to work for Ralph Nader in the area of consumer aviation problems.

One explanation for the inconsistency of training for public interest work is the haphazard nature of the actual hiring process. Far too often, getting a job in a public interest group is more dependent on "who you know, not what you know." Time and again, interviewees said that they were able to apply for a job only because a friend told them about it, or that when a job opened up they were considered for it because they already knew someone in the organization. This type of informal communication network does not always work to bring forth the best applicants for ostensibly specialized jobs.

Party and Ideology. The public interest activists are strongly oriented toward the Democratic Party. Sixty-four percent of the sample identifies with the Democrats, as opposed to 42% of the general public when measured by the Gallup Poll.[21] Although the number of people who consider themselves independents has been rising in recent years, the percentage of independents in the sample is relatively small (19% vs. 31% in the Gallup Poll), especially considering the conventional wisdom that it is best for lobbyists to avoid partisan identification.[22] Only 10% of the public interest lobbyists label themselves as Republicans.

[21] *Gallup Opinion Index* (May 1973), pp. 14-15. This period of time coincides with the last part of the interviewing.
[22] Milbrath, *The Washington Lobbyists*, pp. 76-79. Milbrath found 26% of his Washington lobbyists to be independents. Survey data from this time (1956-1957) shows this to be above the rate of independents in the population. See James L. Sundquist, *Dynamics of*

The preference for the Democrats may not so much be indicative of strong partisanship as it is of strong ideological sentiments. The respondents were also asked, "When you compare your own political views with those of other Americans, how would you classify yourself?" The results show a remarkably strong tendency to the left side of the political spectrum (see Table IV-6). Fully 74% of the public interest representatives place themselves in the liberal-to-radical section of the continuum.[23]

TABLE IV-6

Ideology[a]

Conservative	10%
Moderate	4%
Liberal	47%
Left of Center[b]	18%
Radical	9%
"Can't label myself" and "don't think in those terms"	8%
NA	4%
	100% (N = 91)

[a] Self-designation.
[b] Includes "leftist," "left of center," "populist," and "radical-liberal."

Because there are only nine conservatives in the sample, almost all of whom work for the avowedly conservative groups, it must be concluded that, in general, professional

the Party System (Washington, D.C.: Brookings Institution, 1973), pp. 342-354. In further contrast to the public interest lobbyists, Milbrath found about equal proportions of Democrats (39%) and Republicans (36%) in his sample.

[23] Political activists are, in general, more ideological and polar in their issue beliefs. See Herbert McClosky, Paul J. Hoffman, and Rosemary O'Hara, "Issue Conflict and Consensus Among Party Leaders and Followers," American Political Science Review, vol. 54 (June 1960), pp. 406-427. See also Sidney Verba and Norman H. Nie, Participation in America (New York: Harper & Row, 1972), pp. 82-94.

public interest work has a strong bias toward appealing to liberal and very liberal activists. Although it was expected that there would be a natural ideological polarity in the peace-arms and general politics groups, it was also thought that the staffs of the other types of groups might have a broader range of political views. This is clearly not the case.

One interesting footnote to all this is the number of respondents (18%) who placed themselves, without cue,[24] to the left of liberal but to the right of radical. The term "liberal" seems to have fallen on hard times: numerous people who placed themselves in this category did so with some embarrassment, or added a deprecatory remark about the state of the liberals in this country. In between liberal and radical seemed to be a very comfortable niche for many of the respondents, a number of whom adopted former Vice President Agnew's expression of opprobrium for opponents of the Nixon administration and called themselves "radical-liberal."

The public interest lobbyists were further asked to describe any involvement they had had in party politics. Close to half the sample (46%) had not been involved in any electoral activity. A small number (10%) had a record of marginal participation by doing such things as stuffing envelopes at candidate headquarters or working precincts on election day.[25] A substantial proportion of the lobbyists (42%) had been highly active in the past, with involvement ranging from canvassing on a regular basis to managing a campaign. Given the ideological make-up of the sample it is not surprising that most of the campaign work mentioned was done on behalf of liberal, Democratic candidates. Over half of those who had been highly active were veterans of the presidential efforts of Senators Eugene McCarthy and

[24] Respondents were not given a card or list of labels from which they were to pick.

[25] But even this "low" level of activity is in the top 5% or so of the public at large in terms of degree of political participation. See Lester W. Milbrath, *Political Participation* (Chicago: Rand McNally, 1965), pp. 18-19.

George McGovern. A few even took leaves from their jobs
to work for McGovern in the fall of 1972. It should be noted
that respondents rarely spoke of their work as party work,
but rather related their experience in terms of individual
candidates.[26]

One way in which public interest activists are not active
is in the raising of campaign funds.[27] This contrasts to Milbrath's sample, in which 42% of the lobbyists had at one time
been involved in candidate fund raising.[28] Only a handful of
public interest activists mentioned that they had raised
money for candidates. The reason for this is twofold. First,
lobbyists for 501(c)(3) groups cannot raise campaign
money as representatives of their organizations. Second,
contributing money to candidates is seen by the vast majority of public interest organizations as either an unafforda-
ble luxury or an inefficient use of their available resources.

THE JOB

It was noted earlier that the respondents in the sample
were similar in that they all acted as spokesmen for their
groups. Their jobs were described as falling into the three
general categories of director of legislation, director of litigation, and project director. In addition, two-thirds of the
respondents are directors of their Washington office, although in many cases they have only one or two subordi-
nates beneath them. These formal classifications do not say
much about what these people actually do on a day-to-day

[26] Cross-tabulation of the data reveals that a high level of political
activism is significantly related to working for a general politics
group. The level of campaign activity was not in any way related
to ideology; activity was consistent across the spectrum.

[27] There are a few obvious exceptions to this, such as the representatives of the Americans for Constitutional Action, the National
Committee for an Effective Congress, and Council for a Livable
World. These groups are primarily conduits for campaign funds for
congressional candidates. See Chapter VIII.

[28] Milbrath, *The Washington Lobbyists*, p. 383 and pp. 282-286.

basis. A more analytical set of categories might be helpful in understanding the different roles that are played by public interest lobbyists.

Job Description. All the public interest representatives are trying to do the same thing, namely, influence government and attentive publics. The kind of work they do to achieve that end varies widely. Organizational size is a key factor in determining the scope of a lobbyist's work. In the smaller organizations, it is likely that the lobbyist will also be director of the group and be obligated to assume many different duties. In the middle-size groups, the lobbyist will tend to specialize in real advocacy work, but may have some supervisory responsibilities for other staff personnel as well. In the large organizations, the experienced lobbyists will probably be more knowledgeable generalists than specialists in any single substantive area because of the organization's wide interests. Their work will involve directing the work of other, more specialized, lobbyists on the staff. The type of work public interest lobbyists perform may be divided into four different organizational roles.[29]

1. Jack-of-all-trades. The most prevalent array of duties for the lobbyists is, in fact, almost all of the duties. Earlier discussion revealed that one-fourth of the groups in the sample had no more than a single, full-time professional. In those organizations with two or three staff professionals, few of the activists are given the luxury of functioning only in a liaison and lobbying capacity. Rather, these representatives find themselves spending large amounts of time doing fund raising, writing for the organization's newsletter, handling office correspondence, and in numerous other administrative duties.

Quite naturally, the respondents in this category spoke a great deal of their frustrations in not being able to devote

[29] Another way of looking at lobbyist roles may be found in Samuel C. Patterson's "The Role of the Lobbyist: The Case of Oklahoma," *Journal of Politics*, vol. 25 (February 1963), pp. 72-92.

more time to substantive work. The interviewees indicated that what suffers more than the amount of time going into communicating with the government, is the lack of time put into related research. These lobbyists usually do little research on their own, and they rely heavily on research supplied by other groups or by another office of their own organization.

2. Advocate. An almost equally common role found is that of advocate. These are persons who are working nearly full time in communicating with people in government and in other interest groups, and in doing support research for their efforts. The advocates are usually found in the middle- or large-size groups, and they are afforded the opportunity to specialize in their work. Their newsletter and administrative duties tend not to be burdensome.

3. Strategist. A somewhat less frequently adopted role than advocate is that of the strategist, which is found in the larger organizations. These representatives have important duties in directing the work of others and in developing overall strategy for the organization's advocacy efforts. Although almost all of the public interest lobbyists are active in organizational policy making, the strategists are more involved than most. The strategists also do direct lobbying and advocacy work, but it is likely to be in the context of a coordinator or planner of the effort at hand.

4. Community organizer. A small percentage of the activists are concerned more with activating the rank-and-file of their organization than with direct communication with government. Their work consists primarily of organizing members of *ad hoc* groups, putting together demonstrations, or catalyzing action among existing local organizations.[30]

[30] It was extremely difficult to code the lobbyists along a descriptive classification of their jobs because public interest representatives do so many different things for their individual organizations. Even with the jack-of-all-trades category, there is still considerable overlap among the other three role types. The quantitative breakdown is offered with a great deal of caution: jacks-of-all-trades, 37%; ad-

No typology could ever do justice to the extraordinary range of activities undertaken by public interest lobbyists. It is impossible to draw a composite "day in the life" of the representatives in the sample. If there is a common thread that runs through their individual, daily work, it is a sense of urgency that propels the lobbyists back and forth between the three or four major tasks for which they have taken responsibility. It is a constant struggle for the public interest lobbyists to keep from crossing the thin line between maximizing their output and spreading themselves too thin.

Commitment and Income. One of the more surprising findings of Lester Milbrath's study is that 60% of the Washington lobbyists said that they were only "mildly" or "weakly" committed to the cause they espoused.[31] This lack of commitment may be explained, in part, by the structure of the sample, which contained a large number of independent lawyers who worked on a fee or retainer basis and were not members of the staffs of the organizations. In their study of state legislature lobbyists, Zeigler and Baer found relatively strong commitment to the goals of the organization in slightly more than half of their sample. Predictably, they found strong commitment to be related to being an officer in the organization and to not being a lawyer.[32] Sixty-one percent of DeVries' sample of Michigan lobbyists said that the policy positions they advocated had been a "very important factor" in their decision to represent the group.[33]

The pattern of degree of commitment is quite dissimilar

---

vocates, 30%; strategists, 23%; community organizers, 7%; other, 3%. For a comprehensive look at the job of being a lobbyist, see Dexter, *How Organizations Are Represented in Washington.*

[31] Milbrath adds that he feels lobbyists are likely to overreport their commitment because "many lobbyists feel that it is important to be sincerely committed to what they are doing if they expect to be trusted and listened to." *The Washington Lobbyists,* p. 109.

[32] Zeigler and Baer, *Lobbying,* pp. 64-66.

[33] DeVries, *The Michigan Lobbyist,* p. 89.

for public interest lobbyists. If there was one thing that was clear from the respondents' attitudes during the interviews, it was that their work is not "just a job." There was not a single activist who gave any indication of anything but strong commitment to organizational goals. All in all, commitment ranged from merely strong to fanatical.

Indicative of the commitment to organizational policy is the personal sacrifice that many public interest activists make to work for their groups. Low salaries, long hours, and uncertainty over the future existence of the organization are job conditions often associated with public interest work. For some, the sacrifice has been extraordinary. One antiwar activist reminisces about his career:

> I was going to law school nights and working days when the war broke out. I completed school in 1966 and I passed the bar the same year. During this time I became active in the antiwar movement in the Cleveland area. I didn't have an organization so I started one. It was called "Get Out Now" and what it did was to get speakers and arrange forums to express our view. I continued to practice law but I eventually gave up my position with the local group. Before the April 24, 1971, demonstration I was working for _____ and they asked me to come to Washington for the three weeks prior, and I did. At the demonstration there were a half million people. I'd never seen anything like it; so I decided to work full time at this. I went back to Cleveland and closed my law practice and finished up my affairs there; then I came back here to work full time.

This man's salary is less than $7500 per year.

In some cases, the difference between the amount of money actually earned by public interest activists and the amount they could earn elsewhere is dramatic. One environmental lawyer remarked in his interview that he had just turned down a job in a private interest group for $10,000 a year more than he was currently making. "I couldn't sleep at night if I took it," he said, with a touch of self-righteousness in explaining his altruism. Another environmentalist, who had considerable job experience, said he turned down a job offer in private industry that would have paid him $55,000, more than double his present salary. "It's just a matter of conscience," he stated. Still one more example is a lawyer who left one of Washington's most prestigious law firms as a full partner to work for a consumer and environmental affairs group. His pay was at least half of his former salary.[34]

Personal and economic sacrifice are practically prerequisites for working for Ralph Nader. One Nader employee, who had just graduated from law school, was making only $5000 per year at the time of his interview. A director of one of the Nader satellites quit his job with a well-known Wall Street law firm to work for Nader for less than $10,000 a year. A few of the "well-paid" Nader lieutenants, men with wives and children, make around $15,000 annually, but they also have a great deal of experience and expertise and could be making much more elsewhere. When asked about his future career plans, one of these better-paid Nader workers could only say, "I don't know, financially this is becoming increasingly difficult." Six months later, he quit Nader to accept a position with a liberal, consumer-oriented Senator.[35]

The distribution of salaries is a wide one, reflecting a broad range of organizational resources and organizational priorities (see Table IV-7). Although Ralph Nader might feel that for $15,000 it is better to have two $7500-a-year employees with little experience, other group directors are

[34] A few other lobbyists said that because of financial difficulties within the organization, they had taken a pay cut within the past couple of years. Others mentioned that they had not been paid on a regular basis in recent months because of financial exigencies.

[35] In contrast to the Nader workers, top Common Cause employees are very well paid. Three top executive officers, right below Chairman John Gardner, make in the neighborhood of $100,000 between them. Gardner was working without remuneration, but now accepts $7500 per year for expenses.

TABLE IV-7

Income

Volunteer, no salary	2%	(2)
Under $5,000	7%	(6)
$5,000–$9,999	19%	(16)
$10,000–$14,999	20%	(17)
$15,000–$19,999	27%	(23)
$20,000–$24,999	12%	(10)
$25,000+	12%	(10)
	99%ᵃ	(N = 84)ᵇ

ᵃ Rounding error.
ᵇ Full-time employees only.

of the opinion that it is important to have an older person with experience and are willing to pay a more competitive salary.[36] Thus, there is a balance in the sample, with 26% earning less than $10,000 annually, and 24% earning a respectable $20,000 or more.

The personal income measure is not the only sign of personal hardship that public interest lobbyists may endure. Long working hours were frequently cited in the interviews.[37] Yet talk about long hours seemed to be as much "bragging" as it was complaining, because the respondents

[36] The personification of personal self-sacrifice is, of course, Ralph Nader. His ascetic life style has undoubtedly added to his credibility as a spokesman for the public interest. See Robert F. Buckhorn, *Nader: The People's Lawyer* (Englewood Cliffs, N.J.: Prentice-Hall, 1972); Hays Gorey, *Nader and the Power of Everyman* (New York: Grosset and Dunlop, 1975); Charles McCarry, *Citizen Nader* (New York: Saturday Review Press, 1972); David Sanford, *Me and Ralph: Is Nader Unsafe for America?* (Washington, D.C.: New Republic Book Company, 1976); and Thomas Whiteside's two-part "A Countervailing Force," *New Yorker*, October 8, 1973, pp. 50-111, and October 15, 1973, pp. 46-101.

[37] Whiteside found that the long working hours had strained the marriages of many Nader aides. One Nader lieutenant told him that he could think of eight or nine marital breakups of Nader workers within the past few years. "A Countervailing Force," October 15, 1973, p. 72.

seemed to reveal this in part to show how committed they were to the cause. In some of the smaller groups the longer hours are compensated for, to a small degree, by a bit of freedom in determining work hours. Workers in these organizations, where there are traces of countercultural and antibureaucratic sentiments, will often come in at 10 a.m. or later, but work into the early evening.

An interesting sidelight to this discussion is that it is downright difficult to get a job in a public interest group. Despite drawbacks from some of the positions, there is no dearth of eager applicants. Among young people, the jobs are highly prized because they offer an opportunity to get paid for working on or against the "system." Although organizations do not always get the perfect individual for the job, openings do not stay unfilled for long.

In sum, public interest groups attract zealous and devoted workers. It is difficult to evaluate the role of personal salaries, because many public interest representatives receive a fair and substantial wage, whereas just as many others are significantly underpaid. It can be concluded that salary is not a primary motivating factor for entering public interest work, but it may be an important reason for leaving it. Salary is largely a function of organizational resources, and it is not necessarily related to merit or capabilities. Salary does seem to be moderately correlated with work experience. It needs to be remembered, however, that the real rewards of public interest lobbying are not in getting rich—and chances of fame are slim—but, rather, in being able to fight for the "right" causes.

FUTURE AND CAREER

The job satisfaction of public interest activists is extremely high. Although material compensation is not always large, solidary and purposive incentives seem to be consistently strong inducements. Many respondents did express frustration at not being able to have more influence with the government, or not having more resources at their disposal, but only a few spoke of real dissatisfaction with the actual work they did.

Despite the fact that the lobbyists appeared to be relatively happy in their jobs, many of them seemed uncertain about public interest work as a career (see Table IV-8). When the public interest activists were asked about future plans, about half (53%) said that they were planning to stay in the type of work they were doing.[38] Only 9% of the respondents were intending to leave their present jobs, and the remainder (38%) were undecided about their future.

Career plans are strongly related to the age of the activists. Those lobbyists who are 30 or older are much more likely to have decided to continue in their present work. In contrast, over three-quarters of the activists younger than 30 were either planning to leave their jobs or were undecided about their vocational plans.[39] It is not surprising that the younger representatives are less committed to public interest lobbying as a life's work.[40] The young will tend to have less in the way of family responsibilities and may feel fewer pressures to choose a formal career. Most respondents who were leaving public interest work, or were thinking of it, fell into two general categories. First, there were those who consciously felt that they should try their hands at a

[38] Because the intent was to tap career intentions, respondents were asked if they would "like to continue in this type of work" rather than asking them if they wanted to stay in their present job for the rest of their career.

[39] Another factor that appears to be related to career plans is organizational stability. Quite expectedly, those in groups where there was some question of the organization's survival tended to be more uncertain about their own plans. Yet, again, the question asked referred to their future with regard to the type of work they were doing, not to the specific job.

[40] Writing of aspiring politicians, Joseph Schlesinger notes: "the attainment of public office at an early age represents a less costly investment than later entry into a public office career. Requiring no formal training like medicine and the law, politics is an inexpensive trial run for those whose interests are vague." Schlesinger, *Ambition and Politics*, p. 176.

TABLE IV-8
Future Plans

Future	Age					Total
	20–29	30–39	40–49	50–59	60+	
Yes, rest of career	21% (5)	54% (18)	53% (9)	100% (11)	83% (5)	53% (48)
Planning to stay but undecided about future	37% (9)	21% (7)	35% (6)	—	—	24% (22)
Planning to leave	21% (5)	6% (2)	6% (1)	—	—	9% (8)
Undecided about future	21% (5)	18% (6)	6% (1)	—	17% (1)	14% (13)
Total	100% (24)	99%ᵃ (33)	100% (17)	100% (11)	100% (6)	100% (N = 91)

ᵃ Rounding error.

number of things before determining what they wanted to do with the rest of their lives. Second, there were those who were genuinely undecided about what they were going to do. There were only a few, like the following antiwar lobbyist, who have simply "had it" with public interest work.

It's not just working in an office nine-to-five. It's weekends, it's nights—it just takes up so much of my time. I'd like to reverse my priorities. I think you reach a saturation point. My personality isn't geared to this.

There are two contradictory themes running through this analysis. At the same time as there is a high degree of job satisfaction throughout the sample, there are relatively indeterminate career orientations for close to half of the activists. One problem that arises in trying to explain indecisiveness toward public interest careers is that the concept of a public interest "career" is rather amorphous. The occupational role of public interest lobbyist is not one that is popularly understood, nor are there clear expectations of how one is supposed to build a career in public interest work.[41]

The culture of public interest lobbying is very much characterized by a "here-and-now" quality. Staff personnel tend not to work on long-term projects, but rather are usually concerned with the crises that the organization faces during the current day, week, or month. In addition, it is unlikely that the lobbyists are doing work that will lead to advancement within the organization. There are few rungs to be climbed within a public interest group. Consequently, the work they are doing is probably the same type of work they will be doing in five years. These factors would not seem to encourage careerism in public interest work.

The question may be asked as to what are the futures of those in the sample who are not going to be career public interest activists. One thing for certain is that this group of lobbyists did not see their job as a stepping stone to a good

[41] See Zeigler and Baer's discussion of lobbying as a nonprofession, *Lobbying*, pp. 62-66.

job in government or to elective office.[42] Only a single respondent said he was thinking of running for office some day. A few did mention that they might like to go into government, but many more said that they had just left and would never go back. Follow-up questions asked of those leaving, or thinking of leaving public interest work, elicited little in the way of definite plans or objectives.[43]

The fact that so large a portion of the sample is young, and that 65% of the lobbyists had been employed for less than three years at the time of the interviews, makes it difficult to discuss authoritatively the career patterns of public interest activists. It is possible that the present group of activists will, despite their indecision, develop into career public interest lobbyists. The youth and inexperience of a large portion of the activists, low salaries in many of the organizations, the instability and impermanence of others, and the lack of structured opportunities within organizations are variables that seemingly work against an increased tendency toward careerism in public interest work.

CONCLUSION

Public interest work does not seem to fit well into common patterns of political ambition. Rather, activists seem to choose public interest work as an alternative to more traditionally ambition-oriented careers such as public office. The reasons why individuals go into public interest work are a complex combination of factors, such as strong ideological commitment to a cause, the appeals of life and work styles with a relative amount of freedom, and opportunity

[42] It must be remembered that this disavowal of interest in governmental work came during the years of the Nixon administration. Had a liberal Democrat been in power, the predominantly liberal lobbyists might not have been so negative about this possibility. At the time, though, they just did not see this as a realistic alternative.

[43] An exception to this are five young people who had made arrangements to return to school. Two of the five were conscientious objectors who did their alternative service in public interest work.

and luck in finding a job. Some of the stratum of the population that wants to make a vocation of politics may do so through public office or government work, but there are others who will find public interest lobbying much more appealing.[44] It is also possible that public interest work may attract some who might not otherwise be active in politics.

The importance of discussing careerism is predicated on the assumption that career activists are a more valuable organizational resource than are younger, inexperienced lobbyists who do public interest work for a couple of years and then leave. Previous studies of lobbying suggest that substantive or process expertise is a most valued quality in a Washington representative. Because the comparative data on public interest lobbyists show that they are much less likely to acquire prior expertise in government, on-the-job experience becomes an even more significant variable. Public interest lobbyists, however, are much less experienced in their work than are their private interest counterparts. Follow-up research will be necessary to determine if, over time, public interest groups develop a more experienced cadre of workers.

The individual skills of a lobbyist become even more significant in low-resource organizations that have only one or two staff professionals. For many groups, there is little in the way of financial, membership, or staff resources to back up their Washington office. In these cases, the value of representatives who have issue expertise, procedural know-how, and the battle scars of "front-line" experience becomes magnified. Lobbyists with only a year or two of experience are predominant, however, in low- as well as high-resource public interest groups.

At the same time that the relative lack of job experience of the lobbyists lowers the potential capabilities of the pub-

---

[44] Schlesinger writes, "The most salient characteristic of the system is the proliferation of outlets for political ambition." Public interest work is just one outlet outside of all the elective office opportunity structures. *Ambition and Politics*, p. 16.

lic interest groups, there are other factors that may work to counterbalance this. The public interest representatives display an extremely high commitment to their work. What they lack in skill and knowledge may be made up for, in part, by simple hard work. For the most part, these people are zealots, and they derive a great deal of satisfaction from their jobs. In contrast to the more mildly committed private interest lobbyists, the public interest activists are more likely to seek out the work they are doing, rather than merely to "drift" into it.

CHAPTER V

Speaking for Those Who Can't:
The Fund for Animals

"Animals Have Rights, Too"—*Fund Slogan*

A little over 20 years ago, while vacationing in Nogales, Mexico, an American tourist named Cleveland Amory paid a dollar to sit in the hot sun to watch a bullfight. Unlike most of the other spectators, however, Amory found nothing sporting or even skillful in the matadors' methodic stalking and stabbing of the bulls. Amory recalls, "I saw not a single bull who entered the arena have any desire to do anything but find a way out."

The event so disturbed Amory that he proceeded to become active in a number of humane organizations. As he became more and more interested in animal protection work, however, he became more and more dissatisfied with the existing organizations. He felt that the organizations with which he was familiar were not having an impact and that the money being raised was being squandered on high salaries and overhead. In 1967 he decided to start his own organization, the Fund for Animals, and he opened up an office on West 57th Street in New York City.

AN ORGANIZATION FOR THE ANIMALS

Although plans for the group were somewhat indefinite, it was not because Amory did not know what he wanted to do, but rather that he wanted to do so much. One thing, however, was clear in Amory's mind: the organization would not be limited to educational endeavors. The Fund was to be action-oriented and would do more than just document existing problems. From the stray alley cat to the endangered polar bear, there had already been too much talk and too little positive assistance. In short, Amory says that he started the Fund because "I wanted to put some cleats on the little old ladies in tennis shoes."

Amory, a large and somewhat gruff-looking individual, is soft spoken only when describing the beauty or tenderness of an animal. He is otherwise a sardonic man who has never been able to understand why mankind is so oblivious to the pain and suffering it inflicts on God's other creatures. Now in his 50s, Amory, aside from his work with animals, is well known as an author, social critic, and TV celebrity.[1] Currently he is probably best known for the "Review" column he writes for *TV Guide*, which has a circulation of 17 million.[2]

Amory devotes approximately three-quarters of his time to the Fund. He uses his other work as a means of supporting himself so that he can work for the Fund without remuneration. In addition to this, he contributes $2000 to $4000 of his own money to the Fund each year.

The most serious problem of any public interest group is securing sufficient funds to maintain itself. The Fund has had to compete for the "conservation dollar" not only with such well-known, established groups as the Audubon Society and the National Wildlife Federation, but also with other animal protection groups, such as Defenders of Wildlife, Friends of Animals, and the Humane Society of the United States.

It is largely through Amory's personal efforts that the Fund has been able to raise the money it has—approximately $300,000 in 1972. Individual memberships in the or-

[1] Among his works are *The Proper Bostonians* (New York: E. P. Dutton, 1947); *The Last Resorts* (New York: Harper, 1952); and *Who Killed Society?* (New York: Harper, 1960). His most recent book, *Man Kind?* (New York: Harper & Row, 1974), deals with the mistreatment of animals and the lack of concern for their preservation.

[2] He also writes a column, "Curmudgeon-at-Large," for the *Saturday Review*.

ganization have been stimulated primarily through Amory's appearances on TV talk shows, his lectures, and from newspaper and magazine advertisements. The TV talk shows have been particularly successful for the Fund, and Amory has appeared on a number of occasions on shows such as those of Johnny Carson, Dinah Shore, and Dick Cavett (a Fund board member). In addition to the national programs, Amory is booked on local talk shows whenever he is traveling.

Despite the fact that the group has grown to an estimated 35,000 members, fund raising remains an enormously time-consuming task for Amory and his staff. The "members," those who have contributed at one time or another and receive the Fund *Bulletin*, are not big contributors. The standard membership fee is a modest $10. "There's no such thing as a $5 membership," says Amory, "because it costs you $5 to get the $10." Although larger contributions are encouraged, the small gifts are so predominant that anything over $50 warrants a personal thank-you note from Cleveland Amory. The group also "sells" buttons and bumper stickers emblazoned with their slogan, "Animals Have Rights, Too," and women's long party skirts that are decorated with the face of a lion on the front.[3] Occasionally they will make a special appeal, such as offering lithograph prints of a snow leopard for $100 apiece and then auctioning off the donated original.

The growth of the organization has been impressive, and the membership tripled in the last half of 1971 and 1972. The Fund has not received a great deal of support from foundations, and although they will continue to solicit foundation money, Amory feels that expanding their financial base will be dependent on a growth in membership and an increase in the number of large contributions.[4] The Fund,

[3] The organization's tax exemption prevents it from legally selling merchandise; they ask for contributions for the particular item instead.
[4] The Fund has 501(c)(3) status, so contributions from individuals are tax deductible. The group recently received a small foundation

however, has decided not to use direct mail appeals for membership because the staff doubts that it would be successful enough to pay the "seeding" costs of such an operation. Rather, they will rely on their traditional methods of stimulating membership with more personal effort on Amory's part in soliciting large contributions.[5]

Amory decided to call the organization the "Fund for Animals" because he thought it would be a good name to use on TV. People would hear him talk about the "Fund" and would realize that they should send money. Later he regretted the decision: "It was damn stupid of me, people probably think that because we're a 'fund' we already have money." The one salvation he finds for the name is that it is so peculiar that at least it sticks in people's minds.

The growth of the Fund's income over the past five years has been matched by a growth in the number of projects the group has taken on, as well as by an increase in the number of Fund employees. In addition to hiring a full-time Washington representative, the Fund hired a traveling field director who works on animal birth control and inspects zoos and animal shelters. Supplementing the Washington and New York offices are a number of regional offices which have sprung up in the past two years, often on the initiative of local Fund members.[6] Most of these offices are staffed en-

---

grant to support an educational campaign on behalf of endangered whales.

[5] Individuals who, by reason of one of Amory's appearances, an ad in a newspaper or magazine, or some other stimulus, write to the Fund headquarters inquiring about membership or additional information are sent a copy of the latest Fund *Bulletin*. The *Bulletin* always contains a membership coupon which lists various suggested sums, in ascending order, that may be contributed. Amory says of the fundraising task that lies ahead of him, "So far we've been gentle about it. I intend to tell our rich donors that if they are really going to help the animals then they're going to have to give up their colleges, their old charities. They're going to have to put their money where their mouth is."

[6] The Fund has regional groups in Atlanta; Los Angeles; West Palm Beach, Florida; Chicago; New Orleans; Corpus Christi, Texas; Baltimore; Detroit; Kansas City; and San Francisco. These "offices"

tirely by volunteer labor. Amory has increased his own New
York staff to five full-time assistants.

There is no real limit to the range of projects the Fund
will undertake. The Fund's national office is interested in
doing anything that will stop the inhumane treatment of
animals. Not only do they take on projects of their own, but
they also channel part of their limited funds into programs
of other organizations that they feel need their support.
They have a Fund for Animals Emergency Room in New
York City for stray and abandoned animals. They have
given money to save coyotes in Colorado as well as to save
wildlife in Israel. Since the opening of their Washington
office, prodding the federal government to save endangered
species has become a major Fund objective.

The Fund also does a great deal of educational work.
They publish a series of small pamphlets entitled "So You
Want to *Do* Something About _____" (Trapping, Kangaroos and Wallabies, the Tennessee Walking Horse, etc.),
which instruct the readers on actions they may take to help
the animals. They also publish fact sheets and send *Special
Bulletins* to their members on issues of importance. Dis-
seminating information about animal birth control and
spaying is also of major concern. Information booths and
exhibits are set up at various fairs around the country. Sometimes a Fund representative will bring a live animal to a
TV show or other event to try to educate people about that
particular species. Before their recent deaths, two wolves,
Jethro and Clem, were taken to places such as the F.A.O.
Schwarz toy store in New York and the front lawn of the
Interior Department in Washington for the purpose of showing people that wolves are not the vicious beasts portrayed
in Little Red Riding Hood.[7]

---

vary in formality, and many consist of individuals working out of their
homes.

[7] Jethro received the Fund's Animal of the Year award for 1971.
The inscription on his plaque read, "Wolf without peer and animal
ambassador extraordinary, an ambassador without portfolio or collar

Nominal authority over the organization lies in the hands of an Executive Board of Directors. Although the board does meet from time to time and a few of its members are active in the organization, important decisions regarding the undertaking or development of Fund projects are usually made by Amory. Assisting the Executive Board is a National Board of about 35 celebrities, such as Helen Gurley Brown, Doris Day, Jack Parr, Andrew Wyeth, and Richard Bach. The National Board has no authority, but the members are used for publicity and fund-raising purposes and their names are listed on the Fund's stationery.

The organization holds no convention, and members have no voting rights or other formal means of "input" into the decision-making process. Members are, of course, kept abreast of Fund activities through the quarterly *Bulletin* and the issue-oriented *Special Bulletins*. The four-page *Bulletin* is an amalgam of articles about recent Fund activities and news concerning the mistreatment of certain species.

It is important to emphasize the role of solidary incentives in the organization of the Fund for Animals.[8] The love of helping animals, accomplishing that task, and peer-group approval are the main rewards for working for the Fund. The priorities of the organization almost seem to be a case of "animals first, people second." The Fund made a donation to the Greek SPCA so that it could stay open on weekends; yet one of the full-time staff assistants in New York was making only $75 a week at the time. Another Fund employee, because of financial exigencies, was recently cut

who has traveled the country from coast to coast, with patience, understanding, and fortitude, to plead the cause of animals everywhere." Jethro and Clem met an untimely death after an appearance on the Dick Cavett show. Chicken necks laced with strychnine were given to the wolves while they were in a parked van. A retired insurance clerk known as "the cat woman" was later arrested for the crime. "Cat Lover Hated Wolves?" *Washington Post*, August 2, 1973, p. B4.

[8] See Peter B. Clark and James Q. Wilson, "Incentive Systems: A Theory of Organizations," *Administrative Science Quarterly*, vol. 6 (September 1961), pp. 129-166.

back in salary from $100 a week to just $50; but as soon as Amory can find the right person to hire, he is going to send him to Spain to try to change the laws regarding bullfights. The solidary incentives are even more significant in the regional offices, where very few of the workers are paid. One of the jobs the New York office must perform is assuaging the feelings of their numerous volunteers around the country. In the words of one New York staffer, "Somebody will call because they don't feel wanted, so we have to talk to them. You know, there's personalities involved . . . people just want to feel that they're part of the organization." The most valuable nonmaterial reward seems to be a word of encouragement or a pat on the back from Cleveland Amory. Conversely, nothing is worse than a real or imagined personal snub from Amory.

The Washington Office. Although Cleveland Amory had been thinking of opening a Washington office for some time, he waited until he found just the right person to run it. Amory wanted somebody who was not only capable but also one who was totally dedicated to helping animals. In the spring of 1972, Amory offered the job to Lewis Regenstein. Amory met Lew Regenstein through Regenstein's work as the Washington representative of the Committee for Humane Legislation (CHL). The Committee for Humane Legislation is the lobbying arm of the Friends of Animals. The Friends of Animals set up the CHL so that it could protect its own 501(c)(3) status, which prohibits it from any "substantial" lobbying.

Of all the other national groups, the Friends of Animals is most similar to the Fund in its constituency and its objectives.[9] The New York-based Friends of Animals was started

---

[9] At the same time, there are an almost endless number of animal-related organizations around the country that compete for members with groups such as the Fund for Animals or Friends of Animals. A representative sample might include the Society for the Preservation of Birds of Prey (Pacific Palisades, California), Friends of the Sea Otter (Big Sur, California), National Catholic Society for Animal Welfare (New York); Save the Dolphin (San Francisco), National

in 1957 by Ms. Alice Herrington, who still heads the organization. Ms. Herrington has not only led the organization for the past 15 years, but she has totally dominated it. Although this type of individual rule is a common pattern among public interest groups, Ms. Herrington's leadership has not been characterized by her creativity or tact. In her zeal to protect animals, she has managed to offend a fair number of human beings by her dogmatism and unwillingness to compromise. During the fight over an Ocean Marine Mammal Protection bill during the 92nd Congress, Ms. Herrington denounced all the organizations that opposed her version of the legislation as "assassins unlimited." Her list of assassins included such legitimate conservation groups as the Izaak Walton League and the Citizens Committee on Natural Resources, as well as management groups like the Sport Fishing Institute and the National Rifle Association.[10] Yet despite the many personal criticisms that are made of Ms. Herrington, there are few who will deny that she has done a great deal for animals.

Although the Committee for Humane Legislation may be a separate organization in the eyes of the Internal Revenue Service, it has come to be a *de facto* Washington office of the Friends of Animals. The CHL was originally designed to be a coalition of many conservation groups. It soon be-

---

Association for Humane Legislation (St. Petersburg, Florida), and the Committee for the Preservation of the Tule Elk (Los Angeles). In addition, the countless local and state humane societies and SPCAs attract a considerable share of the resources committed to the animal protection movement each year.

[10] An extremely interesting attack and "exposé" on the Friends of Animals and the Fund for Animals is Margaret G. Nichols' "Alice (and Friends) in Disneyland," *Field and Stream* (May 1972), pp. 65ff. Both groups are detested by hunting enthusiasts because of the strong antihunting emphasis of the organizations. In another article in the *American Rifleman*, the Fund for Animals and the North American Association for the Preservation of Predatory Animals are criticized for inhumane treatment of animals for exhibiting and keeping captive two naturally wild timber wolves (Jethro and Clem). "Putting on the Bite for Wolves," *American Rifleman* (July 1972), p. 23. In fact, both wolves were born in captivity and were never naturally wild.

came apparent to all concerned that Ms. Herrington would control this group as she did Friends of Animals.

Cleveland Amory was involved in the early stages of the CHL's formation and was appointed Vice President—Ms. Herrington was President. He became dissatisfied as he realized that Ms. Herrington was running the CHL single-handed. Amory soon knew that he was not going to have any effective say in the decision making of the CHL and, consequently, that the Fund would have to open up its own office in Washington.

Lewis Regenstein did his undergraduate work in political science at the University of Pennsylvania and later did work toward a master's degree in the same subject at Emory. Now 30 years old, Regenstein was born and raised in Atlanta and still speaks with a distinctive southern drawl. After he graduated from college, Regenstein went to work as an intelligence officer in the CIA. He worked for the CIA for three years until, on a trip to New York for a wedding, he stopped in to see Alice Herrington. He had never met Ms. Herrington, but he had read some of her work and he wanted to tell her how much he admired what she was doing. Ms. Herrington told Regenstein that she was opening a Washington office (the CHL) and asked him if he would consider taking the job. He accepted on the spot and proceeded to open the CHL office in May of 1971.

Although he took a drastic cut in pay to work for Ms. Herrington, he discovered that he had found something that he really loved doing. Although he had enjoyed his work with the CIA and had been told that he was welcome back, he knew that conservation work was too important to him to leave. In his year at the CHL, he concentrated on the Ocean Marine Mammal Protection bill. The legislation, first known as the Harris-Pryor bill, was enacted into law at the end of the 92nd Congress.[11] Regenstein monitored the

[11] Public Law 92-522. Regenstein had left the CHL by the time the bill was in its final stages, but continued his work at the Fund for Animals.

bill as it progressed slowly through both houses and worked particularly hard on trying to keep weakening amendments from being adopted in subcommittee and committee. The bill, as passed by Congress, provides a moratorium on the killing of dolphins, dugongs, porpoises, manatees, sea otters, sea lions, polar bears, whales, walruses, and seals. In addition, the legislation established a Marine Mammal Commission and a Committee of Scientific Advisers to assist the relevant government agencies in making future decisions on the fate of these animals.[12] Regenstein's most notable contribution to the fight for a strong bill was a scathing guest editorial in the *Washington Post* in which he accused Senate Subcommittee on Oceans and Atmosphere Chairman Ernest Hollings (D., S.C.) of bowing to the special interest of furriers and riddling the bill with loopholes.[13]

Although Regenstein was enjoying his work, he was not entirely satisfied working for Ms. Herrington. As the first year wore on, he was becoming increasingly irritated at Ms. Herrington's unilateral decision making. Sensing that Regenstein was unhappy, Cleveland Amory decided to offer him a job working for the Fund. Amory says, "I never went to him before, only when I knew he was unhappy." Regenstein accepted Amory's offer, which not only gave him more money, but more important, it gave him greater independence. In April 1972, Regenstein opened the Washington office of the Fund for Animals.

Prior to leaving the Committee on Humane Legislation, Regenstein had acquired a valuable volunteer, Ms. Marian Newman. Ms. Newman, the wife of a young physician, had

[12] Although most conservationists consider the law a relatively good piece of legislation, Ms. Herrington thought it to be so weak that she never endorsed it.

[13] Lewis Regenstein, "A Last Chance for Ocean Mammals?" *Washington Post*, May 31, 1972, p. A16. Regenstein was working for the Fund by this time. He later updated the situation in a guest editorial for the *Washington Star-News*, "Deciding the Fate of Sea Animals," July 16, 1972, p. D-3. For Regenstein's later account of this battle, see his book, *The Politics of Extinction* (New York: Macmillan, 1975), pp. 50-117.

moved to Washington, shortly after the CHL opened, from Chapel Hill, North Carolina, where her husband had finished a residency. She had grown tired of her work as a speech pathologist, and before moving she wrote to Alice Herrington asking about volunteer work in the Washington area. Ms. Herrington passed her note on to Lew Regenstein, who wrote Ms. Newman back inviting her to work with him at the CHL.

When Regenstein left the CHL, he asked Amory if Ms. Newman could come with him to the Fund office. For Ms. Newman, the decision to leave the CHL was an easy one. The Fund offered her a small salary, and she preferred to remain with Regenstein rather than with Alice Herrington, who, despite the fact that Ms. Newman worked for free, had shown little appreciation of her work.

The Fund rented a floor (four rooms) of a renovated row house in Washington's Dupont Circle area. Two of the rooms serve as Regenstein's bachelor living quarters, and the other two constitute the Fund's Washington office. The Fund's office reflects their general lack of resources: the furniture is old, and there is little in the office of comfort or luxury. Posters and pictures of various animals give the otherwise drab office a bit of color. On one set of bookshelves, there are samples of "gourmet" food products made from endangered species, such as kangaroo tail soup, whale meat (barbecue and regular), and dog food made with whale meat. On another set of bookshelves, there is a small library of animal-related books and congressional hearings.

The unusual combination of locating his living quarters and his office together works out extremely well for Regenstein. By nature he is a "night owl," and he does much of his work for the Fund in the early hours of the morning. There has come to be little difference between his personal and his private life, as he works both day and night and often on the weekends, too. Although he sets his own schedule, working on animal protection is for Regenstein a matter of moving from one emergency to another. Like Amory, his work for the Fund is not a job or a vocation, but rather it is a passion. Regenstein said of his job:

> I once told someone what I wanted out of a job: I wanted to sleep as late as I want, work as late as I want, not have to commute, do something I love and get paid for it. My friend laughed, but this is it. I love it.

The Washington office of the Fund is characterized by both inefficiency and productivity. It is productive because of the long hours put in by Regenstein. In addition, Ms. Newman works for many more hours than her meager salary warrants.[14] Yet the extra hours put in by both must make up for a number of less efficient aspects of the office's operation.

A great deal of the day-in, day-out work is sending out information such as copies of Regenstein's articles or letters to public officials. The Fund office, however, does not own a Xerox machine, and many hours a week are spent going to and from the printer. A great deal of time is also wasted each week at the typewriter. Neither Regenstein nor Ms. Newman type very well, and on a number of occasions, as much as two labor hours have been spent retyping a letter until it was error-free. The priorities of the national office have dictated that funds are better spent elsewhere than on a Xerox machine or a part-time typist for the Washington office. The shoestring budget of the Washington office is typified by a remark made by Regenstein while ordering some stationery over the phone: "Hang the expense, let's go ahead and get $5 worth."

The lack of resources is also reflected in the office's information gathering, which tends to be haphazard at best. Regenstein scans and clips *The New York Times* and the *Washington Post* every morning. Much of the information collected comes by word of mouth, usually over the phone. The Washington office receives a few journals or magazines

[14] At the time Ms. Newman was working three to four days a week in the office with work at home as well.

in the environment and wildlife field. Neither Regenstein nor Ms. Newman have any real background in ecology or biology other than what they have learned on the job.

The relationship between the Washington office and the New York headquarters is a rather casual one, as the Washington office possesses a great deal of independence. Although there are nominal lines of authority with Amory in command, Regenstein is free, for all intents and purposes, to do what he wants. Although they communicate frequently, Regenstein does not clear his activities with Amory and is under no pressure to do so.[15] The independence afforded Regenstein is considered by Amory to be beneficial to the organization. He is fiercely proud of the people who work for him and prides himself on picking individuals whom he can trust to work independently of him. In Amory's words, "I don't know where [field director] Jim Hendrick is today, or what Lewis is doing, but I know whatever they're doing, I'll back them."

Both the people in New York and those in Washington consider their offices to be a sort of "antibureaucracy." Because the offices are tiny (six people in New York, two in Washington), they are provided with the luxury of informality and there is no need for organizational line charts. Both offices contrast themselves favorably with larger groups, such as the Audubon Society and the National Wildlife Federation, which they consider to be inefficient and ineffective. As one New York staffer put it, "We don't want an organization in which when you want something done you have to send intraoffice memorandums. We want people out doing things."

Ideally Regenstein and Ms. Newman work independently on different projects, but this is true only part of the time. Because of the crisis or emergency atmosphere of the office, Ms. Newman often helps Regenstein with the projects he

[15] There seems to be very little strain between the two offices. The one minor complaint I did hear from people in both offices was that their own work was not really appreciated by the other office.

has undertaken. Her role is not that of a secretary, however, although she does somewhat more of the "busy work," such as typing and running errands, than does Regenstein. There is a virtual lack of planning in the office. Decisions are made on a day-to-day basis in response to what Regenstein regards as emergencies that must be taken care of immediately. To understand better the decision making, planning, and general operation of the Fund's Washington office, it might be helpful to examine some of their specific projects and activities.

THE WOLVES IN MINNESOTA

During the period of mid-November to mid-December 1972, the Fund office was primarily concerned with the plight of the Eastern timber wolf. The last sizable group of timber wolves left in the continental United States is indigenous to the area in and around Minnesota's Superior National Forest.[16] There are no precise figures as to how many Eastern timber wolves are left in Minnesota, but government estimates are that between 500 to 1000 wolves remain. Some environmentalists claim that 500 is an optimistic figure and that there may be 300 or fewer wolves left in Minnesota.

The Eastern timber wolf (*Canis lupus lycaon*) appears on the Department of Interior's Endangered Species List. The Endangered Species Conservation Act of 1969 did not, however, prohibit the individual states from setting their own policies with regard to animal management and hunting.[17]

[16] Eastern timber wolves are also to be found in Canada. There are an estimated 20 to 30 timber wolves on Michigan's Isle Royale in Lake Superior.

[17] The Endangered Species Act of 1969 (Public Law 91-135) has since been superseded by the Endangered Species Act of 1973 (Public Law 93-205). The 1969 law was strongest in its application to animals of foreign countries. No furs or other by-products of an endangered species could be imported into the country. Although some states did follow the Interior Department's lead and prohibited hunting of federally listed endangered species, the law did not contain any legal

The State of Minnesota did not agree with the Interior Department's opinion of the wolf's status and did not move to protect the animal from hunters and trappers. Acting on its own in 1969, however, the U.S. Forest Service (Department of Agriculture) declared a moratorium on the killing of wolves in the federally supervised Superior National Forest. The Forest Service said that the moratorium would continue until the state came up with a management plan for the timber wolves.

The Minnesota Department of Natural Resources disputed the Forest Service's decision and questioned its legality. The state subsequently wrote to the Department of Interior recommending that the Eastern timber wolf be taken off the Endangered Species List. The State of Minnesota has traditionally considered the wolf to be a bothersome varmint, and until 1965, the state paid a bounty on wolves. Despite their disagreement with the Forest Service's decision, the state Department of Natural Resources acquiesced, and a research team headed by L. David Mech, an acknowledged wolf expert,[18] began work on a management plan, two years in the making, which was released in September 1972.

Lewis Regenstein first became actively interested in the problems of the timber wolves at about the same time as the Canadian government announced a plan to reduce the wolf population in Quebec province. Contrary to the dearth of wolves in the continental United States, Quebec wildlife officials felt that a surplus of the predators had caused the deer population to reach a dangerously low level. As an in-

---

sanctions to protect native animals. The 1973 law, however, is considerably stronger. It is now a federal crime to buy, sell, import, or export any endangered species or products made from them. The act provides a scale of fines for those who violate the regulations set forth by Interior to protect individual species. It also adds a new category, "threatened," to the endangered/plentiful classification. Rules may be set to control the hunting and trapping of threatened animals so that they will not be reduced to endangered status.

[18] See L. David Mech, *The Wolf* (Garden City, N.Y.: Natural History Press, 1970).

centive to hunters to go out and shoot a wolf, the Quebec Tourism, Fish and Game Department offered 50 wolf jaws set in acrylic and inscribed with the hunter's name. All one had to do to become eligible to win one of the jaws was to deliver a carcass of a wolf (or coyote) to a game warden. After this "hunting season" was completed, 600 steel traps would be spread over the heavily populated wolf areas to reduce the animal's numbers further.

Regenstein, outraged at the plan, decided to try to publicize it in the hope that like-minded conservationists would generate letters of protest to the Canadian authorities. Regenstein first wrote to Minister of Tourism, Game, and Fish Claude Simard and to the Prime Minister of Quebec, Robert Bourassa, telling them that the Fund was "shocked" to learn of the plans for a "massive wolf kill." He was then successful in getting the Canadian Press wire service and the UPI to pick up the story from their Washington bureau, which quoted Regenstein's letters extensively. The Quebec wildlife officials denied that the plan was of the scale charged by the various conservation groups,[19] and they refused to stop its implementation.[20]

Regenstein, now aware of the Minnesota management plan, decided that he would continue his work on behalf of the timber wolves. Wanting to do some writing on the subject, he twice tried to interest *The New York Times* in a piece on wolves, but he received no encouragement. He was, however, able to get an article accepted for publication in the magazine put out by Defenders of Wildlife, another conservation group. Although it was not his first choice, *De-*

---

[19] A more active effort was taken by the Canadian and American Wolf Defenders. The group, which is headed by Araby Colton of Carmel Valley, California, put out a special bulletin alerting members to the plan and told them to write to Minister Simard. To Regenstein's dismay, however, the bulletin was inaccurate in its claim that Quebec wanted to kill *all* the wolves in the selected area. They also said that 600 trucks full of traps would follow the hunt, when it was really 600 traps that would be dropped.

[20] Later, Quebec fish and game officials admitted that the hunt was a failure because not enough hunters were interested.

fenders of Wildlife News would enable him to reach an audience that was very much interested in endangered species. It was Regenstein's intent to stimulate letters to government officials who could act to save the threatened species. Because the article dealt with all the wolves of North America, Regenstein included the addresses of Minnesota Governor Wendell Anderson, Alaska Governor William Egan, Interior Secretary Rogers C. B. Morton, and Quebec Prime Minister Bourassa, with a plea to write to these men expressing concern.

Regenstein's article, written in late October, discussed the problems of both the Eastern timber wolf and the red wolf (*Canis rufus*), which is native to the southwestern United States.[21] His major point, aside from the wolves' endangerment, was that the wolf has been unfairly maligned as a useless and troublesome animal:

> It is difficult to understand why man has waged such a remorseless war on these unique and valuable creatures. Wolves play a vital role in maintaining nature's balance and in keeping herds of deer, elk, and moose at desirable population levels. By preying mainly on the very old and young, the sick, and the lame, they eliminate excess animals from the herd. This insures that the forage and food supply is not exhausted, which could result in the death of the entire herd. Wolves also help prevent large scale die-offs from starvation by keeping ungulates (hooved animals) on the move in winter; and by removing dis-

[21] The red wolf is also seriously threatened with extinction. These animals have been hunted relentlessly because they are suspected of being predators of livestock. Red wolves only rarely attack adult cattle or other livestock. Despite federal and state "control" programs, the species has been nearly wiped out. Between 1960 and 1963, a federal program was responsible for having 10,275 red wolves killed in Arkansas, Oklahoma, and Texas. The population has been reduced to an estimated 300 or less, and red wolves have began to mate with coyotes, producing a hybrid and threatening the species even further. See Steve Seater, "The Red Wolf at Bay," *Not Man Apart*, December 1972, p. 7 (publication of Friends of the Earth).

eased animals, wolves keep the herds healthy and prevent epidemics. Another important function is in removing the unwary and less-intelligent animals. By culling out these biologically inferior individuals, wolves are thought to be a significant factor in the evolution of a healthy ungulate population.[22]

Regenstein also covered, in brief, the highly evolved structure of wolf packs, which are characterized by rigorous "pecking" orders in terms of leadership and authority. The second half of the article contained summaries of the condition of wolves and their chances for survival in Minnesota, Alaska, the southwestern United States, and Canada.

Despite the fact that it was a well-written essay that was sure to provoke letters from incensed readers, it lacked the immediacy of a newspaper article—it wouldn't appear for more than a month. The more Regenstein thought about the problem, the more he was convinced that the situation demanded immediate action.

The "emergency" nature of the problem had been fueled by the issuance of the Minnesota management plan the month before. The management plan had been approved by Travis S. Roberts, Regional Director of the U.S. Interior Department's Bureau of Sport Fisheries and Wildlife, and by Harold E. Anderson, the U.S. Forest Service's Supervisor of the Superior National Forest. All that was needed to put the plan into effect was the passage of an enabling act by the Minnesota legislature, which would convene in early 1973. Given the state's antagonistic attitude toward the wolf in the past, it became clear to Regenstein that drastic measures were now necessary.

Because the taking of wolves was unregulated prior to the Forest Service's moratorium, the Minnesota management plan was an improvement over the previous situation in that it would control the hunting and trapping of wolves. What

[22] Lewis Regenstein, "A Last Chance for America's Wolves," *Defenders of Wildlife News*, November 1972, p. 477.

was most surprising about the proposed plan was its optimism concerning the wolf's continued survival. Although government estimates were that there could be as few as 500 wolves left, the plan would have permitted the taking of 150 to 200 a year. Part of the Superior National Forest would be set aside as an inviolable sanctuary where wolves could not be taken. Other parts of the national forest, however, would be opened up to hunters and trappers. In most parts of the area covered by the management plan, there would be a six-month open season on wolves, but in some regions the animal could be killed year-round.

During the Forest Service moratorium, the wolf population appeared to remain static. Thus it seemed problematic to Regenstein and many other conservationists that the wolf population could withstand a harvest of 150 to 200 a year. Regenstein felt strongly that there should be a complete moratorium on the taking of wolves throughout the state.[23]

Regenstein was hopeful that the Bureau of Sport Fisheries and Wildlife in Washington would come out against the plan. Although this would not have prevented the plan's implementation, it might have influenced the state Department of Natural Resources or the state legislature to make changes in the proposal. The immediate obstacle to Interior Department disapproval of the management plan was the fact that the regional Sport Fisheries and Wildlife office had already endorsed the plan. For the national Bureau to reject the plan would mean, in effect, publicly criticizing their regional office.

During the middle part of November, Regenstein made initial inquiries concerning the management plan to a sympathetic bureaucrat at the Bureau of Sport Fisheries and Wildlife. The official had not been aware of the specifics of the plan, but promised Regenstein that he would find out as much as possible. Later in the same week, he informed

[23] The one exception he was willing to make was for the live trapping of wolves in areas where they were allegedly harming livestock.

Regenstein that a decision on the management plan was pending. The following week, however, Regenstein learned that no decision would be immediately forthcoming.

Regenstein was extremely upset and concluded that the only recourse left was to, in his words, "blast 'em." This meant getting out a press release on the wolves in Minnesota with the intent of forcing the Interior Department to take a stand. Regenstein made this decision on the Monday before Thanksgiving, and he wrote the release and planned its distribution over the holiday weekend. On that same Monday, Regenstein leaked the story to Jack Anderson, who used it the next day on his radio show. Anderson told his audience:

> The last 500 of the Eastern timber wolves roam the Federal and state forest lands of Minnesota. These gaunt, grey beasts are gradually being killed off by hunters and trappers. Now, in the guise of establishing a sanctuary, Federal authorities have approved a plan which may let them be killed off at an even faster rate. Ironically, some officials fighting to save the wolves were kept in the dark about the new slaughter plan and only found out about it from the Fund for Animals.[24]

On Monday morning, November 27, the press release was printed up, and by that afternoon Marian Newman and a volunteer were hand delivering it.[25] The two Fund workers delivered about 40 of the releases to such places as the *Washington Post, The New York Times* Washington office, the AP and UPI wire services, and to important out-of-town newspapers with offices in the National Press Building. In addition to this, more than 300 press releases were mailed out to Interior Department officials; additional newspapers

[24] Transcript (mimeo), Jack Anderson radio broadcast, November 21, 1972.

[25] Whenever feasible, Regenstein has important letters, articles, and press releases hand delivered. The purpose of this is to draw attention to the delivered object that it might not otherwise receive.

across the country, including 25 Minnesota papers; other conservation groups; Fund regional offices; Minnesota Congresspersons; and to various other individuals Regenstein wanted to reach.

It took three days to get all the press releases delivered and mailed out. This was, in part, due to the need to type the more than 300 envelopes with the addresses as well as return addresses (because the Fund cannot afford printed envelopes) on the one working typewriter in the office. More important, there was no master mailing list, but rather Regenstein and his assistants had to make it up as they went along.

The release itself was rather blunt, and it directly attacked the Department of Interior, Assistant Secretary Nathaniel Reed of the Bureau of Sport Fisheries and Wildlife, and the Minnesota Department of Natural Resources. The text ran two pages, single-spaced, and a cover sheet contained a summary of the text. The first paragraph set the tone of the release:

> The Fund for Animals revealed today that the U.S. Department of Interior, the U.S. Forest Service, and the State of Minnesota had agreed on a plan to virtually destroy the last Eastern Timber Wolf population remaining in the United States. Unless this project can be defeated or amended and prompt protective measures adopted, these animals will be threatened with extinction.[26]

Regenstein went on to describe the plan, its implications, and the valuable role played by the wolf in the ecology of the forest. He stated that protests concerning the plan should be directed at Governor Anderson and Interior Secretary Morton. Unless the plan was rescinded, the release warned, "the day will not be far off when the last Eastern Timber Wolf, howling in loneliness, will lift its voice in the night, only to be answered by silence."

[26] News Release, the Fund for Animals, November 28, 1972, p. 1.

Because the Fund does not subscribe to a clipping service, it is impossible to know how many newspapers picked up the story on the Minnesota management plan. United Press International, however, did write a sympathetic story from the press release which was sent out across the country. One of the newspapers that used the UPI story was *The New York Times*, which ran it in the December 3 Sunday edition.[27] Despite two hand deliveries and a phone call from Regenstein, a *Washington Post* environmental reporter never wrote the story up.[28] Other papers that did run the story included the *Chicago Sun-Times* and the *Chicago Tribune*.

Four days after the release was issued, Regenstein received a call from a high Interior Department official who told him, off the record, that the plan did indeed need changing. He told Regenstein that the big problem inhibiting action on their part was a fear of straining relations with their regional office. He asked Regenstein's advice as to how Interior might proceed on the matter without appearing to be critical of their regional office. Over the weekend, Regenstein wrote a carefully composed letter in which he suggested that the best course of action for Interior to take would be to call for a moratorium on the taking of wolves while at the same time praising the good parts of the plan

[27] "Plan to Preserve Wolves Termed Danger to Them," *The New York Times*, December 3, 1972, p. 108. Little over a year later, however, *The Times* would publish a piece on its Op-Ed page by Dick Maw, a writer on ecology and wildlife from Minnesota, that claimed that the number of wolves in the Superior National Forest was "grossly" underestimated. Maw argued that the resident wolves were decimating the deer herd, and professional trappers, therefore, should be allowed to take a percentage of wolves each year. "Taking Stock of Wolves," *The New York Times*, December 10, 1973, p. 37.

[28] Two weeks after the Department of Interior had announced that it was not in favor of the plan, another *Post* reporter, C. Boyd Pfeiffer, the outdoors columnist on the sports page, wrote a column on the timber wolves that was highly critical of the state plan. The article was based on the press release and a telephone conversation with Regenstein. "Plan to 'Help' Could Wipe Out Minnesota Wolves," *Washington Post*, December 19, 1972, p. D8.

(e.g., the sanctuary). Furthermore, Regenstein reasoned that if Interior came out against the plan, the focus of attention would then shift to the Minnesota Department of Natural Resources.

On the following Tuesday, Regenstein received a call from Deputy Secretary of Interior E. U. "Buff" Bohlen, who told him that Interior had decided to come out against the plan. The official Interior Department position would read:

> We believe that the best course of action is a moratorium on the taking of all wolves, with the possible exception of those preying on livestock until a nationwide recovery plan is implemented.

A week later, Interior affirmed this position in a press release. Regenstein was obviously pleased with Interior's action, but he believed it to be only a small victory, because it appeared at the time that the ultimate decision on the plan was still to be made by the State of Minnesota.[29]

It would be inaccurate to draw a simple cause-and-effect relationship between the Fund's activities and the Interior Department's decision not to back the Minnesota management plan. It may very well be that Interior would have made the same decision had the Fund not shown an interest in the wolves. Without overstating its influence, however, two things can be said on behalf of the Fund's actions. First, the Fund must receive some credit for getting Interior to act as "fast" as it did in rejecting the plan. Second, the bad publicity generated toward Interior became an additional factor that had to be included in the final evaluation

[29] Additional authority to protect the wolves was given to the Interior Department by the passage of the Endangered Species Act of 1973. See *supra*, note 17. In mid-1974 the Department of Interior announced that the Minnesota timber wolves were now completely protected by the federal government because they were listed in the Convention on Nature Protection and Wildlife Preservation in the Western Hemisphere. See Regenstein, *The Politics of Extinction*, p. 178.

of the plan by that Department. Interestingly, the Fund's views were never solicited until after it publicly criticized the Interior Department.

Additional Activities. Although the work to save the wolves in Minnesota was the most extensive Fund project during the period of observation, a number of other activities undertaken by the office are also of interest. One such effort also involved wolves. In mid-November, Ms. Newman was informed that a fashion show benefit for the Cancer Research Pulmonary Disease Division of Washington's Georgetown University Hospital would include furs made from wolf pelts. Ms. Newman had a great deal of trouble getting anybody with authority over the affair either to confirm or deny this. Finally, on November 27, the day of the event, Ms. Newman was told by one of the organizers that no wolf fur coats would be modeled in the show.

Despite the denial, however, a wolf coat was modeled in the show. *Washington Post* society reporter Nina Hyde, who had previously been contacted by the Fund office, ridiculed the show in the next morning's paper. Her article, "Redskins in Wolf's Clothing" (some of the coats were modeled by Washington Redskin football players), criticized the show both for its insensitivity to endangered species and for the general incompetence of the organizers. Ms. Newman was quoted in the article as alleging that the Fund had been deceived by the organizers.[30]

Although discrediting one fashion show is, in and of itself, of minor importance, the above example is illustrative of an ongoing effort by the Fund to reeducate women in their attitude toward fur coats. Quite simply, the Fund for Animals is trying to make people realize that a fur coat is made from animals that were killed expressly for their fur. In terms of wild animals, trapping not only endangers many

[30] Nina Hyde, "Redskins in Wolf's Clothing," *Washington Post,* November 28, 1972, p. B3.

species but is immoral because of the pain and suffering that is inflicted upon the animals.[31] Officially, the Fund neither condones nor opposes the raising of fur-bearing animals in captivity for commercial purposes, although privately the staff members are against this also.

Probably the most successful effort by the Fund in their attempt to change American culture with regard to fur coats was a two-page advertisement against the use of animal fur for women's coats. One page was a full-color picture of five TV and movie stars (all of whom were Fund National Board members) wearing fake fur coats and the other page had statements from the stars as to why they could not, in good conscience, wear real fur.[32] The ad contained both a plug for the sponsor, the E. F. Timme Company, a manufacturer of fake fur, and a solicitation for the Fund for Animals. The ad ran in *The New York Times, Esquire, Newsweek, Look, McCall's,* and *New York.*[33]

Attacking the fur industry is a continuing interest of Regenstein's. He has written a number of articles on the subject, and he willingly gives his time and information to other environmentalists who are working in the area. He is particularly concerned about exposing the Foundation for Environmental Education, which is ostensibly a conservation organization, but was set up and continues to be supported financially by the fur industry.[34] Because of declining sales, furriers, suspecting that bad publicity from conservationists was partly responsible for the slump, set the organi-

[31] Most animals in the United States are trapped with steel leg traps, which crush the animal's leg in a vise-like grip. Some animals will twist off or chew the remains of their leg. Because the traps cannot be selective, many animals of no use to the fur trapper will be caught in the traps and die for no reason. See Amory, *Man Kind?*, pp. 198ff.

[32] The Fund stars are Mary Tyler Moore, Amanda Blake, Doris Day, Jayne Meadows, and Angie Dickinson.

[33] The ad, however, was rejected by the *New Yorker, Harper's Bazaar,* and *Vogue.* Regenstein suspects that it was rejected by these magazines because they all carry a lot of fur advertisements.

[34] See Lewis Regenstein, "Fur Industry Fights Back," *Not Man Apart,* December 1972, p. 9.

zation up to tell their side of the environmental story with regard to fur-bearing animals.

Regenstein also spent a couple of days in early December trying to generate interest in the case of Fred Zeehandelaar, a New York importer of wild animals, who was indicted for violating the Endangered Species Act of 1969.[35] Zeehandelaar was accused of falsely dating a check to indicate that he had placed an order for 20 live cheetahs before the spotted cats had been placed on the Endangered Species List. Regenstein wrote to the U.S. Attorney for the Southern District of New York and to the prosecuting attorney expressing his interest in the case.

Regenstein said in his letter that if Zeehandelaar was convicted, it was important to punish him to the full extent of the law so as to deter future potential violators. He also sent a letter and materials on the matter to about 40 other conservationists asking them to take an interest and to write to the U.S. Attorney in New York. Otherwise, Regenstein warned in his form letter, Zeehandelaar, if convicted, "could get off with a light fine and/or suspended sentence, as has happened to alligator poachers. . . ." Zeehandelaar was later convicted and given three months in jail and fined $5000.[36]

Ms. Newman continued working on the problems of kangaroos and wallabies, on which she had concentrated since she started working at the Committee for Humane Legislation. The kangaroo and wallaby populations have declined rapidly, and some species have become extinct. Ms. Newman's major objective was to get various kangaroo species placed on the Endangered Species List, which would have eliminated the lucrative American market for kangaroo pelts. The Interior Department had taken Ms. Newman's materials and information under consideration, but they had not yet moved to place the animals on the list.

At somewhat of an impasse during the late fall, Ms. New-

[35] "Importer Indicted as Cheetah Cheater," *The New York Times*, December 7, 1972, p. 57.
[36] *Conservation News*, December 15, 1973, p. 14.

man had decided to try to get the state of New York to place the kangaroo on its own Endangered Species List, because most of the imported pelts go to furriers in New York City. She had also decided to prepare a mailing, urging protective action, to newly elected Australian Members of Parliament after the parliamentary election in late November. For the most part, the kangaroos had to take a back seat during November and December, as Ms. Newman spent most of her time helping Regenstein with other projects, particularly the wolf press release. Six months later, though, Ms. Newman's dedication and perseverance finally paid off as the Department of the Interior placed nine Australian marsupials on the Endangered Species List. She even received a personal tribute to her tireless work on behalf of kangaroos and wallabies when Secretary of the Interior Rogers C. B. Morton said in his statement announcing the decision that "A great deal of credit for the increased interest in kangaroos is due to the efforts of Mrs. Marian Newman who works for the Fund for Animals."[37]

THE FUND AS AN INTEREST GROUP

The Fund for Animals is an organization that does not have a great deal of visibility. Although those knowledgeable in wildlife matters are aware of the group, the Fund does not have the reputation of well-established environmental organizations such as the Sierra Club or the National Wildlife Federation. And although lack of resources is a characteristic problem of public interest groups, the Fund's Washington office, with one full-time and one part-time employee, is more limited than most. Consequently, for these and other reasons, the Fund's office in Washington is often dependent on the press in its attempts to influence government.

Regenstein and Ms. Newman simply do not see themselves as having the necessary influence to lobby administra-

---

[37] News Release, Fish and Wildlife Service, Department of the Interior, June 1, 1973, p. 2.

tors or others without using the press as a means of "pressure." In their relations with the Department of Interior, for example, it is their feeling that all they would get from exclusive direct lobbying is a lot of rhetoric from insincere bureaucrats. Both Fund workers are terribly cynical about the willingness of Interior Department officials to make decisions favorable to animals that are in any sense controversial.

Regenstein is far more comfortable in the role of a writer and publicist than as an administrative or congressional lobbyist. He spends a great deal of his time writing, submitting, and distributing his articles. Regenstein's favorite outlets for his written work are *The New York Times* and the *Washington Post*. The two newspapers have not always been receptive to his overtures, particularly *The Times*, which has rejected four or five of his submissions to the Sunday *Magazine* or the Op-Ed page. He has had more luck with the *Post*, which has published a number of his articles on subjects such as spotted cats, wild horses, mountain lions, and ocean mammals. Both he and Ms. Newman have also written on occasion for Washington's evening newspaper, the *Star-News*.

In addition to newspapers, Regenstein publishes in environmental magazines such as *Not Man Apart, Defenders of Wildlife News, Environmental Quality Magazine*, and *Environmental Action*. Both his magazine and newspaper articles tend to be short, untechnical, and polemical. He is always careful to identify "villains" by name, and often he openly encourages his readers to write to officials concerning a particular policy. Ms. Newman, who has written a few articles on her specialty, kangaroos and wallabies, reflects the same general style in her work.

In sum, there is a threefold purpose in the Fund's articles, news releases, and otherwise inspired news stories. The first reason is, of course, to draw attention to the existing problem. The second purpose is to encourage the readers to write to the relevant policy makers expressing a strong conservationist viewpoint. Third, the Fund tries to put governmental officials "on the spot" to a point of embarrassment by revealing their seemingly antianimal position.

What "power" or "pressure" the Fund is able to bring to bear is thus due largely to their ability to portray policy makers in a negative light in the printed media. Sometimes, as in the case of the Eastern timber wolves, the press is used to try to influence an upcoming decision. At other times the Washington office makes the effort for the purpose of preventing a recurrence of something they find outrageous. Such was the case when they distributed a press release (subsequently picked up by Jack Anderson) exposing former Secretary of Commerce Maurice Stans for his effort to obtain special permits for a friend to hunt endangered spotted cats.

Optimally, the Fund would like their use of press exposure to be potentially threatening enough to cause greater concern for conservationist viewpoints in governmental decision making. Yet the Fund office still has a great deal of trouble in getting their view into print in what they consider to be the right places. Endangered cheetahs or blue whales are not subjects that newspapers and nonenvironmental magazines will always deem important enough to cover. As in the case of the Eastern timber wolf, the *Washington Post*, considered vitally important by the Washington office for any publicity campaign, did not publish an article on the subject until after the Interior Department had changed its position.

Although Regenstein would undoubtedly like to have greater influence in Interior Department policy making, he has serious reservations about developing the type of warm working relationship that might seemingly facilitate this. He feels that overly friendly relations could lead to a "cooptation" of the Fund that would reduce its ability to act without compromise.[38] Rather, Regenstein sees the role of

---

[38] Philip Selznick defines "cooptation" as "*the process of absorbing new elements into the leadership or policy-determining structure of an organization as a means of averting threats to its stability or*

the Fund as more of an adversary than as a cooperating "client." It is important to Regenstein that people in the Interior Department know that he will criticize them without regard to personal friendship. Regenstein expressed his philosophy in the following terms:

> It does no good to cultivate them because they'll tell you, "Lew, we agree with you, but if we do anything more than we are we'll get [Assistant Secretary of Interior] Nat Reed fired. The sheep ranchers are pressing us, there's nothing we can do." Now you've got to get them so they say to the sheep ranchers, "We've got to do this because the conservationists are pressing us."

After the Interior Department had rejected the Minnesota management plan, Regenstein received a very conciliatory letter from a high Interior Department official. The Interior bureaucrat told Regenstein that from now on he wanted the Fund to have more "input" in Interior policy making and that Regenstein should call him personally anytime the Fund wanted to express an opinion on a matter. Although he admitted that "it was a nice gesture," Regenstein was unimpressed. He wrote a strong reply to the Interior official questioning certain stands the man had taken in the past:

> Even if you feel—out of political necessity—that there should be a potential loophole for trophy hunters in the new endangered species act, it is disappointing to see someone who should know better give such a vigorous blanket defense to the concept of hunting threatened animals. . . . I am particularly distressed when I see you stray from your usually sensible statements and speak nonsense.

Regenstein was, in effect, serving notice that any rapprochement between the two would not lessen the Fund's zeal in criticizing Interior for not effectively protecting animals.

Neither Amory nor Regenstein see increasing the administrative or congressional lobbying capabilities of the Washington office as a Fund priority. When asked what he would do with a hypothetical million-dollar foundation grant, Regenstein replied that he would spend it on a nationwide advertising campaign. "I'd pick three endangered species: the whales, the dolphins, and the wolves, and concentrate on them." When asked if he would spend at least some of the money on enlarging his staff, hiring a lawyer, for example, he said, "No, I'd put that far down the list. Maybe I'd get one person who could type and take shorthand."

Amory feels that any increase in funding should be used on programs outside of the United States. "Basically the animal work abroad is more abundant. I know they're still throwing cats off the roof here in New York and they're still skinning raccoons in Alabama, but there is much more to do worldwide." He later mused, "Take Africa, what a job that's going to be . . . and Mexico, I'll sleep a lot better when I know we have a formidable program going there." For Amory, to do anything less than attack the animal problem on every level and in every part of the world would be to shirk the Fund's duty.

CHAPTER VI

"Fighting the Fights That Others Don't"—The Women's International League for Peace and Freedom

IF it is the conventional wisdom that political interest groups become more conservative as they grow older, the Women's International League for Peace and Freedom is an exception to the "rule."[1] The hopes, objectives, and philosophy of the organization are just as radical as they were when pacifist Jane Addams helped to found the WILPF more than 50 years ago. From World War I through the Vietnam War, the group has worked against what they regard as the immorality and insanity of human warfare.

The Women's International League has been trying to stop war since 1915, when more than 1000 women from 12 countries met at The Hague to devise strategies to bring World War I to an end. The assembled women vowed to work beyond the current conflict for a Society of Nations and for universal disarmament. Jane Addams, leader of the U.S. delegation to the conference, became the organization's first president. A U.S. Section of the League was soon established, and a few years later an auxiliary legislative office was opened in Washington, D.C. The WILPF opened the office because they thought it was important that there be a "peace lobby" in the nation's capital. Dorothy Detzer, WILPF lobbyist from 1925 to 1945, noted in her memoirs the struggle that lay ahead for the group:

> the realization of this good society would surely be postponed as long as men's genius and energy and wealth were centered primarily on the pursuits of war. Man had

[1] See Theodore J. Lowi, *The Politics of Disorder* (New York: Basic Books, 1971).

to lose his life in peace in order to find it. Peace would not be handed to him like sweets on a platter; peace had to be won.[2]

THE ANTIWARS LOBBY

The WILPF remains today as an international organization with sections in 20 different countries and a headquarters in Geneva. In the United States, the WILPF Section has about 10,000 members and 155 local chapters. Despite its name, the organization is now open to both sexes, and there are approximately 1500 male members in the United States. The U.S. Section has its main office in Philadelphia, where 10 full-time employees and a half-dozen volunteers and part-time staff direct the national organization.

Dorothy Steffens, Executive Director of the WILPF, says that of the 155 chapters, "Only about half are active. The rest just hold meetings on occasion. Some even have trouble getting a chairperson."[3] Ms. Steffens stresses, however, that the emphasis in the WILPF is on local activism. "It's easy to get caught up in the Washington syndrome. It's not going to happen there. It'll happen because of pressure in the local communities. Washington is the last place to react. It's counterproductive to place all your energies there."

Ms. Steffens, now in her 50s and a long-time member of WILPF, was living in England with her husband when the National Board asked her to become executive director. The

[2] Dorothy Detzer, *Appointment on the Hill* (New York: Henry Holt, 1948).

[3] The local chapter in Washington holds regular meetings, but otherwise it is relatively inactive. The chapter is composed mostly of middle-aged white women who are bent more toward discussion than activism. One of the workers in the legislative office said of them regretfully, "In between meetings they hold board meetings to discuss what went on at the last meeting. When the Vietnam Veterans Against the War came to town to demonstrate they made sandwiches for them." The legislative office is currently setting up another local chapter, which they hope will take a much more activist approach to national and local D.C. policy matters.

position had become vacant becasue of the ill health of Glenna Johnson. After some hesitation, Ms. Steffens and her husband, a university professor, decided that, because of the critical nature of the times, it was important for her to take the position. At some sacrifice, the couple moved to Philadelphia, and Ms. Steffens took over WILPF's helm in July 1971.

In looking back over the past decade, Ms. Steffens feels that the organization has changed considerably. Of particular importance is the increasing work being done on the local level. "We've come out of a quiet period. . . . We got busy in the local communities; we stopped pushing paper around." Despite the WILPF's traditional image—it has been investigated in the past for "subversive" activities by the FBI and by the old House Un-American Activities Committee[4]—Ms. Steffens believes that the WILPF has become even more radical in the past few years. "We've supported the Black Panthers. We were very strong in our support of Angela Davis. We're now backing the American Indian Movement."

One unwelcome change that has accompanied Ms. Steffens' tenure is increasing financial instability. During the 1971-1972 fiscal year (September-September), the WILPF was forced to cut its expenditures back to $172,000. This is roughly $50,000 less than the budget of two years earlier. Twenty percent of the WILPF budget is allocated to the legislative office in Washington. Much of the financial cutback was achieved by reducing the number of staff positions in the Philadelphia office. Even the Executive Director's salary of $10,500 was cut. Indicative of the poor financial situation is that Ms. Steffens must sometimes pay her own train fare when she travels to Washington on WILPF business.

The basic WILPF dues are $10 ($5 for students) and $15 for a married couple. This accounts, however, for only

[4] It was later called the Internal Security Committee and has since been abolished altogether.

42% of the WILPF's income. The rest of their money must be raised primarily from additional contributions from the membership, and Ms. Steffens finds that she must now spend 25% of her time on fund raising.[5] The individual chapters do not pay any dues to the national organization.

The League's international office in Geneva is in similar financial straits, because its major source of income is contributions from the U.S. Section. The U.S. Section, despite its own financial problems and the weakness of most other national sections, feels that it is important to maintain the international nature of the organization. Indeed, the U.S. Section strives to keep in contact with similar women's groups in other countries outside of the WILPF structure. They have very warm relations with the East Berlin-based Women's International Democratic Federation, which has a membership in the millions. Ms. Steffens calls it the "Communist counterpart to WILPF." They also keep in contact with the Soviet Women's Committee, and during the war they were in touch with the Women's Union of North Vietnam.

The legislative office of the WILPF operates out of a basement at 120 Maryland Avenue, NE, in Washington. If nothing else, the office is close to power: it is across the street from the Supreme Court and less than a half block from the grounds of the Capitol. The office itself is a mélange of political posters; yellow, blue, green, and orange file cabinets; old wooden desks; and memorable "Doonesbury" comic strips Scotch-taped for posterity to countless locations. Guarding the entrance to the office is a black wood coffin filled with the names of Vietnam War dead on individual file cards, which was used in an antiwar march some years ago.

The successor to such notable WILPF lobbyists as Doro-

---

[5] Contributions above and beyond the payment of dues constitute 39% of the WILPF's income. The remainder of their money comes from a number of other sources, such as from the sale of educational materials and the sale of WILPF trinkets.

thy Detzer and Annalee Stewart[6] is Roselie Riechman. A shy, soft-spoken woman of 28, Ms. Riechman hardly fits the stereotype of the tough, smooth-talking Capitol Hill lobbyist. Her background is in social work. After graduating from Temple University in English Literature, she worked for VISTA before coming to Washington, where she did community work for an agency in Southeast Washington. Ms. Riechman applied for the job at the legislative office in early 1971 when she saw it advertised in a small community newspaper, the *D.C. Gazette.*

There are two other WILPF employees who work in the Washington office. Bill Samuel, now in his mid-20s, came to work in the office in 1969 as a summer intern after graduating from Wilmington College in Ohio. His older sister, Pat, worked in the legislative office, but left to work for the Philadelphia headquarters in November 1970. The younger Samuel, who left graduate school after a semester and returned to the WILPF as a secretary, was then promoted to "legislative associate." Samuel, a Quaker, is deeply committed to his ideals, and he returned his draft card to the Selective Service after receiving a medical deferment. His primary job is doing research and writing for the office's *Legislative Bulletin* and for *Peace and Freedom,* the monthly newsletter of the national organization. He is also active as coordinator for the Washington War Tax Reistance, which advocates the withholding of portions of personal income tax and telephone excise tax payments as a form of protest against military spending. His "organization"—a small group of activists who meet occasionally—is nominally affiliated with the national War Tax Resistance based in Kansas City.

Martha "Marti" Powers left Illinois College in her sophomore year and moved to Washington to find work. She bounced around from job to job—nine in all—in 1970 before she was hired to do clerical work for the legislative office

[6] The Rev. Dr. Stewart served as the president of the U.S. Section from 1946 to 1950. From 1950 to 1970, she served with some prominence as a lobbyist for the WILPF.

in January 1971. Ms. Powers still performs the duties of "office manager" and does more clerical work than the other two, but she now has additional responsibilities for working on special projects and writing for the *Legislative Bulletin*.

None of the three is formally in charge of the day-to-day workings of the office. Rather, there seems to be a conscious effort by all three to maintain an atmosphere of equality and independence. The office is not, however, characterized entirely by informality. Although there are only three people on the staff, a prearranged staff meeting is held each week. At the meetings, the three discuss what they have been working on, what they will be working on, settle questions of office routine, and air any personal grievances they may have. One person takes notes at the meetings, later writes them up in the form of minutes, gives the minutes to the other two for comments and corrections, types up the edited version, sends one copy to the Philadelphia office, and places one copy in the permanent files. Ms. Riechman says of the meetings, "You'd think because there are only three of us here, we wouldn't need them, but we find that one person would tell something to one of us and forget to tell the third. This way we make sure that this doesn't happen."

A major responsibility of the office is putting out the *Legislative Bulletin*, which, when the Congress is in session, comes out on a monthly basis. The *Bulletin* is mailed to about 500 people, including chapter leaders, National Board members, and other WILPF activists. It is edited with the hope that local leaders will pass on the information to the rank-and-file on the issues of interest to the individual chapter. The *Bulletin* is typed onto stencils by Samuel and Ms. Powers and sent by first-class mail after it is mimeographed on a decrepit, but still functioning machine.

The *Bulletin* averages between 8 and 10 single-spaced pages and deals with specific pieces of legislation before the Congress. Because WILPF members are interested in such a diverse number of policy areas, the legislative office feels obligated to cover as many issues as possible. It not only reviews "peace" issues such as military spending and nuclear disarmament, but it also includes domestic subjects, such as welfare reform and civil liberties legislation. Each edition contains a dozen or so articles and, at the end of each piece, there is an "Action" paragraph that instructs WILPF members about what to do if they would like to try to influence the particular policy outcome. Usually this takes the form of urging WILPF members to write their own Congresspersons in support of, or against, specific pieces of legislation. Because Samuel has the primary responsibility for doing the research for the *Bulletin*, he spends more than an hour each day reading and clipping the *Washington Post*. He also spends time each day looking through the newsletters of other liberal groups that come into the WILPF office. In addition, he makes limited use of official government documents and congressional hearings.

Formal policy for the organization is set by the WILPF's National Board. The Board is made up of 35 to 40 WILPF members, most of whom are elected on a geographic basis. Meetings are held three times a year and are scheduled in various parts of the country to enable different local chapter members to meet with the national officers and to participate in those business sessions that are open to them. One of the three annual meetings serves as a national convention, and all WILPF members are invited to participate, because there is no delegate structure.[7]

The WILPF positions on important political issues are debated thoroughly at the National Board meetings, and long hours are taken to facilitate a fair hearing of all points of view. Despite the detailed discussions that go on, the policy resolutions are purposely broad so that they represent as wide a consensus as possible. Directives to the Wash-

[7] The WILPF is planning to cut back regular board meetings to one every other year. In alternate years, the board will meet at the biennial convention. The new emphasis in the WILPF is on regional meetings of local chapter personnel.

ington office instructing it to work on particular pieces of legislation are infrequent. Rather, it is left to Ms. Riechman and her associates to interpret the organization's priorities and to develop related legislative strategy.

As with any public interest lobbyist, the issues Ms. Riechman "should" be working on far exceed her time and resources. Even within the limits of issues she considers to be WILPF priorities, there are countless bills, demonstrations, and coalitions to which she could devote her time. For Ms. Riechman, the problem of defining what a peace lobbyist should be is one with which she has continued to struggle since she first took the job. A basic conflict is choosing among working on legislation, working on demonstrations, and working on getting information out to WILPF members. She knows that as a lobbyist her primary job should be distributing information to congressional offices. However, much of the legislation for which the WILPF works— such as converting military spending to domestic purposes —has little chance of quick enactment and can be rationalized only on the grounds that efforts now may help to effect a gradual change in "climate" that will eventually lead to policy changes. Consequently, there is a great deal of temptation for her to work on activating people at the grass roots, or on arranging nonviolent political demonstrations that may bring more attention to the WILPF's point of view than more conventional forms of lobbying.

The decision as to how she should allocate her time is complicated by the role she thinks she must play in the coalitions that arise to work on specific issues. Generally, it is the feeling of those in the peace movement that what strength they have comes from their numbers. In addition, staffs are too small and financial resources too limited for most groups to be able to arrange a demonstration or major lobbying effort without the assistance of similarly committed groups. Some of these coalitions, such as the Coalition on National Priorities and Military Policy, are formal, ongoing organizations. Most coalitions, however, are *ad hoc* working arrangements for a particular project.

Ms. Riechman feels strongly that the Women's International League can accomplish little on its own and that it is important for her to cooperate in both permanent and *ad hoc* coalitions. She believes that coalitions are both an efficient means of obtaining information and a good place to work out ideas and political strategies. During 1973 the WILPF held membership in both the Coalition on National Priorities and Military Policy and the Coalition to Stop Funding the War, and Ms. Riechman attended biweekly meetings of both. She also feels obligated to work in *ad hoc* coalitions when other groups ask the WILPF to participate.

Her work in coalitions is terribly time consuming, and occasionally her sense of duty to participate goes against her better judgment. For example, during the week of February 26, 1973 (the beginning of a five-week period of observation), she received a request from another peace organization to aid them in a demonstration protesting the Thieu regime's treatment of political prisoners in South Vietnam. Despite some misgivings about the competence of the organizers, Ms. Riechman immediately agreed, because she thought the issue to be an important one.

Ms. Riechman spent a good part of the week trying to get members of Congress to speak before the demonstrators, who were scheduled to march to the Capitol on March 2. The WILPF office also made arrangements with the Capitol police for a demonstration site on the west steps of the Capitol. On the day of the rally, Ms. Riechman was startled to find only 30 protesters at the Capitol—her coalition partners had told her there would be 500 people. The leaders of the demonstration forgot which side of the Capitol Ms. Riechman had told them they had permission to use, and they assembled on the east side instead of the west side. Congressman John Conyers (D., Mich.), who WILPF had arranged to be the primary speaker at the demonstration, proceeded to the west steps, found nothing, and returned to the House floor.[8] Later, Ms. Riechman lamented, "The

[8] Fortunately, another Representative, Bertram Podell (D., N.Y.), was able to find the marchers and to give a short speech on the issue.

worst thing about it, aside from the fact that we spent so much time working on this, is that we used our name. We told congressional offices that we were helping to sponsor this."

Ms. Riechman wishes that there was more direct communication between rank-and-file WILPF members and the legislative office. It would better enable her to gauge the priorities of the members. More important, though, she feels that it would help her if she knew which Congresspersons the members were writing to.[9] She does not like to contact offices of congressional districts that do not contain a WILPF chapter. It is Ms. Riechman's opinion that she can be most effective when she is acting on behalf of WILPF members who have already written to their Congresspersons. In her words, "It's not the lobbyists who move the Congressmen, it's the constituents."[10]

In her first two years at WILPF, Ms. Riechman concentrated on the Vietnam War and related issues. She was very active in helping to organize the Ring-Around-the-Congress protest that took place on June 22, 1972. The leader of the protest was folksinger Joan Baez. Her notoriety helped to draw attention to the demonstration, but it was a group of Washington-based activists, including Ms. Riechman, who did most of the organizing and legwork for the protest. The

[9] In the *Legislative Bulletin* and at National Board meetings, she has urged members to send her a carbon copy of any letter they send to their representatives in Congress. To her frustration, however, she receives carbons of only a fraction of those letters sent by WILPF members.

[10] To try to improve her access to congressional offices, Ms. Riechman sent out a questionnaire to WILPF chapter heads in which she asked them if there was anyone in the local chapter who personally knew their Representative or Senator. Her objective was to build up a directory of names of members who could help her in working with different offices. Less than a quarter of the chapters responded to the questionnaire. Ms. Riechman's vocational perspective, which leads her to the conclusion that constituency influence is much more important than lobbying influence, is supported by recent research on Congress. See John W. Kingdon, *Congressmen's Voting Decisions* (New York: Harper & Row, 1973).

Ring-Around-the-Congress was designed to bring thousands of demonstrators to Washington who would march to the Capitol grounds and form a symbolic ring of citizens surrounding the Capitol itself. Unfortunately for the organizers, the demonstration fell during a week of torrential rains from Hurricane Agnes, and this surely decreased attendance, which was limited to about 2000 people.

One of her major concerns with the war in Vietnam was the issue of political prisoners. Ms. Riechman worked particularly hard in the case of Madame Ngo Ba Thanh, who was jailed in September 1971 after she participated in a demonstration protesting the presidential election in which Nguyen Van Thieu was the only candidate.[11] Mme. Thanh is a graduate of Columbia University Law School, a member of the WILPF, and until her jailing was the leader of the peace-oriented Vietnamese Women's Movement for the Right to Live.

Mme. Thanh did not receive proper medical treatment while in jail and became so ill that she had to be carried on a stretcher to her trial on March 22, 1972. During the trial, Mme. Thanh had an asthmatic attack, and her heart momentarily stopped beating. An article describing all this was carried in the following day's *New York Times*.[12] After reading the account and fearing for Mme. Thanh's life, Ms. Riechman, Ms. Steffens, and Bea Milwe, a WILPF activist from Connecticut, decided to go to the South Vietnamese Embassy to inquire about Mme. Thanh. Ms. Riechman was extremely upset over Mme. Thanh's condition, and she was determined not to leave the Embassy until the South Vietnamese provided information about her. Ms. Riechman recalls the visit to the Embassy:

[11] Mme. Thanh was charged with engaging in "activities harmful to the national security," organizing an "illegal organization," and passing out printed matter that "undermines the anticommunist potential of the people." "Women Arrested for Mme. Thanh," *Peace and Freedom*, May 1972, p. 1.

[12] "Trial of Ailing Critic of Saigon Put Off Indefinitely," *The New York Times*, March 23, 1972, p. 2.

I had read the story in the *Times* and I decided the night before that if it came to that, and if there was press there, I would allow myself to be arrested. . . . When we went to the Embassy the next day there were a number of us but they would only let three of us in. They wouldn't give us any definite information so I suggested to Dorothy and Bea that we stay. And we did. This man kept trying to talk us out of staying. During all this another man kept coming in and whispering into the man's ear. We thought they were going to take us away any minute. We knew, however, that they wanted us to leave voluntarily because there was press outside and it would be embarrassing to them if we were arrested. When the police did come, they were really nice; I mean, they were opening doors for us. I guess it was because we all looked so middle class. Well, I was wearing slacks, but Dorothy and Bea, two middle-aged women, were all dressed up. Then, when we got to the police station, seven or eight of my friends called because I was supposed to be someplace else. When I got these calls, they escorted me to the phone. How many people do you know of that get to answer the phone when they're in jail?

Despite all this, the confrontation and arrest at the Embassy received no major press coverage. "It didn't even make the *Post*," complained Ms. Riechman. Both she and Ms. Steffens, however, believe that the efforts of the WILPF, along with the little press coverage that her case did receive, were instrumental in keeping the South Vietnamese woman alive. WILPF members across the country wrote countless letters to the South Vietnamese Embassy, to their Senators and Representatives, and to the State Department, concerning Mme. Thanh. Because of the attention drawn to Mme. Thanh's case, it would have been very bad publicity for the Saigon government if she had died, and she did obtain a minimum of medical attention after her trial. Mme. Thanh remained in prison at an undisclosed location until August 1973, when former President Thieu finally ordered her release.[13]

CONGRESS AND THE TWO FRENCHMEN

Another WILPF activity involved two French schoolteachers, Jean-Pierre Debris and Andre Menras, who, when they found themselves facing the draft, chose the French government's alternative *La Cooperation* educational exchange program. The two were assigned to South Vietnam and they went to Danang, where they worked for two years. Debris taught mathematics at a high school, and Menras was an instructor at a primary school.

The two men claim that when they left France they had no preconceived notions about the South Vietnamese government. Their first-hand observations of the government headed by President Nguyen Van Thieu led them quickly to abandon their apolitical attitudes. They found the Thieu regime to be unbelievably tyrannical and corrupt, but despite their growing outrage, they kept silent for two years. Finally their consciences dictated that they must speak out against what they had been seeing. On July 25, 1970, the two Frenchmen climbed up the monument adjacent to the National Assembly building in Saigon and unfurled a Viet Cong flag. They also handed out leaflets, printed in Vietnamese, which urged immediate peace. Police and MP's

[13] Thomas Lippman, "Freed Vietnam Neutralist Returns to Political Wars," *Washington Post*, August 25, 1973, p. A11. Ms. Riechman and the entire WILPF organization are extremely proud of the role they played in publicizing the Ngo Ba Thanh case. The legislative office generated 60 to 70 letters from individual members of Congress to the State Department on Mme. Thanh's behalf. Ms. Riechman and others in the WILPF felt that Mme. Thanh's outrageous treatment and persecution would draw attention to the larger problem of political prisoners. Prior to Mme. Thanh's release, Ms. Riechman said, "She's a symbol, that's why we're working so strenuously for her."

quickly surrounded the two, and they beat them as they dragged them off to jail.

The two were incarcerated in Saigon's Chi Hoa prison. At their trial—at which they were not allowed to speak—Debris was sentenced to four years in prison and Menras to three. To their surprise, the French government made no effort to secure their release.[14] It was not until pressure from French public opinion began to mount that Foreign Minister Maurice Schumann began to make inquiries on their behalf. For reasons known only to Saigon, Debris and Menras were released ahead of schedule on December 29, 1972, just prior to the January cease-fire.

The two Frenchmen suspect that the Thieu regime released them so that they would not continue to witness the reclassification of prisoners that had begun. "Reclassification" was the process by which the South Vietnamese government allegedly changed the official status of "political" prisoners to common criminals. Because the cease-fire agreement provided for the release of political prisoners—those charged with acts of sabotage, espionage, or being supporters of the Viet Cong—reclassification was viewed at the time as a means by which Thieu could keep his opponents in jail.[15]

On the day of their release, Debris and Menras were immediately expelled from the country and put on a plane bound for Paris. The two men's involvement, however, did not stop with their release. They resolved to do all that they

[14] With appreciable cynicism, the two men believe that the French government was slow to act because there were large French-owned landholdings in South Vietnam and, thus, the French government did not want to anger President Thieu.

[15] The accord technically provided for those prisoners who could be identified as belonging to one side or the other. As Sylvan Fox pointed out, "no provision is made for the thousands of non-Communist, anti-Government prisoners held by Saigon because it considers them politically dangerous." "4 South Vietnamese Describe Torture in Prison's Tiger Cage," *The New York Times*, March 3, 1973, p. 7.

could to expose the situation in the South Vietnamese jails. Before the year 1973 was out, they would travel all over the world telling of their experiences at Chi Hoa. They began their speaking tour in Paris where, on January 20, they addressed an assembled 5000 people. The following excerpts from a transcript of the event detail some of the brutal torture and abuses they witnessed:

> But that day, the first day of Tet, they could come down into the prison yard. So we saw, the whole jail saw, for the first time, these hundred prisoners from the tiger cages.
>
> And in what condition! They had to crawl down, because they couldn't walk anymore; their knees had been broken. They dragged themselves along the ground with little wooden benches they had made. In the sun they had to close their eyes completely because they'd been blinded from so many years of darkness. Their faces were haggard and lined, their bodies gaunt and emaciated. They were wearing tattered prison uniforms, the standard black pajamas.
>
> ✻   ✻   ✻
>
> They even mixed the Catholic students with members of the National Liberation Front, so they could be classified as communists and all the political prisoners were mixed with ordinary ones. Then they took away the files of these prisoners, so that no one will be able to prove that they were political prisoners, and not ordinary criminals.
>
> ✻   ✻   ✻
>
> Then, there is what the police call the "plane trip." After the victim's wrists have been tied together behind his back, a long, very strong rope is inserted through the cords around his wrists, while the other end is attached to a pulley on the ceiling. By pulling on the rope the police can make the victim swing in the air by his wrists, which have been tied together behind his back. The ef-

fects of this action are heightened by an occasional black-jacking, or cigarette burn on the more sensitive parts of the body, particularly the genitals.

* * *

There is yet another form of torture, which is practiced on war prisoners. The prisoner is stripped naked and made to sit on a chair with a hole in the seat. A lighted oil lamp—making it possible to raise and lower the flame —is placed underneath the chair.

If the prisoner refuses to talk, the flame is raised higher and higher, until it burns the anus. Some 75 percent of the prisoners tortured in this manner do not survive since the only possibility of saving them would be operation on the abdomen that would permit the intestine to function normally.[16]

After their appearances in Paris, Debris and Menras began to travel through Europe, with stops in Switzerland, Belgium, Luxembourg, Italy, and England. At the end of this tour, they were asked to come to the United States by Amnesty International, an organization that works for the release of political prisoners throughout the world. Amnesty International was naturally concerned with the South Vietnamese prisoners, and they felt that it was vital for Debris and Menras to speak to the American public.

The U.S. affiliate of Amnesty International, with headquarters in New York City, and the International Assembly of Christians, based in Minneapolis, coordinated the tour of the two Frenchmen.[17] The speaking tour, beginning on

[16] Jean-Pierre Debris and Andre Menras, "Terror in Thieu's Prisons," reprinted by the American Friends Service Committee, Philadelphia, Pennsylvania, n.d.

[17] Amnesty International picked up the expenses, mostly plane fares, for Debris and Menras. The two were housed in private homes in the different cities they visited. People working for the International Assembly of Christians spun off another group, the International Committee to Free South Vietnamese Political Prisoners from Detention and Torture, to work on the problem beyond the visit of Debris and Menras.

March 5 in New York, included stops in Detroit, Cleveland, Chicago, Minneapolis-St. Paul, Phoenix, Denver, Los Angeles, San Francisco, Philadelphia, Washington, D.C., and Boston. In each of these cities local peace activists were put in charge of scheduling engagements for the two former prisoners.

The people at the two organizations sponsoring the tour knew that Ms. Riechman was interested in the political prisoner issue, and they rightfully assumed, after talking to her informally, that she would be willing to work on the project. Ms. Riechman did not know of her actual appointment until she received a Xeroxed list of "contact" people in all the cities, which was sent to her by the International Assembly of Christians. This happened less than three weeks before the Frenchmen were scheduled for their Washington stop. Ms. Riechman, however, never questioned that it was her obligation to do all she could for Debris and Menras.

The other "contact" person for Washington was Chris Jenkins of the Indochina Resource Center. Jenkins, a tall, bearded, rather quiet man of 30, went to Vietnam with the International Voluntary Service organization after he graduated from Stanford University. After two years, he returned to the United States and enrolled in a master's degree program in Asian Studies at the University of California at Berkeley. At the same time he began to be active in the antiwar movement. By the time he began working for the Indochina Resource Center, a group that specializes in conducting and distributing research on war-related issues, he had become quite interested in the problem of political prisoners.

Jenkins and Ms. Riechman spoke on the phone a number of times in what became a slow "feeling out" process as each tried to gauge how much work the other was willing to do. At first, each seemed to hope that the other would take command of the effort. Little was being accomplished this way, and they agreed to hold a meeting and invite others who might be interested in working on the Washington visit. Subsequently, two other individuals, Edith Villastrigo of Women's Strike for Peace[18] and Becky Mullin, an intern at the Friends Committee on National Legislation, joined the developing coalition. Although others gave of their time on occasion, it was these four who did the majority of work on the Debris and Menras visit.

Three meetings of this working group were held prior to the arrival of the two Frenchmen on Sunday evening, March 18. At the first meeting, on March 2, Ms. Riechman, with uncharacteristic forcefulness, directed the discussion, and she exacted commitments from the others to do specific tasks. Out of the meeting developed a consensus that the general goals should be gaining press coverage and getting the two Frenchmen maximum exposure on Capitol Hill. The two broad objectives could, of course, be tied together, but there was some disagreement as to how this could be done. A long time was spent discussing the feasibility of having the two Frenchmen testify before a congressional hearing. It was agreed that it would be hard to get them before a committee, because no directly related hearings were scheduled for the two days Debris and Menras would be in town. Despite this, the group felt that hearings should be the first priority, because the congressional testimony would add considerable credibility to their stories and it would put them "officially" on record.

The work was divided within the group, with Ms. Riechman taking the major responsibility for arranging Capitol Hill appearances. Ms. Mullin would also work on the Congress, and Ms. Villastrigo would work both on the Congress and on the press. Chris Jenkins would devote his time to the press and to gathering background data on political prisoners that could be distributed in conjunction with the Frenchmen's appearances.

[18] Women's Strike for Peace, headquartered in New York, does not maintain a Washington office. Washington area members are in contact with one another and do some work together on antiwar issues.

The visits and phone calls to congressional offices tended to be rather unfocused at first. The chances for an appearance before a congressional committee diminished quickly when Ms. Riechman's best hope, Representative Don Fraser (D., Minn.) was found to be unwilling to commit himself to doing anything on the Frenchmen's behalf. Fraser is a member of the House Foreign Affairs Committee. In addition to his being one of the most steadfast liberals in the House, his Minneapolis district includes the International Assembly of Christians' office, and activists in that organization had worked with Fraser before on other issues.[19]

By the time of the second meeting on March 7, Ms. Riechman had just about given up on trying to get Debris and Menras before a congressional committee. The group generally felt that if hearings could not be arranged, then the next priority should be a press conference sponsored by a Representative or Senator. Chris Jenkins reported that Cora Weiss, a noted peace advocate and director of Women's Strike for Peace, had called him from New York and told him that another activist, Vinnie McGee, had called Senator Clifford Case's (R., N.J.) office with regard to the Frenchmen's visit. John Marks, an aide to the Senator, had agreed to sponsor a luncheon for congressional aides with Debris and Menras as guest speakers. This caught all in the working group by surprise, but all were quite pleased, because this was the first real success with either the press or the Congress.

Further plans were made at the meeting to contact various elements of the press. The group was spurred on by the fact that Amnesty International had arranged an interview for Debris and Menras with *New York Times* columnist Tom Wicker on March 6. Wicker's column appeared in the

[19] Ms. Riechman did not work on the Senate Foreign Relations Committee because Sandy Gottlieb, director of SANE in Washington and on the National Board of Amnesty International, had told Amnesty International that he would work on getting the two Frenchmen before that committee. In the end, he was unable to arrange anything.

March 11 Sunday *Times* and was syndicated by *The New York Times* wire service. Wicker wrote a sympathetic column, and he emphasized the implications of reclassification for the cease-fire. In part he wrote:

> there was one element of the Menras-Debris account that needs repetition, if only because it could bode trouble for the cease-fire agreements now uneasily in force. They contend, with a wealth of eyewitness detail, that the Thieu Government is systematically forging records and callously shifting bodies about from prison to prison, so that thousands of its political captives can be reported as common criminals and kept in jail, cease-fire or no cease-fire.
>
> Aside from questions of compassion and justice this effort by the Thieu regime to hold on to its civilian political prisoners . . . is a direct violation of the Paris accords.[20]

The group decided to make two Washington columnists, Mary McGrory of the *Washington Star-News* and Nicholas Von Hoffman of the *Post*, primary targets for press coverage. McGrory, who would win a Pulitzer Prize in 1975, is a widely respected reporter whose columns are usually analyses of, or reflections on, important national problems. Von Hoffman, more of an iconoclast than a leftist,[21] writes polemics intended to reach readers' emotions as well as their minds. He often writes columns about individuals who have been treated unfairly by an action or inaction of the government. Both McGrory and Von Hoffman are nationally syndicated. In addition to these two, the group constructed a list of other newspaper, TV, and radio reporters who were to be contacted on behalf of the Frenchmen.

The work on trying to arrange a press conference was

---

[20] Tom Wicker, "The Other Prisoners," *The New York Times*, March 11, 1973, p. E15.

[21] For example, the day after former President Harry Truman died, Von Hoffman wrote a column that was critical of Truman.

terribly frustrating for Ms. Riechman and Ms. Villastrigo. For the Congress, the issue of political prisoners was largely a "nonissue." Because the cease-fire had been signed less than two months earlier and American POWs were being released during this time, the feeling that one got on Capitol Hill was that members of Congress and aides just wanted to forget about South Vietnam. Members of Congress can pay only marginal attention to the majority of issues they face,[22] and the relief most people felt at finally "getting out" of the war made it that much more difficult to make political prisoners a visible issue.

On top of this problem of congressional lack of interest, Ms. Riechman and Ms. Villastrigo found themselves in serious disagreement over how they should approach House and Senate offices concerning the two Frenchmen. Ms. Villastrigo, a stern, matronly woman, had no compunction about coming right out and asking a congressional aide if his boss would hold a press conference. During lunch on their second day of working together, Ms. Riechman tried to convince her that she was using a faulty strategy by being so forward. "You're giving them an excuse to say 'no,' Edith. You've got to feel them out, see if they're interested. They're sharp people; if they're interested they'll ask, 'what can we do?'" Mrs. Villastrigo quickly brushed aside the criticism, "Look, I don't want to waste my time. After all, what are we here for? I want to go into these offices and talk turkey. I want them to know just where I stand."

The day wore on without success. Ms. Villastrigo continued to ask legislative and administrative assistants if their office would be willing to sponsor a press conference. An aide to Senator Walter Huddleston (D., Ky.) told the two lobbyists, "No, I don't think he'd be interested." A legislative assistant to Senator Joseph Biden (D., Del.) said, "Well,

[22] The classic statement on members of Congress and the problem of marginal attention is Lewis Anthony Dexter, "The Representative and His District," *Human Organization*, vol. 16 (Spring 1957), pp. 2-13.

you know, freshman Senators just don't go around calling press conferences." Finally, when Ms. Villastrigo insisted that they go to the office of Senator Marlow Cook (R., Ky.), Ms. Riechman felt that she was completely wasting her time. She thought that the moderate Cook was an unlikely candidate to host a press conference where American complicity in South Vietnam's political repression would be the major topic. Consequently, she told Ms. Villastrigo that it would be better if they worked independently, and Ms. Villastrigo was left to go to Senator Cook's office by herself.

Prior to the next meeting of the group, Ms. Riechman concentrated on the House and, in particular, on the Foreign Affairs Committee's Subcommittee on Asian and Pacific Affairs.[23] Robert Nix (D., Pa.), a nine-term Congressman from Philadelphia, had just taken over the chairmanship of the subcommittee at the beginning of the 93rd Congress in January. Nix has always maintained a low profile in House affairs, and he has focused much of his efforts on serving requests of his urban, mostly black, constituents.

Ms. Riechman knew that there was little chance of Nix holding a press conference for Debris and Menras, but she had three objectives in seeking him out. First, she wanted to provide him with information on the political prisoner issue so that, if and when legislation did come before his subcommittee, he would have it at his disposal. Second, she felt that it was important to let him know that people were concerned about the issue. To that end, Ms. Riechman generated some letters that week from WILPF members in Nix's district that asked him to become active on the political prisoner question. Third, before Ms. Riechman could go to the other Democrats in the subcommittee, Lee Hamilton, Lester Wolff, and Leo Ryan, she needed to be able to tell them that their chairperson would not be doing anything

[23] The House Government Operations Subcommittee on Foreign Government Operations was another possibility. Norman Cornish, an aide to the subcommittee chairperson, William Moorhead (D., Pa.), was unreceptive to Ms. Riechman, however, when she made initial feelers concerning the Frenchmen's visit.

with regard to Debris and Menras. The three would be sensitive toward doing something that might "upstage" Nix, who had yet to hold his first organizational meeting of the subcommittee.

Ms. Riechman approached Nix through his subcommittee aide, Tom Kennedy. When Ms. Riechman asked Kennedy if Nix might be able to see the two Frenchmen on Monday or Tuesday of the next week, Kennedy replied that it would be unlikely. Although Kennedy did not mention it, Nix is a "member" of the "Tuesday-Thursday club" and does not usually commute into Washington until Tuesday afternoon. Kennedy, however, offered to meet with Debris and Menras, and said that he would prepare a memo on the meeting for Nix afterwards. Ms. Riechman agreed, and a time was set for Monday morning.

Ms. Riechman proceeded to approach the offices of Congressmen Hamilton, Wolff, and Ryan. To her dismay, however, none of these offices showed any substantive interest in the two Frenchmen. Other offices of liberal Congresspersons were equally unresponsive, and by the time of the third meeting on March 13, a press conference had yet to be arranged.

The people who had been working on the Frenchmen's visit were joined at their meeting by Sandy Persons, staff director of Members of Congress for Peace Through Law (MCPL). MCPL is a liberal, bipartisan group of Congresspersons from both houses who meet from time to time to hear speakers on matters of peace and war.[24] On March 12, Persons called Chris Jenkins and told him that MCPL would like to have Debris and Menras speak at one of their forums.

Persons explained to the working group that he had re-

[24] At the beginning of the 93rd Congress, 92 Representatives and 32 Senators were members of MCPL by virtue of paying their $10 fee. The rest of the money, which goes for supporting a small research staff and an office near the Capitol, comes from private donors. For a brief description and history of MCPL, see Congressional Quarterly's *Guide to the Congress of the United States* (Washington, D.C.: Congressional Quarterly, 1971), pp. 610-612.

ceived a call the day before from Martha Platt, a contributor to MCPL, who had housed Debris and Menras while they were in Minneapolis. Ms. Platt told Persons about the two Frenchmen and, after about 20 minutes, she convinced him that he should schedule an MCPL meeting for the two. Ms. Riechman saw the MCPL meeting as an opportunity for press coverage. She raised the subject with Persons, but he quickly dismissed the idea. He emphasized that MCPL gatherings are low-key affairs. "Our purpose is to allow the members, regardless of party or seniority, regardless of anything, to come and do their thing."

Because there was still no Congressperson to sponsor a press conference, contingency plans were made by the group to sponsor their own press conference if Ms. Riechman and Ms. Villastrigo could not get anybody by the end of the week. It was reported at the meeting that both Mary McGrory and Nicholas Von Hoffman had expressed an interest in doing a column on Debris and Menras, but neither had made a firm commitment. Other reporters who had been approached, such as Richard Dudman of the *St. Louis Post-Dispatch*, William Raspberry of the *Washington Post*, and syndicated columnist Jack Anderson, had indicated that they would not be covering the story. Arrangements had been made for Debris and Menras to appear on a local Washington TV talk show, "Panorama," which airs during the lunch hour.

On the remaining three working days before the two Frenchmen arrived, things began to fall into place for their Capitol Hill visits. Although Ms. Riechman had been critical of Ms. Villastrigo's lobbying approach, it was Ms. Villastrigo who finally produced a sponsor for a press conference: liberal New York Congressperson Bertram Podell. In addition, Ms. Riechman received a call from Amy Augustus of Amnesty International, who told her that a member of her organization had written, on behalf of Debris and Menras, to Senator George McGovern (D., S.D.) and Representative Paul McCloskey (R., Calif.). The two Congresspersons, both long and vociferous opponents of American involvement in Southeast Asia, agreed to meet personally with the two Frenchmen.

Debris and Menras arrived in Washington on Sunday night, March 18, and they were immediately taken to a wine-and-cheese reception in a private home in the fashionable Georgetown section of the city (see Table VI-1). The guests were activists in the antiwar movement, and the

TABLE VI-1

Schedule for Jean-Pierre Debris and Andre Menras

Sunday, March 18

7:30 p.m.   Reception for "movement" people in Georgetown

Monday, March 19

10:00 a.m.   Meeting with Tom Kennedy, House Foreign Affairs Committee aide to Rep. Robert Nix

11:00 a.m.   Meeting with Rep. Paul McCloskey

12:00 noon   Luncheon for Congressional staff sponsored by Senator Clifford Case's office

2:00 p.m.   Meeting with Senator George McGovern

3:00 p.m.   Meeting with Norman Cornish, Government Operations Committee aide

4:00 p.m.   Meeting with David Rossiter, aide to Senator Edward Brooke

Tuesday, March 20

10:00 a.m.   Press conference sponsored by Rep. Bertram Podell

12:30 p.m.   Appearance on "Panorama" television program

3:30 p.m.   Appearance before Members of Congress for Peace Through Law

4:30 p.m.   Radio interview with the Canadian Broadcasting Corporation

5:30 p.m.   Meeting with church youth activists

9:30 p.m.   Flight from National Airport to Boston

---

two Frenchmen gave a brief, informal presentation. The real lobbying began early the next day when Ms. Riechman led the two up the east steps of the Capitol shortly before 10 a.m.

Their first meeting was with Congressperson Nix's aide, Tom Kennedy. Kennedy led the two out of his subcommittee staff office near the rotunda to the House members' dining room, where Debris and Menras told their story over coffee. The two, with some emotion, began to tell of their imprisonment and of the reclassification of political prisoners. Kennedy took notes as they gave him the names of specific political prisoners, such as Tran Thi Huoung, who was illegally arrested after the cease-fire; Truong Dinh Dzu, who had run for President against Thieu;[25] and Duoung Van Sau, just 7 years of age. They also told him about an American firm, RMK-BRJ,[26] which, they alleged, was continuing to manufacture tiger cages for President Thieu.[27]

After the two had finished their presentation, Kennedy began to describe the role Congressperson Nix could play in the upcoming foreign aid authorization hearings that the House Foreign Affairs Committee would hold. Debris and Menras showed little patience with Kennedy's explanation

[25] Dzu was released less than two weeks later, on March 27, 1973, after five years in prison. Dzu's crime was advocating negotiations with the Viet Cong.

[26] Raymond, Morrison, Knudson-Brown, Root, and Jones. See Holmes Brown and Don Luce, *Hostages of War* (Washington, D.C.: Indochina Mobile Education Project, 1973), p. 43.

[27] Tiger cages are small stone compartments, approximately five feet by nine feet, with bars across the top. Prisoners are often shackled within them so that they cannot stand up. They came to light in 1970 when two American Congresspersons, Augustus Hawkins and William Anderson, "discovered" them in the Con Son Island prison camp. The Congresspersons were led to the tiger cages by a congressional aide, Thomas Harkins, and Don Luce, director of the International Volunteer Service. The resulting exposé in late 1970 prompted the South Vietnamese government to announce that they were discontinuing usage of the tiger cages. See Brown and Luce, *ibid.*, pp. 36-43; Jacques Leslie, " 'Tiger Cage' Victims Cite S. Viet Torture," *Washington Post*, March 4, 1973, p. A17; and Sylvan Fox, "4 South Vietnamese Describe Torture in Prison Tiger Cage."

of the complex appropriations process, and their eyes started to roam about the room. Finally, Debris interjected a suggestion that they would repeat constantly during their two days on Capitol Hill, "Couldn't the Congressmen ask Thieu, when he comes to Washington, about the political prisoners, about why they haven't been released under the agreement?" Kennedy, knowing that hostile members of Congress would get nowhere near Thieu during his scheduled visit to Washington in early April, mumbled, "Oh, when he's here, he'll just go to some boring diplomatic teas." Debris shot back plaintively, "But the questions can be asked *diplomatically!*"[28]

The meeting with Representative McCloskey was next on the Frenchmen's schedule, and Ms. Riechman led the two to his office, where they were to meet Ms. Villastrigo. When they arrived at McCloskey's suite in the Cannon Office Building, they also found two Yale University students, Ed Baily and Mike Lattemore, who had been at the party the night before. The two had heard from Cora Weiss about the Frenchmen's visit to Washington, and they decided to make a documentary film on it.[29] Ms. Riechman had realized the night before that Baily and Lattemore might cause some problems during the congressional meetings, and she specifically asked them to clear with her any filming they planned to do so that she could make sure it would not bother any Congressperson who might be present. To her consternation, McCloskey's staff had already given them

[28] President Nixon decided to meet Thieu for their talks at the Western White House in San Clemente, California. Thieu subsequently came to Washington, where he was hosted by Vice President Agnew.

[29] Baily, a graduate student in German, and Lattemore, a sophomore, were on leave from school, and they were trying to get into North Vietnam so that they could make a documentary there. They thought that this would be a worthy interim project, but their purpose was somewhat vague, because they had no sponsor nor any leads as to who might be interested in airing or distributing their film. Lattemore said, "We're doing it for the record, and whatever comes of it—well, we don't know."

tentative permission to film the encounter with the Congressperson. McCloskey arrived from a hearing 15 minutes later and, although he seemed puzzled by the presence of the two filmmakers, let them into his office. He sat at his desk, taking notes with a felt pen, as Debris and Menras, on an adjacent couch, began to recount the story of their arrest:

> *Debris*: We were beaten unconscious.
>
> *McCloskey*: What kind of weapons did they use?
>
> *Debris*: An iron bar; we were kicked and stoned.
>
> *McCloskey*: Any Americans there?
>
> *Debris*: Yes, they took pictures. American journalists.
>
> *McCloskey*: Where was this, by the Caravelle Hotel?
>
> *Debris*: Yes. We were interrogated for five days, but they didn't torture us. They did torture a Vietnamese in front of us.
>
> *McCloskey*: How?
>
> *Debris*: They poured soapy water on his face after they stuck a rag in his mouth. Then they beat him with truncheons.
>
> *McCloskey*: Rubber ones?
>
> *Debris*: I don't know. Black ones. After five days we were taken to prison, held in solitary confinement, no exercise, no sun, no water to wash, only to drink. They beat us a second time on the 8th of December; and a third time on April 26, 1971. This was in cell #183, a new solitary confinement cell. They also sent us to a psychiatric ward of a hospital with lunatics for five days.

The presence of the two cameramen began to irritate McCloskey as Baily and Lattemore bobbed back and forth in front of his desk changing camera angles or moving in for close-ups. The filming of the conversation seemed to create an atmosphere of a staged event rather than of a serious presentation and discussion. After about 20 minutes, the agitated McCloskey called Norman Cornish, a staff member of the Foreign Government Operations Subcommittee of the Government Operations Committee, and told him to meet with Debris and Menras, because the committee should have their story on the record.[30] As he ushered the group out of his office, McCloskey turned to the Frenchmen's escorts and said of their meeting with Cornish, "I don't want anyone else to go. This isn't a publicity event." As soon as they got out into the hallway, Ms. Riechman told Baily and Lattemore that they would have to ask her permission before they filmed any more meetings. Subsequently she did not let them cover anything else on Capitol Hill with the exception of the press conference, which, of course, was open to all.

Ms. Riechman and Ms. Villastrigo took the two Frenchmen back across Independence Avenue to a small room in the Capitol, where the luncheon sponsored by Senator Case's office was being held. The organizers were pleased to find columnist Mary McGrory in attendance; she took copious notes during the affair. After a moving presentation by Debris and Menras, some of the 30 or so staff aides asked questions, and then the meeting broke up. Ms. Riechman was discouraged by the lack of resolve on the part of the staffers. "They were the people who were already aware of this issue. That was good, but I just didn't see any determination to do anything on this."

At 2:00 p.m., Senator George McGovern welcomed Debris and Menras and their escorts into his personal office. McGovern sat passively in an armchair while the two former prisoners began telling him of their experience. His interest perked up, however, after he asked them if any of the South Vietnamese people who had met with him in a Saigon church in September 1971 had later been put in jail. Menras answered affirmatively, which upset McGovern, and the Senator tried to get as much information as possible about the peace sympathizers who had been imprisoned.

McGovern asked them how many political prisoners there

[30] See *supra*, note 23.

were, and he was startled when Debris estimated 200,000. McGovern noted, "That's an awful lot of prisoners. Joliet is one of our biggest prisons. They have 2000 prisoners; that's 100 Joliets." As Menras began to describe how young women are raped and tortured, a loud buzzer rang a single time, indicating that a roll call vote was taking place on the Senate floor. As he rose to leave, Ms. Villastrigo asked, "Senator, what can we do about this problem?" The former Democratic presidential nominee replied as he gathered some papers on his desk, "Oh, I think we'll have to do something on the Senate floor."[31] He asked Debris and Menras to stay and give more information to his secretary, and then he left for the vote.

Debris and Menras were next taken to the Rayburn House Office Building, where they met in a basement room with Foreign Operations Subcommittee staffer Norman Cornish. Ms. Riechman told Cornish that McCloskey said he should see the two in private, but Cornish dismissed this with a wave of the hand and invited the escorts in. Although McCloskey had instructed Cornish to "get this on file," Cornish did not take a single note and, indeed, he did most of the talking. He told them bluntly that they were wasting their time with him. Cornish stated, "The people on this committee already know the situation. They've backed legislation to end aid to Thieu and had it defeated on the floor. You already have 12 supporters on this committee; you should be going to the other 420 or so Representatives and 100 Senators."

Debris and Menras sat patiently as Cornish described how hard he had worked on the issue of political repression by Saigon and how fruitless that work had been. When Cornish began to tell the two Frenchmen about the current constitutional crisis between the executive and legislative branches, Ms. Riechman announced that they were late for the next appointment and would have to leave. Cornish concluded, "All I can do is wish you good luck."

[31] Earlier, he had said that he was going to look into the specific cases of those people who had been jailed after meeting with him.

Debris and Menras, dejected because of Cornish's attitude and weary from an already long day, slowly made their way back across the Capitol to the Russell Senate Office Building, where they met with David Rossiter, an aide to Senator Edward Brooke (R., Mass.). Brooke, accompanied by Rossiter, was leaving shortly to go to South Vietnam.[32] The two Frenchmen's spirits revived quickly when Rossiter told them that Brooke was planning to ask the Saigon government about specific political prisoners. They eagerly accepted Rossiter's invitation to give him names of prisoners to inquire about. Speaking rapidly in French, the two deliberated over which names they should include. After putting down a dozen names, they agonized over the list and finally circled a few prisoners they were particularly concerned for. Their session with Rossiter ended around 5:30 p.m., and their long day of lobbying finally ended.

After dinner at the home of Chris Jenkins and a good night's rest, Debris and Menras were back on Capitol Hill Tuesday morning for their 10:00 a.m. press conference. Approximately 40 people crowded into a small room in the Cannon Building. Most of the people gathered, however, were antiwar activists, individuals who had worked on arranging the Frenchmen's trip, and congressional staffers. In all, there were about 10 reporters and cameramen present. Congressperson Podell's office had got Representatives Abzug (D., N.Y.), Drinan (D., Mass.), Moakley (D., Mass.), and Rosenthal (D., N.Y.) to cosponsor the press conference, but only Abzug and Moakley showed up.[33] A few minutes after 10 a.m., Podell began the conference by reading from a prepared statement:

[32] Brooke also intended to go to North Vietnam, but after arriving in South Vietnam he was denied entry to Hanoi.

[33] Ms. Riechman had purposely avoided asking Congressperson Abzug to host the press conference. She felt that because Ms. Abzug is so strident and is identified with so many radical causes, her sponsorship might work to discredit the two Frenchmen. Ms. Villastrigo disagreed and later complained to Ms. Riechman, "When we went around, looking for a news conference and we said leave Bella alone, we were wrong. The important thing is to get the information out, and Bella always gets the press."

thousands of political prisoners crowd South Vietnamese jails, men whose only crime is their opposition to the Thieu government. These men symbolize for the future of Vietnam what our POWs symbolize for America: an end to the years of long conflict. There can be no hopes for a settlement while they remain jailed for their beliefs.

After Congressperson Abzug spoke for a few minutes, Andre Menras began to recite their story and their accusations. He opened by stating:

We witnessed the killing of the people and the destruction of the landscape. We've seen the killing of the foreigners: Americans, Thais, Koreans, New Zealanders, and Filipinos. As human beings we could not keep silent in front of all these killings.

The two spoke for about 20 minutes and, after a few questions, the rather uninspiring press conference broke up.

The two were transported across town for their appearance on the "Panorama" show at 12:30 p.m. Host Maury Povich asked a few initial questions, but then was content to let Debris speak on his own. The Frenchmen were on camera for 15 minutes. At the end of the show, Debris and Menras got back into Chris Jenkins' Volkswagen van and were taken back to Capitol Hill for their MCPL meeting.

Arriving a few minutes late at the ornate Speaker's Dining Room in the Capitol, the two found it nearly empty. Along with MCPL Chairperson John Seiberling (D., Ohio), there were only two other members of Congress, Don Edwards (D., Calif.) and Don Fraser, and a few staff aides present.[34]

[34] Congressperson James A. Burke, a conservative Democrat from Massachusetts, arrived in the middle of the meeting. Burke was strikingly unsympathetic to stories concerning the torture of political prisoners by the Thieu regime. When Chairperson Seiberling politely asked Burke his opinion on the matter, Burke hemmed and hawed for a bit and then recalled Japanese atrocities in World War II. "You got to realize we're dealing with a whole different type of people here."

Although MCPL meetings are characteristically small—averaging 8 or 10 members of Congress—Sandy Persons was clearly embarrassed by the small turnout.

Debris and Menras repeated the presentation they had given hundreds of times over the past few months. The two former prisoners were completely exhausted by this time, and neither spoke with a great deal of force or enthusiasm. The meeting mercifully ended after about a half hour. The two men were then quickly interviewed by a correspondent for the Canadian Broadcasting Corporation for radio. After a cup of tea at the WILPF office, Debris and Menras spoke one last time at a gathering of some church youth meeting in the Methodist Building, adjacent to the WILPF.

Both Debris and Menras were somewhat frustrated and confused by their encounters with the Congress. They had little way of gauging how effective they had been. Menras summed up the two days: "I have learned to be careful. People act sympathetic but when they walk out, they do not act. I think the people we met with at the Congress were good people. But they will not act. I would call it 'passive resistance.'" Menras was not totally pessimistic, however. He told the peace activists who had organized the Washington tour, "Washington was the best of all American cities. The people here knew the most about the prisons."

Before they left that night, the Frenchmen and their American companions were heartened by the appearance of Mary McGrory's column in the evening Star-News.[35] Although she was not optimistic about Congress reducing aid to Thieu, McGrory eloquently reported the points Debris and Menras made at the luncheon. The Frenchmen were also informed that, despite the fact that he did not hear them speak or interview them, Nicholas Von Hoffman had written a column on them that would appear in the follow-

ing morning's *Post*.[36] Von Hoffman wrote the column from
the printed material, particularly their Paris statement,[37]
sent to him by Chris Jenkins.[38]

As soon as dinner was over, Chris Jenkins and Rosalie
Riechman took the two to Washington's National Airport,
where they were met by Edith Villastrigo. After receiving
an emotional hug by Ms. Villastrigo, Jean-Pierre Debris
and Andre Menras boarded their plane for Boston. Their
appearances in Boston would be followed by a tour of
Canada, and then Japan, Germany, Holland, and Sweden.
For Debris and Menras, long-range career plans had been
put aside. They had too many friends who were still in South
Vietnamese jails and whose lives they must try to save.

Debris and Menras created something less than a stir
during their two days in Washington. The two newspaper
columns and their television appearance brought only a
modicum of publicity to their cause. Most of the people to
whom they talked were already openly critical of the Thieu
regime. In light of the recent disengagement of American
troops from South Vietnam and a natural tendency of people
to want to forget about Vietnam, it might have been unrealistic to think that they could have attracted more attention than they did. The tour of the two Frenchmen might
best be thought of as an opening skirmish in the fight peace
groups planned to wage to eliminate American aid to what
they considered to be a corrupt, tyrannical government in
South Vietnam. The fight for the release of the political
prisoners and against American aid would never be "won"
by the peace groups until the collapse of the Saigon regime
in the spring of 1975.

[36] Nicholas Von Hoffman, "Between the Halves and Have-Nots,"
Washington Post, March 21, 1973, p. B1.

[37] See *supra*, note 16, and accompanying text.

[38] The Frenchmen would not learn that their press conference
had failed to produce the exposure the organizers had hoped for.
The WILPF legislative office received no wire service story clippings
and the two Washington papers did not have news stories in addition
to the columns.

THE WILPF AS AN INTEREST GROUP

The effort to publicize the plight of political prisoners in South Vietnam by the Women's International League for Peace and Freedom during the first part of 1973 was far from a complete success. The Capitol Hill tour of Debris and Menras was, of course, only one small chapter in the struggle against the Vietnam War in which the WILPF had been engaged for so many years. There were only a few short-term victories, such as the survival and eventual release of Mme. Ngo Ba Thanh, but countless frustrations and disappointments as the American involvement in Indochina continued until the bitter end.

What can be said about the role of the WILPF during the Vietnam war era? One can speak with some confidence about the contribution of the entire antiwar movement in forcing a deescalation and final withdrawal of American troops. It is rather difficult to isolate the individual influence of the WILPF within this larger cast of actors, but the WILPF certainly made some small, if immeasurable, contribution to the overall accomplishments of the antiwar movement. At the same time, the WILPF was never able to establish itself as a national leader within the antiwar sector. Despite the fact that it has been a staunch radical organization since 1915, newer groups such as the New Mobe, the People's Coalition for Peace and Justice, and the National Peace Action Coalition sprang up to guide those Americans who opposed the war. As entrepreneurs, the WILPF fared poorly; during the past decade thousands of people were drawn to new, left-leaning organizations, while WILPF membership showed little increase.

Part of the problem the Washington office faces in its lobbying efforts is simply the issues on which it chooses to work. To criticize the legislative office as ineffective is, in large part, to criticize it for devoting time and effort to policy matters that are going to be difficult to influence. The choice of issues by Ms. Riechman and her associates comes not from foolishness or naiveté, but rather from a deep, ideological conviction. Given the extent of the American commitment to the Thieu regime, the WILPF's chances of bringing about extensive pressure by the Nixon administration on Saigon to liberalize its political prisoner policy were quite slim. The humanitarian instincts of the WILPF could not, however, permit them to stop their work in this thankless area. There were too many people whose lives were in danger and whose chances for survival hinged on publicity generated in the press or by the intervention of individual members of Congress.

It must be pointed out, however, that the problems of the legislative office extend far beyond issue selection. Most significantly, the WILPF office has not become a source of information for congressional offices. Lobbying is not only a process of an interest group transmitting information to government, but frequently it is a two-way relationship, with the government approaching organizations they trust and rely upon for needed data. The WILPF has not, however, developed a reputation for expertise and useful data on specific topics. The legislative office has not consistently been a place to which congressional aides can turn for assistance or advice on legislation, hearings, or reports on which they are working. The information Ms. Riechman does provide to congressional aides when she approaches them is usually put together and printed by other liberal groups, such as the Friends Committee on National Legislation, the Coalition on National Priorities and Military Policy, and the Indochina Resource Center. The research that Bill Samuel does is primarily for the *Legislative Bulletin* and *Peace and Freedom*, but both publications carry a preponderance of information that is available in the *Washington Post*.

It could be argued that the WILPF would be a much stronger interest group if the local chapters worked closely with the Philadelphia and Washington offices in a coordinated effort on one or two issues a year. This, of course, is not the case. Local chapters work on a plethora of national, state, and local issues. Ms. Steffens says with some amusement, "This is something that the Soviet women who come to visit can't understand. There are no directives in WILPF."[39] Ms. Steffens makes a strong defense for not focusing the entire organization on a few national issues:

> Some people are going to be more interested in some issues than in others. Sure, we would have to be more efficient if we were a business corporation. But, while we'd gain efficiency, we'd lose people who might work on an issue just because they're interested in it, not because WILPF is pushing it.

Although their financial future is uncertain, the WILPF will, no doubt, struggle on. The WILPF activists around the country are a strongly committed group, and the end of the Vietnam War will not diminish their zeal. Their global goals—an end to war and true justice for all—are Utopian, so the Women's International League will be around for a long time to come.

[39] Exchange visits are held by the U.S. Section of WILPF and the Soviet Women's Committee. The most recent discussions were held in San Diego, California, in December 1972.

CHAPTER VII

Communication and Decision Making

THE number of issues and subissues on which public interest groups would like to work is always far in excess of the number on which they are actually able to become active. Each group must decide how it will commit its limited resources. The organizations must not only choose the issues on which they will lobby, but they must also determine, consciously or otherwise, how much of their resources to allocate and the manner in which the resources will be expended. This chapter and the two that follow will discuss these processes of organizational choice. The present chapter will examine decision making as it relates to the choice of specific issues for lobbying. The subsequent chapters will analyze the selection of tactics and strategies of influence associated with advocacy efforts.

Any discussion of organizational behavior must deal with the relationship of the organization to its clients or constituents. In what ways do central decision makers and constituents communicate with each other? For most public interest groups, a very significant channel of communication is the organization's publication. Publications not only reveal what information organizations feel is useful and interesting to their audiences, but they can also offer insights into the way professional staffs view the role of the memberships and the functions of the organizations themselves.

Communication and intelligence in an organization flow not only from top to bottom, but the other way around as well. A central purpose of this chapter is to examine the means by which the desires and preferences of constituents are conveyed to public interest group decision makers. To what extent do the rank-and-file influence organizational decisions? At the same time, the other components of the decision-making process must be analyzed. In particular, the relationship between the professional staffs and governing bodies of the groups must be outlined. Who is actually making the decisions concerning the issue choices of the public interest lobbies?

PUBLICATIONS

The publications of public interest groups are aimed at one or more of four audiences. First, a publication may be intended to reach the entire formal membership. It is usually the case in membership groups that each individual who pays dues or makes a contribution receives a magazine or newsletter. A second audience may be an active or mobilizable public within the organizational membership. These are people who generally are more active than the average member. The organization considers that they are more likely to write letters to members of Congress when asked or to work on stimulating grass-roots activity when they are contacted.[1] Third, the interest groups—often those without membership—may want to reach an attentive public outside the organization. Attentive publics are groups of individuals that maintain a salient concern on certain issues.[2] For example, a civil rights group such as the Center for National Policy Review, which does not have a membership, sends its newsletter to other civil rights organizations and interested individuals. Fourth, groups may send their publications directly to the government officials and staff personnel who deal with the related issues.[3] Usually, this audience is approached in conjunction with at least one of the other three.

[1] On the concept of a "mobilizable public" within an interest group, see James N. Rosenau, *Citizenship Between Elections* (New York: The Free Press, 1974).

[2] See Francis E. Rourke, *Bureaucracy, Politics, and Public Policy* (Boston: Little, Brown, 1969), pp. 12-24.

[3] On lobbying conceptualized as direct and indirect communication between lobbyists, through channels, and government officials, see Lester W. Milbrath, *The Washington Lobbyists* (Chicago: Rand McNally, 1963).

A variety of styles and formats are used by public interest groups in their offerings. Of the sample of 83 groups, more than a dozen print *magazines*, which are distinguished by high-quality paper, photographs, a highly stylized presentation, and which contain a variety of material (feature articles, editorials, news from Washington, letters to the editor, and internal organization news and gossip). A smaller number of groups publish a *newspaper*. The content does not usually differ much from the magazine format, but the cheaper printing costs outweigh the need for a more attractive package such as the magazine. The most frequently used vehicle is the *newsletter*. These have fewer pages, are often folded rather than stapled, and tend to use low-quality paper. Newsletters tend to carry less in the way of in-depth feature articles, concentrating instead on more concise news and data summaries. Finally, there are *alerts*, which are put out as need be. They are printed cheaply, usually number only a page or two in length, and generally are mailed to selected members or attentive publics to inform them of an important upcoming vote in the Congress. Alerts are more than advisory in nature; they are also an appeal to readers to write letters and to activate others.

An organization's primary use of one of these types of publication by no means precludes the publication of another. Indeed, a third of the public interest groups are responsible for more than a single publication (see Table VII-1). Obviously, the amount of financial resources available to a group is an important, if not determining, factor in the quantity and frequency of publications (see Table VII-2).[4] Almost all of the organizations that publish a magazine also publish a more selectively circulated newsletter.

---

[4] Harold Wilensky writes, "*The more an organization depends on the unity and support of persons, groups, factions, or parties within its membership for the achievement of its central goals, the more resources it will devote to the intelligence function and the more of those resources will be spent on experts whom we might call 'internal communications specialists.'*" *Organizational Intelligence* (New York: Basic Books, 1967), p. 13.

TABLE VII-1

Publications

Magazine/newspaper and newsletter	22%	(18)
Newsletter and alerts	11%	(9)
Magazines or newsletter only[a]	39%	(32)
Alerts only	4%	(3)
Annual report only	4%	(3)
None	20%	(17)
NA	1%	(1)
	101%[b]	(N = 83)

[a] Primarily newsletters only.
[b] Rounding error.

Although the frequency and format of the publications is of interest, it is their content that is of most significance. The central question to be asked is how much useful information is made available by these organizations to their membership and specialized audiences? Answering this is not a matter of just finding out which organizations do investigative work or sponsor original research. Organizations can perform the equally useful functions of summarizing

TABLE VII-2

Frequency[a]

Biweekly	6%	(4)
Monthly	40%	(25)
Bimonthly	19%	(12)
Quarterly	16%	(10)
Irregularly	17%	(11)
NA	2%	(1)
	100%	(N = 63)

[a] Most frequently issued publication (excludes annual-report-only organizations).

and interpreting the research of others, or publicizing what is "on the record" in government documents.[5]

The conclusion reached from a thorough examination of samples of each group's publications is that public interest groups do an excellent job of putting forth data that are of value to their intended audiences. Of the three-quarters of the sample that publish something more than an annual report, the vast majority print highly factual, issue-oriented publications. There are only a few groups, such as the Washington Peace Center, that issue a newsletter that is concerned with news—such as fund-raising matters, schedules of meetings and events, and gossip—that is pertinent only to the organization. From the rank-and-file member, who seeks symbolic reassurance that the organization is doing good work, to the congressional staffer, who wants background material for upcoming committee hearings, the publications seem to serve their various audiences creditably. A few examples of some of the better publications will illustrate the value of public interest journals.

The *Defense Monitor*. One of the more unusual of the new public interest groups is the Center for Defense Information. Started in the spring of 1972 by a retired Navy admiral, Gene LaRocque, the group's purpose is to fight military waste. Because LaRocque was a career military officer and is hardly the image of a leftist critic, and because the professional staff is composed of other career military officers and "think tank" veterans, the Center has gained a great deal of respect in a relatively short period of time.[6]

[5] One poverty-civil rights worker spoke at length on the value of reading the record, "I learned something from I. F. Stone who said, 'Don't depend on insiders, read government handouts.' So I went to sleep reading horrible USDA reports, but we found out what was going on in the USDA and we knew more about what was going on in the USDA than they did."

[6] For a brief description of the organization and the *Defense Monitor*, see Duncan L. Clarke, "Congress, Interest Groups, and the U.S. Arms Control and Disarmament Agency," paper delivered at the annual meeting of the International Studies Association, New York,

Much of this respect derives from the Center's exceptionally good newsletter, the *Defense Monitor*, which comes out six times a year. Although the Center has no real membership—it is supported by foundations and a few large individual contributors—it mails out 8,000 to 10,000 copies of each issue of the *Defense Monitor*. Only a small percentage of these go out unsolicited. Each mailing includes 150 copies sent to Capitol Hill and 260 to the press. Copies even go to the Pentagon and to the White House. Plans by the Center to make the *Defense Monitor* more "readable" hardly seem necessary; currently it is a straightforward, factual presentation of qualitative and quantitative data with a minimum of rhetoric and fulmination. Some of the recent issues have carried impressive overviews of particular defense-related issues. One such issue had a detailed statistical analysis of the U.S. and Soviet navies, with direct comparisons of numerical differences, weapons capabilities, and future construction plans. Another issue dissected the proposal for the B-1 bomber by contrasting its nuclear warhead potential with both the in-use and improvable B-52's. The Center staff concluded that the B-1 bomber will provide only marginal advantages and is not worth its projected cost.

The high quality of the *Defense Monitor* and the reputable nature of the Center staff have given the group a great deal of visibility. The Center's file of newspaper clippings of stories that cite Center views and data is quite impressive. LaRocque, who enjoys being called the "Ralph Nader of the military," is the perfect spokesperson for the group because of his background and demeanor. In his public appearances, LaRocque is low-key, unemotional, and measured in his arguments. There have been only small victories for those who would cut military spending, but the Center and its *Defense Monitor* have supplied Pentagon critics with a surfeit of ammunition.

March 1973; and John Pierson, "A Weather Eye on the Military," *Wall Street Journal*, April 24, 1972, p. 1.

Civil Liberties. The American Civil Liberties Union's *Civil Liberties* is an example of a high-quality public interest publication that is intended primarily for the rank-and-file members of the group. Printed as a newspaper, *Civil Liberties* assumes a highly sophisticated and interested audience. Its subject matter covers a wide spectrum of personal and civil rights questions, and it constantly probes new areas of controversy. *Civil Liberties* is not technical enough to be of great use to public interest lawyers. Rather, it is basically concerned with educating the large (close to 200,000 persons) ACLU membership. Most of *Civil Liberties*, which is published nine times a year, is devoted to three or four very long analytical pieces on major issues of the day.

Recent issues of *Civil Liberties* included a story on the implementation of the "Riot Act" rider to the 1968 Civil Rights Act, an attack on the arbitrary nature of custom searches, an explanation of the ACLU prison reform project, and a discussion of the responsibility of the ACLU in the American Indian civil rights movement. In its tone and approach, *Civil Liberties* is much like popular magazines such as the *New Republic* or the *Nation*. Its basic intention is to create an informed citizenry. It probably does not convince many of the "right" stand on issues, because most of the members surely share the same political predispositions. It does, however, provide readers with a considerable amount of information as well as exposing them to developing issues of which they may not be fully aware.[7]

National Wildlife, International Wildlife, Conservation Report, Conservation News, and *Ranger Rick's.* All five of these publications are put out by the National Wildlife Federation. It is obvious that the environmental group is

---

[7] For a critique of the "biases" of the ACLU and an attack on alleged changes in organizational philosophy, see Joseph W. Bishop, Jr., "Politics and ACLU," *Commentary*, December 1971, pp. 50-58. For a rejoinder to Bishop's criticism, see Aryeh Neier, "Response: Politics and ACLU," mimeograph available from the American Civil Liberties Union, n.d.

able to publish five separate magazines and newsletters because of tremendous financial resources—over $10 million a year. But the National Wildlife Federation takes its educational role seriously, and it tries to serve the needs of different audiences with its different journals.

National Wildlife may be considered the primary publication of the Federation. It goes to approximately 600,000 individuals or "associate" members who pay $6.50 a year for it. Although there are some in-depth, but easy-to-read, articles on environment, the staff of the Federation freely admit that it is the "pretty pictures" that attract subscribers. Each issue of the bimonthly is full of high-quality, glossy, color photos of the flora and fauna of North America. *National Wildlife* is a handsomely packaged magazine, and it is enjoyable just to thumb through. *International Wildlife*, also at $6.50 a year, is set in a format similar to *National Wildlife*, but as the title indicates, its focus is worldwide. It goes to a somewhat smaller audience than *National Wildlife* in alternate months of the year.

Two specialized newsletters aimed at people who have a more professional interest in environmental affairs are *Conservation News* and *Conservation Report*. Both are sent free of charge to those who ask to be put on the mailing lists. *Conservation News* goes out 20 times a year to 50,000 people, including affiliate Federation leaders and activists as well as a wide variety of interested parties outside the organization. It contains a general potpourri of environmental news, book reviews, and current research summaries, with articles only slightly more technical than those in *National Wildlife*. *Conservation Report* is indispensable to any organization or individual that is concerned with environmental legislation. It has a mailing list of 14,000 and comes out 40 times a year. It monitors and analyzes all significant environmental legislation before the Congress, and each issue has 8 or 10 short articles on hearings, committee actions, floor votes, committee reports, and the like.

Possibly the most unusual of all public interest publications is National Wildlife's *Ranger Rick's*, a magazine aimed at elementary school-aged children. It has a phenomenal circulation of about 400,000, close to three times the membership of the Sierra Club. National Wildlife pushes hard at marketing it as a gift that parents and grandparents can give to a small child. A modest $6.00 buys 10 issues a year, all of which contain numerous glossy color photographs of wildlife and nature scenes. Included in each issue is a continuing story, "Ranger Rick and His Friends." Ranger Rick is a precocious raccoon who, in a recent adventure, went to Australia with Ollie Otter, Sammy Squirrel, and Davey Deer. Once there, they met Sidney Koala and a group of indigenous marsupials. An accompanying nonfiction article explained in a serious vein the problems that Australia faces with regard to endangered species, soil erosion, air and water pollution, and solid waste disposal.

CONSTITUENCY RELATIONS

For those groups that have memberships, a magazine or newsletter serves as a means by which the organization communicates with its constituents. These publications enable the professional staffs of the public interest groups to express their views on the issues they deem of most concern to the organization. What must now be examined is the manner in which rank-and-file members are able to convey their views on the issues on which they think the professional staff should be working.

The purpose here is not to ascertain whether or not public interest groups are democratic in their workings. If "democracy" is taken to indicate that constituents have a formal opportunity to select their leaders, it may be stated at the outset that public interest groups are not democratic. Rather, these organizations are quite oligarchic in nature; in all but a few of the groups, the leaders cannot be realistically challenged.[8] This tendency seemingly holds for interest groups in general. Lipset, Trow, and Coleman conclude:

> In few areas of political life is the discrepancy between formal juridical guarantees of democratic procedure and the actual practice of oligarchic rule so marked as in private or voluntary organizations such as trade unions, professional and business associations, veterans' groups, and cooperatives. . . . almost all such organizations are characterized internally by the rule of a one-party oligarchy. That is, one group, which controls the administration, usually retains power indefinitely. . . .[9]

If public interest groups are undemocratic in this sense, they may still be open to the influence of members through processes other than the selection of leaders.[10] An attempt will thus be made to analyze alternative channels of constituency influence.

In examining the organization of public interest groups, what is most interesting is not that they are oligarchic in practice, but that there are not even formal concessions to a democratic structure in a majority of membership groups. As David Truman points out, the organizational structures of interest groups usually take the form of the "democratic mold." Truman notes that without democratic procedures,

[8] The classic statement on political organizations becoming naturally oligarchic is Robert Michels' *Political Parties* (Glencoe, Ill.: The Free Press, 1958). First published in 1911.

[9] Seymour Martin Lipset, Martin Trow, and James Coleman, *Union Democracy* (Garden City, N.Y.: Anchor Books, 1956), p. 1.

[10] James Q. Wilson writes of "democracy" in voluntary organizations, "an organization will be said to be 'democratic' to the degree that it permits members freely to choose officers or policies. An association is 'representative,' but undemocratic, if member interests are congruent with leadership policies but the members do not, as a practical matter, choose these leaders in meaningful elections or participate in the formulation of leadership policies." The question of congruency between leaders (staff) and members is addressed below. *Political Organizations* (New York: Basic Books, 1973), pp. 237-238.

"an organization cannot achieve 'respectability' and 'legitimacy' in the community."[11] Nevertheless, in terms of "statutory influence," 57% of the public interest membership groups have no structure that ostensibly elicits and considers member opinion (see Table VII-3). In response to

TABLE VII-3

Formal Influence

No means	57%	(33)
Delegate structure	17%	(10)
Direct means	26%	(15)
	100%	$(N = 58)^a$

a Membership groups only.

questions concerning constituency relations and organizational policy making, interviewees for these groups were very frank in admitting that their memberships are supportive rather than participatory.[12]

For the remainder of the groups (43%), the most common mechanism by which members can try to influence organizational decisions is through annual or biennial conventions. Some groups have federated structures where the rank-

[11] David B. Truman, *The Governmental Process*, 2nd ed. (New York: Alfred A. Knopf, 1971), p. 129.

[12] The definition of organizational membership used throughout this study is those individuals who have contributed money or dues to a public interest group recently enough to be carried on a group's mailing list. Some groups do, in fact, disclaim any notion of membership, and they label their supporters only as "contributors." Those that call their supporters "members" do not use the term in a consistent fashion. Some just contribute money, but have no say in organizational decisions, whereas other "members" have full voting rights. Thus the distinction is made here between participatory and supportive memberships. The nonmembership groups are those organizations that are funded by foundations, with few or no individual contributors, and those church-related lobbies that have no distinct membership aside from those expressing a denominational affiliation. See Chapter II.

and-file's views can be represented via elected delegates to the meetings. Other organizations have open conventions that all members are free to attend. In a smaller number of groups, members are able to express preferences directly to the professional staff by ballot or by polls. Even if members do not really control their leaders, they do have at least some chance to communicate their sentiments through these outlets. Whether or not these opportunities result in any real influence within the organization will be discussed below.

Within the subsample of participatory membership groups, the seven organizations that are *coalitions* should be distinguished. The structure of these groups facilitates a far greater degree of participation than can be found in the other public interest lobbies. The members of organizations such as the Committee for Congressional Reform are other interest groups. Usually, coalition members have their own representatives in Washington, which gives them a chance to meet periodically with the permanent coalition staff. Consequently, there are frequent meetings held by the coalitions where policy and strategy are debated by representatives of member groups. Although the professional staff retains disproportionate influence, these coalitions are generally the most susceptible and receptive to constituency influence of all the public interest groups.[13]

Participation in the coalitions is fostered not only by the opportunity for close consultation, but also by the dependence of the coalition staff on the resources of member groups. This means more than just financial support. Quite often major advocacy efforts are conditioned on the amount of work the member organization staffs are willing to contribute. One coalition staff lobbyist noted the limitations

[13] For the factors leading to and against cooperative behavior among interest groups, see Donald R. Hall, *Cooperative Lobbying—The Power of Pressure* (Tucson: University of Arizona Press, 1969), pp. 38-128. Formal organization of coalitions is only one form of cooperative behavior. See Chapter IX for a more detailed look at coalition behavior by public interest groups.

upon him: "Realistically, we can only get a big push from the members twice a year. We can get other levels of action from them, of course, but only once or twice a year can we get all the horses going."

The remaining participatory membership groups display varying, but generally low, degrees of constituency influence. The organizations with delegate-convention structures exemplify conformity with the democratic mold. Similar to private interest group organizations—labor unions, for example—conventions are easily controlled by professional staffs.[14] Conventions are policy-ratifying, not policy-making, bodies. Staffs write the resolutions and set the agenda. One environmentalist said cynically of the delegates to his group's convention, "Most of the people don't even know what they're voting on." Despite this, the convention must act as a minor constraint on policy makers; knowing that a controversial resolution may put one on the spot is at least a moderating influence on staff personnel.[15]

In a few organizations, there is some measurable grass-roots influence deriving from the convention process. In the League of Women Voters, resolutions are first solicited from local and state leagues.[16] The professional staff in Washington add their own influence when they synthesize the resolutions into those to be brought before the biennial gathering. At a recent League convention, the delegates actually rejected a proposal by the League national office concerning an internal matter. The national wanted to increase its own funding from a direct membership fee, but the local League delegates later forced a compromise.[17] Overall, the League

[14] See Truman, *The Governmental Process*, pp. 111-155.

[15] The dilemma of having to deal with "power" that is not expressed in "concrete decisions," but that may derive from anticipated reaction, is best expressed by Peter Bachrach and Morton S. Baratz, "Two Faces of Power," *American Political Science Review*, vol. 56 (December 1962), pp. 947-952.

[16] For a profile of the League, see Judith Axler Turner, "League of Women Voters Backs Study with Lobbying to Influence Policy," *National Journal*, May 20, 1972, pp. 860-870.

[17] Mary Russell, "Women's Groups Suddenly Finding Their Purses Are Empty," *Washington Post*, December 3, 1972, p. A8. In 1974,

remains one of the more democratically operated public interest groups.

There are also a very few organizations whose conventions offer members an even more direct role in group policy making. The National Peace Action Coalition has an annual convention that is open to all self-designated members, rather than just to selected delegates. Attendance at these meetings is encouraged, and resolutions are solicited from members on the night prior to the first business session. The resolutions that pass do represent the decisions of those attending, with a minimum of predetermined policy by the organization's leadership. Long-range planning is difficult, and the directives that are passed hold only through the next demonstration. A steering committee must direct the organization through most of the calendar year.

Polls are used to tap member sentiment by a small number of groups, most notably Common Cause, the Liberty Lobby, and the American Security Council. The polls (questionnaires) are not always the most scientifically valid measuring instruments, as questions can be loaded or biased in their wording.[18] The opportunity for expression does exist, however, and surprising results on a given question will always be brought into consideration when leaders develop organizational policy.[19]

---

the League decided to admit men as members with the hope that they would bolster the organization both in terms of finances and volunteer labor. Maria Karagianis, "Men, Minorities, Younger Women—Voters League Changing," *Boston Globe*, May 18, 1975, p. 33.

[18] Some questions from the American Security Council's 1973 National Securities Issue Poll read: "Do you believe that the United States should encourage and help the people in the captive nations in their desire for freedom?"; and "Since the Supreme Court has weakened the old laws, should Congress write new and enforceable laws making it illegal to teach or advocate the overthrow of the government by force and violence?"

[19] In Common Cause, for example, the top issues selected by the members are always placed on the official agenda. The decision of most importance, however, is which issues will get real priority attention, and this decision is influenced much more by the board than by the members. In the 1972 poll, 20,000 of the 200,000 members responded to the questionnaire included in an issue of the newsletter,

The discussion has dwelt on the formal channels of influence in the participatory membership groups. An informal means of communication that can be used by individuals to express their views to membership and nonmembership groups alike is letter writing. People may write for different reasons, but most frequently they probably write to urge a group to take action on a certain issue. Interviewees stressed —often in the context of admitting that their members had no real say in policy decisions—that they were very much aware of sentiment in the mail. Being aware of it and being responsive to it are two different things; there was little evidence of unprompted mail being a real influence on policy making in many organizations.

One place where the mail is of consequence is in the Ralph Nader conglomerate. Despite the Public Citizen apparatus, there are no participatory membership groups among the various Washington satellites. Nader himself has become an unofficial ombudsman for cheated, swindled, abused, and outraged consumers. The mail, much of it addressed "Ralph Nader, Washington, D.C.," goes largely unanswered, but it is read. In addition, it is an important source of information for the consumer product-oriented organizations. The Center for Auto Safety, for example, receives all the complaints Nader gets concerning automobiles. Some of this mail eventually ends up as a data base, documenting defects, for Center campaigns to force recalls of specific models.[20]

In sum, it may be said that in the majority of groups the

Report from Washington. See Theodore Jacqueney, "Common Cause Lobbyists Focus on the Structure and Process of Government," *National Journal,* September 1, 1973, p. 1296. The 1973 poll is in the September 1972 *Report from Washington,* p. 7, and the results are reported in the March 1973 issue, p. 6.

[20] For a sketch of the Center for Auto Safety (p. 19) and its relationship to the entire Nader organization, see Lois G. Wark, "Nader Campaigns for Funds to Expand Activities of his Consumer Action Complex," *The Pressure Groups* (Washington, D.C.: National Journal, 1971), pp. 12-24.

members or constituents have little direct influence on organization leaders. In a pattern similar to that of private interest groups, public interest lobbies are strongly oligarchic. If anything, this tendency may be even more pronounced in public interest groups, where the democratic mold structure, much less real participatory democracy, is largely absent.[21] Still, with or without statutory means of influence, members exert some control over the organization's elites by their potential for negative action. The members can "vote with their feet" by leaving the organization with a nonrenewal of their membership should the group move in a direction that is unacceptable to them. The existence of a membership is, in and of itself, at least a small constraint on the group's policy makers. As Luttbeg and Zeigler point out, "Even in the absence of efficient consultative mechanisms, leaders and followers exist in a functional relationship. That is to say, leaders are limited by the followers' expressed or latent values and expectations."[22]

Given that the objective here was not to determine if "democracy" exists in public interest groups, what then are the implications of the generally low degree of constituency influence? First, the absence of direct representation increases the freedom of staff and governing boards. The latitude given staff permits them to become active on issues and to take positions of which members might not always approve.[23] In some public interest groups, antiwar lobbies,

[21] As Dahl and Lindblom point out in the case of a polyarchical society, regular participation is not as important as the opportunity to participate when the need arises. "The question, then, is not so much whether citizens are active but whether they have the opportunity to exert control through activity when they wish to do so." See Robert A. Dahl and Charles E. Lindblom, *Politics, Economics, and Welfare* (New York: Harper Torchbooks, 1963), p. 312 and, generally, pp. 272-323.

[22] Norman R. Luttbeg and Harmon Zeigler, "Attitude Consensus and Conflict in an Interest Group: An Assessment of Cohesion," *American Political Science Review*, vol. 60 (September 1966), p. 655.

[23] The relationship between leaders and followers is fundamentally affected by the structure of the incentive systems. See, generally, Harmon Zeigler and G. Wayne Peak, *Interest Groups in American*

for example, the attitude difference between leaders and followers is not of great significance. On the other hand, in church groups the differences between leaders and staff and the "person in the pew" is of considerable magnitude. Almost all of the church representatives interviewed acknowledged that the Washington office took much more liberal positions than the parishioners would mandate if they had the opportunity.[24]

The second implication of the lack of constituency influence and representation is that it can affect the public image of a group. Again, Luttbeg and Zeigler write, "Like all political organizations, they are accorded more legitimacy when they can show they are representative of the attitudes and values of a particular segment of society."[25] This is more than just an assumption of political scientists; public interest lobbyists are, in fact, quite concerned about conveying their *representative* role during advocacy efforts. Understandably, church lobbyists, who are the most unrepresentative of the public interest constituencies in the sample, were particularly sensitive to this factor. Many of them mentioned that they like to be accompanied by local ministers from a Congressperson's district or state when lobbying on Capitol Hill. Although members of Congress and administrative personnel have some preconceived notions of which groups' views they value,[26] initial impres-

---

Society, 2nd ed. (Englewood Cliffs, N.J.: Prentice-Hall, 1972), pp. 64-92.

[24] In his organizational analysis of interest groups, Henry J. Pratt found that bureaucratization of the organization has not made the interest groups more conservative *per se*. Rather, he finds evidence to suggest that bureaucratization has fostered professional staffs with continuing reformist impulses. See Henry J. Pratt, "Bureaucracy and Interest Group Behavior: A Study of Three National Organizations," paper delivered at the annual meeting of the American Political Science Association, Washington, D.C., September 1972.

[25] Luttbeg and Zeigler, "Attitude Consensus and Conflict in an Interest Group," p. 655.

[26] See Lewis Anthony Dexter, "The Representative and His District," *Human Organization*, vol. 16 (Spring 1957), pp. 2-13.

sions can certainly be shaped by the perceived representativeness image.[27]

The groups that are most open to criticism of being unrepresentative are, of course, those organizations that have members but no "democratic mold," or that have no members at all. For membership groups, this lack of opportunity for rank-and-file participation runs against the grain of our political culture. It is an accepted norm that political organizations maintain at least the veneer of democratic processes in their internal operation. For those organizations that have no real membership, there is the constant problem of convincing skeptics that they speak for a constituency that is truly supportive of their advocacy efforts.[28]

ADVOCACY DECISIONS

It is now clear that constituents are not the dominant influence in public interest groups. What remains to be discussed is the comparative influence of the professional staffs and governing boards of these organizations. Examining board-staff interaction should provide the necessary information to determine the locus of decision-making power in public interest groups. Once the general patterns of authority are identified, it will then be possible to explore the process by which decision makers choose issues on which to lobby.

Who Governs? The leadership of public interest groups has heretofore been discussed in rather vague terms. Spe-

[27] As V. O. Key writes, "the more completely an organization encompasses its potential membership, the greater is its moral authority when it claims to speak for an interest in society." *Public Opinion and American Democracy* (New York: Alfred A. Knopf, 1961), p. 503.

[28] For legislative lobbying, the lack of a membership has tactical disadvantages. Members of Congress have been shown to be much more responsive to constituents than to Washington representatives. See John W. Kingdon, *Congressmen's Voting Decisions* (New York: Harper & Row, 1973).

cifically, there are two components to the leadership of the
various groups. First, there is the professional staff. These
are the people who are the employees of the organization
and work in the Washington office, or in other headquarters
and branch offices, on a day-to-day basis. Second, almost
all of the groups have boards of directors. These boards have
legal responsibility for their organization, but their real influence within the groups varies widely.[29] Members of the
professional staffs are sometimes also members of the governing boards.

A series of responses to questions in the interviews revealed that the professional staffs dominate the policy-making processes of slightly more than two-thirds (69%) of the
public interest groups (see Table VII-4). They are at least

TABLE VII-4

Decision Locus

Staff	69%	(57)
Board	10%	(8)
Shared, staff and board	12%	(10)
Shared, staff, board, and members	10%	(8)
	101%[a]	(N = 83)

[a] Rounding error.

equal participants in all but 10% of the lobbies in the sample.
In terms of deciding which issues to lobby on, allocating
resources between advocacy efforts, formulating major aspects of strategies and tactics, and generally developing
policy positions, the professional staffs tend to be the primary locus of influence.

Concomitantly, the boards of directors tend to have a very
minor leadership role, or no real role at all, in most public
interest groups (see Table VII-5). Although many of the
boards have the statutory responsibility for making major

[29] See Mayer Zald, "The Power and Functions of Boards of Directors," American Journal of Sociology, vol. 75 (June 1969), pp. 97-
111.

TABLE VII-5

Board Role

Primary decision maker	10%	(8)
Shared responsiblity for decision making	22%	(18)
Minor capacity[a]	33%	(27)
Ceremonial	30%	(25)
No board	6%	(5)
	101%[b]	(N = 83)

[a] Fund raising, making occasional contact for staff, etc.
[b] Rounding error.

organizational policy decisions, their "decisions" are often *pro forma* approval of what the staff has already determined. Despite the fact that boards are composed of knowledgeable, and sometimes very expert, people, the quality of personnel is not the determining factor of their intraorganizational influence. Boards can be put together for "show" on letterheads and grant proposals or for fund-raising purposes, as well as for consultative potential.

It can be concluded that the professional staffs of public interest groups have a tremendous amount of freedom. Even where the staff is not the dominant power in decision making, it is often the primary source of policy initiation. That is, the staff begins the process of debate on particular issues before the governing body of the organization.

Although the trend toward staff domination is a strong one, there is significant variation within the sample. Staff dominance is most evident in the consumer and environmental groups. Analysis of the origins of the public interest groups showed that these two group types had the greatest propensity to be responsive to entrepreneurs rather than disturbances.[30] It may very well be that in organizations

[30] See Chapter II. See also, Jeffrey M. Berry, "On the Origins of Public Interest Groups: A Test of Two Theories," *Polity* (forthcoming, 1977).

that are set up around a particular individual, there is less concern for "controlling" the staff and creating a strong countervailing board.

Power that is shared between the professional staff and the board, or between the staff and the board and the members, is more likely to be found in the general politics and peace-arms groups. The peace-arms lobbies tend to be catalyzed by disturbances rather than entrepreneurs, and both types of groups adhere more strongly to the democratic mold structure. It is not as clear why these groups are more likely to have more than a single locus of power. The subsamples of each type show about half as staff-dominated and half with shared responsibility, with strong generalizations not possible. The church-supported lobbies are the least likely to be staff dominated. Movement into new policy areas is likely to be debated in light of church doctrine. Power in these groups is shared with constituency assemblies and smaller governing boards, but the staffs still play a very important policy-initiation role.[31]

It should also be noted that because so many of the organizations are relatively recent in their origins (47% started in the five years preceding the survey), many have yet to go through the transformation that takes place when the leader-founder is no longer present. It is quite often the case that a stronger bureaucratic structure emerges after the demise of the leader of a voluntary organization.[32] This "bureaucratization" may very well include stronger organizational roles for governing boards or even rank-and-file members. Evidence from the survey does, in fact, suggest

[31] For a look at the gradual, but wholesale, involvement of church groups in civil rights legislation, see James L. Adams, *The Growing Church Lobby in Washington* (Grand Rapids, Mich.: William B. Eerdmans, 1970).

[32] For an analysis of the process of organizational development in interest groups, see Theodore J. Lowi, *The Politics of Disorder* (New York: Basic Books, 1971). For a critique of the standard Weber-Michels model, see Mayer Zald and Roberta Ash, "Social Movement Organizations: Growth, Decay, and Change," *Social Forces*, vol. 44 (March 1966), pp. 327-341.

that there is less of a tendency for older organizations to be staff dominated than for newer ones. Consequently, it may be more the "age" of the groups rather than their issue basis of organization that is the more important factor leading to staff domination.

Decision Dynamics. Identifying the decision makers still leaves much of the story untold. What are the actual dynamics of choosing policies and allocating resources to advocacy efforts? The first point to be made should be obvious: not all decisions are the same. Many decisions are automatic responses rather than a comprehensive search for all alternative policies. Automatic responses include not only those associated with minor, routine matters; decisions can also be automatic when an issue comes up that is so central to the group's purpose that there is no question that it will choose to make a large advocacy effort.[33] For example, when a greatly strengthened endangered species law was introduced in the 93rd Congress, no real decision had to be made by the Fund for Animals. There was no doubt that the group would work hard for passage of the legislation.

As in all organizations, decisions in interest groups tend to be incremental in nature.[34] Policy fights with the government rarely have quick endings. Rather, specific policy issues endure over surprising periods of time, sometimes stretching out over many years. As the immediate focus of the specific issue changes, the interest groups adapt their efforts accordingly. Most of the work that groups do on a day-to-day basis consists of following up work they began previously. After the National Committee for an Effective

[33] An automatic response is something of an ideal type, best conceptualized as a pole on a continuum of search and problem solving in decisions. See James G. March and Herbert A. Simon, *Organizations* (New York: Wiley, 1958), pp. 139-140.

[34] See Charles E. Lindblom, "The Science of Muddling Through," *Public Administration Review*, vol. 19 (Spring 1959), pp. 79-88. See also Paul R. Schulman, "Nonincremental Policy Making: Notes Toward an Alternative Paradigm," *American Political Science Review*, vol. 69 (December 1975), pp. 1354-1370.

Congress came so close to getting a new campaign finance
law in the 91st Congress—a bill was vetoed by the President—the work never really stopped even after the enactment of the Federal Election Campaign Act of 1971.[35]
NCEC continued to be active in pressing for new reforms
and, along with a new group, the Center for Public Financing, they worked for the passage of the Federal Election
Campaign Act Amendments of 1974, the most far-reaching
law to date.[36]

The fact that such a large proportion of organizational
decisions are automatic responses or gradual, incremental,
steps still does not answer a fundamental question: what
leads groups to strike out in new areas where the commitment is not really part of previous, ongoing work?[37] Why
does the American Civil Liberties Union start a large-scale
prison rights project, or the Public Citizen Litigation Group
initiate legal action on presidential impoundments, or the
Center for Law and Social Policy begin extensive work on
the rights of mental patients?

Within the constraints of limited available resources, and
within the purview of organizational goals, the interviews
suggest that decisions to move on new issues usually re-
volve around two variables: the expertise and personal interest of the professional staff. Expertise is the competence
of the individual staff members to work on certain issues.

[35] See Robert L. Peabody, Jeffrey M. Berry, William G. Frasure,
and Jerry Goldman, *To Enact a Law: Congress and Campaign Financing* (New York: Praeger, 1972); and Jeffrey M. Berry and Jerry
Goldman, "Congress and Public Policy: A Study of the Federal Election Campaign Act of 1971," *Harvard Journal on Legislation*, vol. 10
(February 1973), pp. 331-365.
[36] Public Law 93-443. This act provides for federal funding of
presidential campaigns and for limitations on the size of individual
contributions.
[37] All decisions are, to some degree, incremental. Groups do logically follow patterns in their issue involvement. But there must be
some distinction between small, gradual steps in a policy effort and
significant undertakings in new areas. For the latter case, the incremental model is not fully adequate. See Lindblom, "The Science
of Muddling Through."

Personal interest is simply the receptiveness and desire of staffers to devote time and energy to specific issues.[38] Some of the interviewees' descriptions of the decision making in their own organizations will illustrate the personal discretion often allowed staffers. A consumer lawyer spoke of his organization:

> The formal answer is that we have a set of criteria. We take cases that if we win there will be significant change in the status quo. It will be a test case in most instances. It should affect a lot of people rather than a few. . . . The informal answer is that it's a highly subjective process. Basically, we do what grabs us.

An environmentalist:

> [It's] pretty much decided by whether or not a staff person is interested in an issue and wants to take it on. Sometimes, if an important bill comes up, and we need somebody on it, we'll ask a person to follow it. Projects of one or two weeks or more are decided upon by that staff person.

An animal-protection worker:

> I guess it's when Pearl and I sit down and we get to feel that things are so terrible that they just can't go on and we have to do something about them.

One of Ralph Nader's close aides:

> Sometimes Ralph decides . . . and he'll give me a problem and ask me if there's a lawsuit involved. That's what makes this job exciting. Another thing that can happen is that people come to us [with a problem]. And, then, if I see something in the paper that makes me mad, I might decide to do something about it.

[38] The flexibility in response to new issues in public interest groups is enhanced by their normally small size and lack of hierarchy. See Wilensky, *Organizational Intelligence*, pp. 42-48. The effect of size and structure on decision making is discussed below.

Another consumer lobbyist:

> Essentially, we're looking for hot pokers to stick up GM's ass.

A public interest lawyer:

> At present our decision making is quite like a law firm. If somebody decides they want to take a case, they circulate a memorandum to the staff. If somebody feels strongly about something, in the past, he has been allowed to do it.

This independence in decision making is, of course, most descriptive of the staff-dominated lobbies. Where power is shared with the board, the individual staffers must go through the consultive mechanisms set up by the organization. As noted earlier, even in these groups the initiative remains with individual staff members. It is the staff who approach the board with issue preferences and projects, not the other way around. In these organizations, clearance is not *pro forma*; the boards may act to modify staff-approved policy. The small number of groups that are actually dominated by a governing board are harder to categorize. The decision-making process is, however, much more collective, with less influence accruing to individual staff and board members.

Decision Making: A Summary Statement. The individual liberty allowed staff lobbyists is both an interesting and a significant finding. But to conclude that nonincremental, nonautomatic decisions simply turn upon the personal interest and personal expertise of staffers surely overstates the case. When one public interest lobbyist said of her group's decision making, "I guess I do what I want," she was certainly describing a freedom of action that she felt. At the same time, however, there may be factors that influence decision making that are not readily apparent to the activists involved. It may be useful here to try to elaborate upon the lobbyists' interview responses by placing decision making in the larger organizational and environmental context within which it takes place.

There is no argument with the central thrust of the public interest lobbyists' observations on decision making. The professional staffs do have great discretion in selecting issues on which to lobby. Nevertheless, it is also true that these decisions are influenced by other variables, such as organizational goals, current resource commitments and capabilities, and the activity of other interest groups. These factors work to structure the alternatives open to the lobbyist at the time he or she is ready to make a decision on a new issue. A brief discussion of these organizational and environmental constraints may help to clarify the manner in which these variables act at least to shape the "agenda" from which the decision makers choose among alternative issues.

The evolution of issue decisions may be traced as far back as the initial goals and purpose of the organizations. Public interest groups may appear to have rather broad concerns (e.g., consumer protection, environment), but most have a more narrow focus (e.g., corporate responsibility, wilderness). For each group there exists a distinct subset of policy areas that are regarded as relevant to organizational objectives and that define the boundaries of any issue search by a lobbyist. Organizational goals are not immutable, of course, but change is usually gradual in nature. For a voluntary association, goal adaptation is rarely radical, as each organization has a reputation for advocacy work on certain issues that it does not want to lose. Even if a group proceeds in a new area, the issues they select will have a logical relationship to the organization's goals as they have been commonly understood in the past.[39]

[39] On goal adaptation in voluntary associations, see David Sills, *The Volunteers* (New York: The Free Press, 1957); Abraham Holtzman, *The Townsend Movement* (New York: Bookman, 1963); and Sheldon L. Messinger, "Organizational Transformation: A Case Study of a Declining Social Movement," *American Sociological Review*, vol. 20 (February 1955), pp. 3-10.

Beyond the confines of organizational goals, a group's choice of new issues is restricted by its current resources and commitments. Although many new issues that develop may relate to an individual group's purpose, some cannot be considered because an advocacy effort would require resources beyond the current capabilities of the organization. Every interest group has an ongoing allocation of personnel and financial resources to particular issues, and the choice of new issues must be made with available resources in mind. This is not to say that a group with only a small amount of resources to be utilized on a new issue cannot decide to act upon a very broad issue that needs extensive lobbying; it can choose to work on such an issue in a minor or limited way. There are times, however, when a group simply cannot realistically consider an issue because it does not have the necessary resources. For example, a group may have its experienced Capitol Hill representatives involved in a major effort to get a bill passed, and it could not take on any new legislative issue without dropping or at least seriously curtailing the first.

The amount of available resources and the nature of ongoing commitments will thus affect the range of issue options open to a public interest group. As already evidenced, the qualifications and expertise of the Washington lobbyists are also important variables in this respect. Most notably, a number of the organizations have no legal advocacy capability because there are no lawyers on the staff nor money with which to hire outside attorneys. These organizations will, as a consequence, avoid issues that would warrant the use of litigation or formal administrative intervention. In more general terms, the expertise of staff members will always work to push the organizations toward some issues and away from others. A lobbyist for an environmental group who has no scientific background would surely hesitate to take on a highly technical issue such as breeder reactors. The same staffer, however, might not think twice about going to work on a straightforward issue such as legislation to ban leg-hold animal traps. In sum, the choice of new issues is strongly influenced by the collective expertise of each lobbying staff.

The choice of new issues by a public interest group is further affected by what may be labeled the "competitive environment." Interest groups are always quite aware of what other like-minded organizations are working on. If one advocacy group with a similar policy preference is making a major lobbying effort on an issue, a second organization will want to avoid duplication and overlap of scarce resources. Public interest groups will often develop identities as the leaders on particular issues. Any group with a potential interest in strip mining, for example, must recognize the extensive lobbying effort made by the Environmental Policy Center in recent years and its unquestioned position as spokesman for those who support strong federal regulation.

It is only natural that public interest groups will seek out issues on which they can make a "name" for themselves. In selecting new issues, the organizations will prefer those underworked by other groups. This tendency is tempered, however, by a group's desire to work on issues they consider to be most important and most critical in their policy area. As a result, groups will still move on issues well covered by other groups, and out of this "competition," coalitions and other cooperative arrangements will often arise.

Although alternatives are shaped and reduced by goals, resources, and the competitive environment, there still remains the individual discretion of the decision makers to choose the specific issues among those that merit review. Ideally, an organization evaluates its priorities as it searches out all possible options open to it.[40] In practice, this is not the case. As was shown earlier, in most of the groups the final choice of issues turns on the personal interest (which

[40] On the ideal of synoptic rationality and the realities of real-world decision making, see Lindblom, "The Science of Muddling Through."

is inextricably tied to personal expertise) of individual staff members.

This overview of the decision-making process has simplified the complex relationship between the variables that have been identified. These factors have been isolated for purposes of analysis, but in reality, of course, they are highly interdependent. One cannot, for example, separate the effect of goals from the final discretion allowed staff decision makers because goals become internalized as the lobbyists adopt their organizational role. Consciously or unconsciously, goals will always be part of the mental calculations that go into issue selection.[41]

A Note on Private Interest Groups. The staff dominance in most public interest groups is particularly interesting in light of the previous research on private interest groups. In his sample of Washington lobbyists, Lester Milbrath found that the staff was the "primary locus of policy leadership" in only 13% of the organizations.[42] There are some basic structural differences in the organization of public interest lobbies and private interest lobbies that explain, in part, this wide disparity in decision-making authority. Private interest representatives are often hired on retainer or for a fixed period and never really become part of the organization. In public interest groups, on the other hand, 30% of them have no memberships, with the professional staff literally being the embodiment of the organization. Many private interest lobbyists tend to be directed in their work by the governing boards of the associations they represent. Although these lobbyists still have considerable freedom in tactical matters, the selection of specific issues on which to act is likely to come from above.

Studies by political scientists indicate that the determina-

[41] See Herbert A. Simon, "On the Concept of Organizational Goal," *Administrative Science Quarterly*, vol. 9 (June 1964), pp. 1-22.

[42] Of those with the available information, the 13% figure includes the loci of leadership designated by Milbrath as "respondent" and "staff." See Milbrath, *The Washington Lobbyists*, pp. 41-46.

tion of political "interests" within private interest groups can be a delicate task, and the lack of policy agreement within private interest groups is often quite surprising. In their study of foreign trade legislation, Bauer, Pool, and Dexter found that their expectations of who would be lobbying were woefully inaccurate. They found that their evaluations of self-interest were not good predictors of whether or not the heads of businesses made efforts to lobby on the foreign trade legislation:

> we would suggest that most significant of all to an understanding of what communication went out from business on foreign trade was neither self-interest nor ideology, but the institutional structures which facilitated or blocked the production of messages.[43]

Furthermore, when they studied trade associations in Washington, they found a pattern of nonaction by interest groups one would think would be most active on foreign trade. Not only were the giant associations such as the National Association of Manufacturers and the Chamber of Commerce immobilized by aspects of the legislation that split the membership, but also specific industry associations such as the National Electrical Manufacturers were similarly inactive. Consequently, specialized *ad hoc* interest groups were set up by interested parties to lobby on the foreign trade matter, although these groups suffered from lack of resources.[44]

It may be that the paralysis of interest group action by established organizations is peculiar to national organizations and large corporations or is associated only with certain types of omnibus measures such as a foreign trade bill. Similar findings, however, were recorded by Edward C. Banfield in his study of political issues in metropolitan Chi-

[43] Raymond A. Bauer, Ithiel de Sola Pool, and Lewis Anthony Dexter, *American Business and Public Policy* (New York: Atherton, 1963), p. 229.

[44] *Ibid.*, pp. 323-399.

cago.[45] Banfield observed that "civic associations," local groups that individually encompassed various social, political, and business interests and were set up for the purpose of promoting the city's welfare, could not act on matters relevant to their ostensible purpose:

> The civic associations that played a part in the cases presented here were generally ineffective because of their preoccupation with their own maintenance. They avoided controversy in order to maintain themselves. Almost without exception, they were split down the middle by the issues raised in these cases. To avoid being weakened (in the conventional formula, "loss of effectiveness"), they did not take positions in important matters. When the proponents or opponents of a position found organization necessary, they usually created *ad hoc* ones. If the *ad hoc* organizations survived to become permanent, they soon became as rigid as the others. . . .[46]

The public interest groups were not found to display a tendency toward policy indecision and immobilization because of disagreement over organizational goals. This is not to say that public interest groups are free from internal conflict concerning policy decisions. A notable example is the split that developed in the Sierra Club over the leadership and policies of David Brower, resulting in Brower's establishing his own group, Friends of the Earth.[47] Consumers Union and the Consumer Federation of America have also suffered from significant internal disputes.[48] Gen-

[45] Edward C. Banfield, *Political Influence* (New York: The Free Press, 1965).

[46] *Ibid.*, p. 297.

[47] See John McPhee, *Conversations with the Archdruid* (New York: Farrar, Straus & Giroux, 1971).

[48] On Consumers Union see, Nancy L. Ross, "Consumers Union Staff Split By Testing vs. Advocacy Issue," *Washington Post*, April 24, 1973, p. A2; and "Nader Quits Consumers Union," *The New York Times*, August 23, 1975, p. 10. On the Consumer Federation of America, see Walterene Swanston, "Consumer Federation of America Waging Spirited Battle for Survival," *National Journal*, July 8, 1972,

erally speaking, though, the sample as a whole did not show a pattern similar to the one described by Banfield, and Bauer, Pool, and Dexter. Most of the public interest groups seemed to be able to move rapidly into new, controversial issue areas without the fear of causing a major dispute within the organization.

Clearly, the difference here is largely attributable to the structure of the public interest groups as compared with the Chicago civic associations and the national trade groups in Washington. The public interest groups, predominantly staff controlled and often set up around the leadership of a single individual, operate under a much different set of organizational constraints. Where decisions over policy are made by boards of directors, with its members representing various constituencies within the organization, the potential for disagreement and indecisiveness appears to be much greater. Size, degree of organizational diversity, and the locus of decision-making power are all relevant variables in explaining the differences to be found between the public interest groups and those studied by Banfield, and Bauer, Pool, and Dexter.

It is not possible to make generalizations on decision making and policy conflicts for public interest groups versus private interest groups *per se*. Comparable survey data on private interest groups does not exist. Not all established private lobbies can be expected to behave in the same manner as the Chicago civic associations or the national trade groups. The conclusion that does emerge, however, is the critical importance of the organizational structure in influencing the selection of issues to be lobbied upon. For public interest groups, advocacy choices must be understood in the context of the staff domination and personalized decision making that characterize so many of the organizations.

pp. 1126-1136. See also Andrew S. McFarland, *Public-Interest Lobbies: Decision-Making on Energy* (Washington, D.C.: American Enterprise Institute, 1976), chaps. 4-6.

CONCLUSION

Some strong behavioral patterns concerning authority and decision making have emerged from the survey of public interest groups. In analyzing the interaction between staff and members, it was found that significant resources are expended for communicating to the public interest group members, but only a minority of the organizations give their members formal opportunities to communicate back. More than half of the membership groups do not even go through the pretense of structuring their organization in a democratic mold so that they would at least have the appearance of being open to constituency influence. It is only in a small number of groups that members of boards of directors have any real input into the decision-making process.

It is clear that the power to choose new issues on which to lobby rests in the hands of the staff members in most of the organizations. The men and women who run the public interest groups do not sit at the apex of large bureaucracies. Fifty-four percent of the Washington offices have three or fewer staff professionals, and 90% have 10 or less.[49] Consequently, these groups, which ostensibly "speak for the people," do so through the voices (and deliberations) of a very few.

The staff domination over the choice of new issues in most groups raises questions of accountability. Would it be better if memberships and boards (particularly in the non-membership groups) were more active? Alternatively, has the potential for influence by the boards and membership bodies been underutilized because staff personnel are careful to choose issues within acceptable boundaries? Using the statistics cited in this chapter, it is easy to accuse the majority of public interest groups of being unrepresentative bodies, where small oligarchies determine organizational

[49] See Table III-5.

policies. At the same time, it is fair to assume that members of public interest groups are people who tend to have a deep commitment to a particular policy area in which their group is working. They are generally informed through organizational publications as to current lobbying efforts, and their financial support is at least some measure of approval. In the final analysis, the important question for the membership groups may not be how representative they are in their decision-making processes, but how well they select issues that will continue to attract contributors.

CHAPTER VIII

The Tactics of Advocacy . . .

BECAUSE almost all public interest organization staffs either dominate or participate as an equal partner in decision making, policy decisions are rarely divorced from decisions concerning strategy and tactics. With their limited resources, groups must try to allocate personnel and money in the most effective and efficient manner. Interest groups have a number of alternative methods of advocacy open to them. This chapter attempts both to describe the available choices and to analyze their use by public interest lobbies.

The selection of particular tactics by public interest groups is affected strongly by predispositions toward basic strategies of influence. *Strategy* may be defined as broad plans of attack, or general approaches to lobbying. *Tactics* are the specific actions taken to advocate certain policy positions.[1] The initial focus here will be on the tactics of advocacy. Subsequently, an explanation of the interrelationship of organizational structure, underlying strategies of influence, and choice of lobbying tactics will be undertaken.

To facilitate the understanding of how public interest lobbyists perceive the effectiveness and value of alternative tactics of influence, interviewees were handed a card listing 10 possible means of lobbying the various institutions of government. Respondents were asked, "Which of these techniques has your organization used in the past?" The interviewees were then told, "It would also be helpful if you could evaluate the effectiveness of those techniques which you have used."[2]

[1] Lester W. Milbrath, *The Washington Lobbyists* (Chicago: Rand McNally, 1963), p. 41.
[2] See Appendix A.

The dynamics of this interview question should be noted. The lobbyists were handed the card as the question was beginning to be read. The interviewees, as could be expected, read down the list before going back to the top and talking, in order, about each method utilized by their group. Thus, there is an implicit comparison in their comments as to what is most and what is least effective in terms of the tactics they use.[3] Secondary or probe questions were used to get beyond responses of just "effective" or "not effective" to more descriptive evaluations of the techniques they used.

For purposes of organization, the different tactics may be grouped into three general categories. First, there are those techniques that are characterized by direct communication between lobbyists and governmental officials. These include private, personal presentations before people in government; testifying before congressional committees; and formal legal action, such as litigation and intervention in administrative proceedings. Second, there are methods by which groups lobby through their constituents. For this cluster of tactics, the professional staffs act as intermediaries, stimulating lobbying by citizens toward their government. They may ask all their members to write letters or to participate in protest demonstrations; or they may ask individual, but highly influential, members or constituents to

[3] Those familiar with the work of Milbrath, *The Washington Lobbyists*, Walter D. DeVries, *The Michigan Lobbyists* (unpublished Ph.D. dissertation, Michigan State University, 1960), and Harmon Zeigler and Michael Baer, *Lobbying* (Belmont, Calif.: Wadsworth, 1969), may question why this study does not use an interval scale to measure the efficacy of lobbying techniques. The above authors asked the lobbyists they interviewed to rate tactics on a scale of 0 to 10 (0 to 8 for Zeigler and Baer) according to their value. It was reasoned that even without the numerical scale, comparisons could easily be made. Respondents were not asked to assign ranking scores because I wanted them to talk at length about why each technique was or was not valuable. It was thought that having them concentrate on assigning a numerical value would put the emphasis in the wrong place and would detract from the qualitative answers. On reflection, this approach seems to have worked quite well.

contact a key policy maker. Third, groups may try to change governmental policy by influencing elections or altering public opinion. The techniques of this sort are contributing money to political campaigns, publishing voting records, releasing research results, and public relations campaigns.

DIRECT LOBBYING

Personal Presentations. Of all the techniques open to public interest representatives, the personal presentation of argument to governmental officials was thought to be the most effective. Over half of the sample (53%) viewed personal, face-to-face lobbying as "very effective" or "effective" (see Table VIII-1). This is not surprising, because it confirms findings of earlier studies by Milbrath, DeVries, and Zeig-

TABLE VIII-1

Tactics of Advocacy

	Very Effective; Effective	Effective with Qualifications[a]	Not Effective	Use but Cannot Evaluate	Do Not Use	Total
Personal presentation	53%	14%	7%	10%	16%	100%
Testifying at congressional hearing	20%	16%	42%	10%	12%	100%
Litigation	29%	12%	5%	5%	49%	100%
Letter writing	47%	8%	4%	9%	32%	100%
Contact by influential member or constituent	34%	11%	1%	16%	38%	100%
Political demonstrations	8%	5%	5%	6%	77%	101%[b]
Contributing money to candidates	6%	—	—	—	94%	100%
Publishing voting records	18%	6%	4%	4%	68%	100%
Releasing research	30%	15%	6%	17%	31%	99%[b]
Public relations	24%	6%	—	9%	62%	101%[b]

[a] For example, "Sometimes yes, sometimes no."
[b] Rounding error.

ler and Baer, all of which showed personal contact to be the most highly regarded lobbying tactic.[4]

Although the question referred to members of Congress agency heads, their respective staffs, or White House personnel, respondents were clearly talking about some actors more than others. Few of the public interest groups had any access at all to any White House staff members. A few representatives of large, liberal groups said that they had had some contact with White House people during the Kennedy-Johnson years, but this lack of access seems to be largely independent of the President in power.[5]

Face-to-face contacts with individuals in the legislative branch occur far more often with staff than with Representatives or Senators. Essentially, getting appointments with members of Congress is not an easy task. Demands on their time are tremendous, and actual meetings with them are often preceded by delays, procrastinations, and postponements. A lobbyist with any experience at all knows that it is usually important to meet with a Congressperson's aide before even trying to see the Congressperson.[6]

[4] Milbrath's mean scores (with DeVries' scores in parentheses) on a scale of 0 to 10 (10 being most effective) are as follows: personal presentation of viewpoint, 8.43 (9.24); presentation of research results, 7.40 (7.00); testifying at hearings, 6.55 (6.64); contact by constituents, 5.90 (3.84); contact by a close friend, 3.76 (2.73); letter and telegram campaigns, 4.55 (1.73); public relations campaigns, 5.55 (4.79); publicizing voting records, 2.05 (0.84); entertaining, 1.59 (2.33); giving a party, 1.24 (1.91); bribery, 0.10 (0.00); contributing money, 1.88 (0.87); campaign work, 2.28 (1.21). There has been considerable change in the list of tactics used for this study, so strict comparisons would not be valid if the public interest responses were converted to interval-scale scores.

[5] This conclusion can be drawn only from that portion (a little over half) of the sample that existed prior to Richard Nixon's inauguration. Most certainly, lack of access to people in the White House is characteristic of most interest groups.

[6] David Kovenock found that of all the communications (premises) a Congressperson receives concerning legislation, approximately 12% come from interest groups. His study of six members of a House subcommittee showed that most communications that come to the attention of a Representative are from sources internal to the House of Representatives. The Congresspersons, however, hear from dif-

Similarly, public interest lobbyists deal much more frequently with bureau staff than with agency heads or Cabi-
net officers. To generalize about what level of hierarchy
the lobbyists communicate with is difficult, because they
meet with the lowest staff researchers on up. The major
variable affecting the rank of officials willing to talk to a
public interest lobbyist seems to be sympathy of the agency toward the group. Obviously, this varies considerably.
Most environmental groups have a minimum of access to
middle- or senior-level people in the Interior Department.
On the other hand, the Agriculture Department was consistently denounced by consumer representatives as being
totally unresponsive to them.[7] The difference between the
two departments is the much more positive attitude by Interior toward the role of public interest (environmental)
groups.

The most persuasive explanation of why face-to-face
lobbying is so popular is found in the work of Lewis Anthony Dexter.[8] Dexter has observed that Washington representatives generally lobby their "friends" in government
and leave their "enemies" alone. Therefore, lobbyists are

ferent sources on different types of issues. See "Influence in the U.S.
House of Representatives: A Statistical Analysis of Communications,"
American Politics Quarterly, vol. 1 (October 1973), pp. 407-464. See
also John W. Kingdon, *Congressmen's Voting Decisions* (New York:
Harper & Row, 1973).

[7] One way in which public interest groups and sympathetic bureaucrats circumvent agencies and departments that are "closed" and
unresponsive to public interest concerns is whistle-blowing. This is
the process by which an official publicly discloses information to
the press, or to a public interest group as an intermediary, which
typically documents a bureaucratic cover-up of a situation embarrassing to the government agency. This will be discussed later in
this chapter.

[8] For his analyses on Congress and lobbyists, see Lewis Anthony
Dexter, *The Sociology and Politics of Congress* (Chicago: Rand
McNally, 1969); *How Organizations Are Represented in Washington*
(Indianapolis, Ind.: Bobbs-Merrill, 1969); and *American Business
and Public Policy* (with Raymond A. Bauer and Ithiel de Sola Pool)
(New York: Atherton, 1963).

usually talking with people with whom they already agree, and their presentations will be positively received.[9] Because lobbyists tend to talk to people who already agree with them, however, it seems incongruous that such high percentages of public and private interest lobbyists feel that it is such an effective activity.

This apparent inconsistency becomes less contradictory if personal lobbying is conceived of as a process of trying to activate sympathetic partisans rather than as a process of persuading the uninformed. Bauer, Pool, and Dexter note, "the most important part of the legislative decision-process was the decision about which decisions to consider."[10] There is a multiplicity of demands on legislators and administrators, and thus much of a lobbyist's work is to overcome "marginal attention" toward his or her issue by governmental policy makers.[11] Quite understandably, lobbyists will think it most efficient to try to arouse the latent concern of those they know to be sympathetic to their group's position.

The work by Dexter and his associates has strongly influenced political scientists' conception of the lobbying process to a point of becoming the conventional wisdom on interest group behavior. The data collected on public in-

[9] Dexter, and Bauer and Pool write, "It is so much easier to carry on activities within the circle of those who agree and encourage you than it is to break out and find potential proselytes, that the day-to-day routine and pressure of business tend to shunt those more painful activities aside. The result is that *the lobbyist becomes in effect a service bureau for those congressmen already agreeing with him, rather than an agent of direct persuasion.*" *American Business and Public Policy*, p. 353. On the implications of legislators having different attitudes toward the role of lobbies and their value to the overall workings of the legislative system, see John C. Wahlke, Heinz Eulau, William Buchanan, and LeRoy C. Ferguson, *The Legislative System* (New York: Wiley, 1962); and Betty Zisk, *Local Interest Politics: A One-Way Street* (Indianapolis, Ind.: Bobbs-Merrill, 1973).

[10] Bauer, Pool, and Dexter, *American Business and Public Policy*, p. 405.

[11] See Dexter, *The Sociology and Politics of Congress*, pp. 131-175.

terest groups indicate, however, that there are two important qualifications that must be made to the conclusions that they have offered.

First, the observation that groups lobby their friends and leave their enemies alone does not strictly hold for public interest groups. It is, to be sure, true that public interest lobbies deal most often with their friends. But it also is true that it is not always characteristic of the public interest groups to leave their opponents alone.

One reason offered as to why Washington representatives concentrate on their friends is that all individuals prefer to be in social situations where people will be friendly to them. Dexter points out that lobbyists, simply because they are human beings, do not want to encounter those who might be hostile to them. Accordingly, they shun offices where they think they may get a cold reception.[12]

Another explanation for lobbyists leaving their opponents alone is that a legislator or administrator who is against you on one issue may be a potential ally on another. Therefore, nothing should be done to alienate policy makers by criticizing them or applying some form of "pressure" to change their views. The thinking of public interest lobbyists seems to stand in contrast to this logic. Often public interest lobbyists will not only try to lobby their foes, but they will angrily denounce them as well when the occasion warrants. Openly criticizing opponents is viewed as a tactical weapon that may cause their foes to think twice about taking an adversary position the next time a policy conflict involving the group arises. Denouncing opponents is intended as a sanction; by exposing an official to the press, an attentive public, or even to his or her own conscience as an enemy of the "public interest," they are attempting to create a potential threat for future issues.

---

[12] Dexter notes that the consequence of this is that the lobbyists skip the offices of people who, although they are not open partisans of a group's views, would genuinely like to hear their position on an issue. *How Organizations Are Represented in Washington,* pp. 66-69.

One example of this type of activity was presented earlier in the case study of the Fund for Animals and their fight with the Department of Interior over the Minnesota management plan for the Eastern timber wolves. After a number of virulent attacks on Interior by Fund lobbyist Lew Regenstein and after Interior had rejected the plan as the Fund desired, a high Department official, and Fund adversary during the conflict, wrote Regenstein a conciliatory letter inviting more Fund participation in the future. Regenstein's response was a scathing letter accusing the man of speaking "nonsense" in the past. His message: the Fund would not be coopted by the Department and it would continue to expose individuals, by name, who were not doing their best to protect wildlife.[13]

Lobbying opponents, through friendly and unfriendly approaches, was found to be a common, not anomalous, trait among public interest groups. There are, of course, administrators and members of Congress who will be considered lost causes and will not be contacted directly, but public interest lobbyists do not avoid people in government just because they are unsympathetic. A representative from a broadcasting group who tried to crash a meeting of the Federal Communications Commission where he knew he would be unwelcome was hardly seeking out those who were already on his side. In short, public interest advocacy extends far beyond a small circle of friends.

An interesting corollary to this pattern of behavior is that public interest groups sometimes treat their friends as if they were enemies when those friends disappoint them. A rather celebrated case at hand is that of Ralph Nader and his associates at the Center for the Study of Responsive Law when they denounced Senator Edmund Muskie (D., Me.), long considered to be one of the hardest-working environmentalists in the Congress, for his record on air pollution legislation. In the book *Vanishing Air*, written by the

[13] See Chapter V.

Nader study group on air pollution and headed by John C. Esposito, Muskie was censured for his lack of commitment to legislating and enforcing strong clean air standards.[14] Muskie, known for his dogged work as chairperson of the Senate Subcommittee on Air and Water Pollution, was a surprising target of criticism because of his reputation as a sympathetic conservationist. Despite this, *Vanishing Air* concluded that Muskie was "out of touch" and urged him to resign his subcommittee chairmanship.[15]

Nader and Esposito amplified their criticism of Muskie at a press conference. Because the charges against Muskie were so startling, attention was diverted from the more substantive aspects of the book. Although releasing research results is a separate tactic of lobbying, the entire task force endeavor was also an effort of personal lobbying.[16] The task force worked closely with legislative and administrative staff in preparing the report, and the final interview with Muskie was as much advocacy as it was a research device.[17]

Common Cause is another group that has little respect for the normal etiquette of Washington lobbying. They have publicly attacked the Democratic House leadership,[18] and they have made extensive efforts to remove committee chairpersons with whom they disagree.[19] Usually reliable

[14] John C. Esposito, *Vanishing Air* (New York: Grossman, 1970), especially pp. 287-298.

[15] *Ibid.*, p. 289.

[16] Obviously, denouncing enemies (and friends) is a strategy that can transcend the single tactic of personal lobbying. Nader groups continue to push for antipollution laws and for enforcement of existing laws, through personal lobbying, testifying, legal action, and research.

[17] The Muskie staff felt that they were betrayed by Esposito and other task force members. After the book's publication, they produced an 85-page rebuttal. Muskie himself accepted the criticism gracefully. See Charles McCarry, *Citizen Nader* (New York: Saturday Review Press, 1972), pp. 199-203.

[18] Shirley Elder, "Showdown Set in House on End-War Move," *Washington Star-News*, August 9, 1972, p. A-10.

[19] Marjorie Hunter, "House Democrats Defeat Liberals in Seniority Fight," *The New York Times*, February 4, 1971, p. 1; and Spencer Rich, "Hill Caucus Kills Attack on Eastland," *Washington Post*,

friends are fair game for criticism when the need arises. One of Common Cause's key lobbyists recounts the following story of how constant harassment, through personal lobbying and letter writing, finally made a "believer" out of a northern Democratic Representative:

_____ is notorious for missing votes—he has a terrible record. There was a key vote coming up on an end-the-war amendment in the committee. _____ said he was going overseas, and he wouldn't stay for the vote. Now the time before, the amendment had failed 20-19 in the Foreign Affairs Committee. So we activated our people in his district and they generated a lot of critical letters. I went and talked to his administrative assistant, who is a good guy. He was embarrassed that this had happened. Fortunately, the meeting was cancelled and the vote wasn't taken.

Now, the next time it came up, I went over and I stood outside the committee room and, frankly, I was pessimistic. I think I stood outside there for 3 hours. Chuck Whalen [R., Ohio] came out and told me to get Bob Steele [R., Conn.] and _____. I went to get Steele, but he was already on his way; somebody had already called him. I went to _____'s office and I asked the secretary if the Congressman was in. She said no, he was off the Hill. I said is there any way of getting him back. She said they already knew of the vote because Bingham [D., N.Y.] had called. I asked if I could see the AA, but she said no, he was in a meeting. I said will you tell him _____ from Common Cause was here and there is an important vote in the Foreign Affairs Committee in a little while. I left rather pessimistically and I went back to the committee room and stood outside. A few

April 14, 1972, p. A11. Their efforts would finally bear fruit in the 94th Congress when some House chairpersons were replaced. Common Cause was popularly accorded a small part of the credit for this development.

minutes later the AA comes running down the hall and
asks me if the vote had been taken. I said no, and he said
the Congressman is on his way and would be there in
five minutes. He soon arrived, and the vote was taken
10 minutes later. The end-the-war amendment passed
20-19, for the first time. It was historic.

The Common Cause lobbyist was very firm in explaining
the moral of this story: criticizing members of Congress
is an effective weapon. To expose a person in his or her
district or state is to strike a sensitive nerve.[20] "When you
get the issue out to the people in the district, the ground
rules change." In sum, the Common Cause philosophy is
that the more they publicly denounce friends and enemies
when they "err," the more they strengthen their hand the
next time around.

A second refinement to the generalization that interest
groups only lobby their friends is that there is a lot more
lobbying of members of Congress who are neither friends
nor enemies than the literature suggests.[21] Public interest
groups devote significant amounts of time to trying to persuade "swing" members of Congress to come over to their
side. This stands in contrast to Bauer, Pool, and Dexter's
observation that "Direct persuasion of uncommitted or opposed congressmen and senators was a minor activity of
the lobbies."[22]

Public interest groups seem to be quite concerned about
pinpointing swing Congresspersons on key committee and

[20] Although it is the conventional wisdom that most Americans
have little idea of what their individual Congresspersons do on the
issues of the day, members of Congress are extremely concerned
about the possibility that negative information is, indeed, reaching
the voters and hurting their chances for reelection. See David R.
Mayhew, *Congress: The Electoral Connection* (New Haven, Conn.:
Yale University Press, 1974).

[21] These refinements relate to the literature on legislative lobbying,
but the behavior patterns of the public interest groups extend to
their advocacy before administrative agencies as well.

[22] Bauer, Pool, and Dexter, *American Business and Public Policy*,
p. 442.

floor votes. A review of newsletters and legislative alerts reveals numerous examples of members and activists being told exactly which Representatives and Senators were "on the fence" and should be written to. Groups working on end-the-war legislation appeared to be particularly proficient at identifying those members of Congress who fell into neither the confirmed hawk nor dove categories. Quite literally, public interest groups do act, on occasion, as "pressure" groups; they muscle their resources available to persuade specific members of Congress that they should vote the "right" way. Clearly, for public interest groups, lobbying is something more than just servicing and activating friends in Congress.

Congressional Hearings. It is easy to see that it is difficult to discuss tactics as isolated techniques of influence. As the above examples of personal lobbying illustrate, groups use different tactics in conjunction with each other during an advocacy effort. This could be no truer than for testifying at congressional hearings, because in and of itself it is thought to be a waste of time. Although respondents were reluctant to label techniques flatly as "not effective," fully 42% did so for congressional testifying. The next highest "not effective" response was only 7%, which was accorded to the personal presentation tactic.

It is somewhat ironic that the most ineffective technique was also the most widely used—88% of the organizations had testified before congressional committees. The reason for this is that despite the fact that testifying does not have a substantive influence, it does seem to have important symbolic value. Appearing at hearings helps to legitimatize further efforts to influence legislation. Public interest groups consider putting their views into the official record (printed reports of committee hearings) as part of the game, or one of the norms of congressional lobbying. Some sample comments:

It is not effective, but we have to do it for the record.

It's important to put your views on the record.

It's of minimal importance. We've got to go on the record, fulfill that obligation.

You have to go on the record.

It's important to go on the record, but it doesn't influence people.

The real sentiment of public interest lobbyists about testimony was expressed by a representative of the League of Women Voters, "It's window dressing; it's what you do with the members before and after." Although the actual testimony given at hearings is rarely of great consequence, committee hearings do represent a significant stage in the legislative process. Hearings do reflect the transference of legislation from the idea stage to the agenda stage where legislation is officially being considered.[23]

For a group trying to get Congress to consider a newly arising issue, the holding of hearings is an extremely important step. Forcing a new issue on the agenda of the committee is no easy task. Unless an interest group senses substantial support within a committee or subcommittee, they are unlikely to expend the considerable resources necessary to push for such hearings.[24] Although the decision to testify at hearings is a minor one, requiring only a small amount of resources and being well worth the benefits of being "on the record," the decision to press a potentially unwilling committee to hold hearings is something else entirely. It will be done only by groups when they feel that an issue is

[23] For an examination of the process by which formative issues reach the agenda stage, see, generally, Roger W. Cobb and Charles D. Elder, *Participation in American Politics: The Dynamics of Agenda Building* (Boston: Allyn and Bacon, 1972).
[24] The trials and tribulations of trying to get an unresponsive subcommittee to hold hearings are described in the case study of the Women's International League for Peace and Freedom and their effort to get Jean-Pierre Debris and Andre Menras before Congress and "on the record." See Chapter VI.

of major consequence and are willing to stick with their effort not only through a single session or a single Congress, but for the duration.[25] The wheels of Congress sometimes turn very, very slowly.

Legal Action. Respondents were specifically asked to comment on the tactic of litigation, but the discussion here will be expanded to include other forms of legal advocacy. The majority of groups that use law suits are also active before administrative agencies writing comments on proposed rules, filing complaints, filing petitions for rule making, and intervening, where allowed, in hearings for rule making, adjudicative proceedings, and rate making.[26] Actual litigation tends to be quite expensive, and it tends to be used as a last resort. Much of the litigation initiated by public interest groups grows out of previous, but unsuccessful, advocacy before administrative agencies.

There are many factors that influence the choice of litigation as a lobbying tool, but one of the most important is whether or not a group is structured to carry out litigation. Not all public interest groups approach policy conflicts with a view that litigation or administrative intervention may be a viable alternative as a tactic of advocacy. Rather, it is primarily an alternative to those groups that have made a conscious, organizational decision to allocate resources to legal work on an ongoing basis. Usually this work is done by in-house counsel, but a small number of groups have relied on outside help.[27]

[25] For example, see the case study of the NCEC and campaign finance in Robert L. Peabody, Jeffrey M. Berry, William G. Frasure, and Jerry Goldman, *To Enact a Law: Congress and Campaign Financing* (New York: Praeger, 1972).

[26] For an overview of public interest group advocacy before administrative agencies, see Ernest Gellhorn, "Public Participation in Administrative Proceedings," *Yale Law Journal,* vol. 81 (January 1972), pp. 359-404.

[27] On litigation as lobbying, see, generally, Clement E. Vose, "Litigation as a Form of Pressure Group Activity," *Annals of the American Academy of Political and Social Science,* vol. 319 (September 1958), pp. 20-31; and L. Harmon Zeigler and G. Wayne Peak, *Interest*

The most extensive utilization of legal advocacy comes, quite expectedly, from those groups specifically set up to lobby the courts and administrative agencies. The *raison d'être* for organizations such as the Natural Resources Defense Council, the Center for Law and Social Policy, and the Public Citizen Litigation Group is to provide the public interest movement with a legal arm. A few of these groups, such as the Institute for Public Interest Representation, initially desired to concentrate solely on administrative advocacy, but found it was necessary to use litigation to back up their efforts.

Legal advocacy is structured not only by organizational capabilities, but also by the rules of standing that govern the right of individuals or groups to bring suit in court or participate in administrative proceedings. Some of the most significant and successful suits brought by public interest groups have, in fact, dealt with the issue of legal standing. Because representation of otherwise unrepresented interests is the primary purpose of public interest groups, these standing decisions are profoundly important to those who advocate increased citizen participation in governmental decision making.[28] Brief descriptions of two landmark standing cases may serve to bring out some of the implications of the liberalization of standing rules.

Groups in American Society, 2nd ed. (Englewood Cliffs, N.J.: Prentice-Hall, 1972). For a case study of a public interest group's legal advocacy, see Carol S. Greenwald, "The Use of Litigation by Common Cause: A Study of the Development of Campaign Finance Reform Legislation," paper delivered at the annual meeting of the American Political Science Association, San Francisco, California, September 1975.

[28] For a comprehensive overview of the legal battle surrounding citizen participation and standing, see Comment, "Public Participation in Federal Administrative Proceedings," *University of Pennsylvania Law Review*, vol. 120 (April 1972), pp. 702-845. See also Karen Orren, "Standing to Sue: Interest Group Conflict in the Federal Courts," *American Political Science Review*, vol. 70 (September 1976), pp. 723-741.

In 1965, the Office of Communication of the United Church of Christ filed a petition before the Federal Communications Commission (FCC) asking that the owners of station WLBT in Jackson, Mississippi, be denied renewal of their broadcast license. The United Church of Christ charged that the station was not serving the needs of the black community and was overtly racist in its operation. Documented evidence in the petition included such items as the fact that the station had a segregated, white-only staff, that it systematically ignored black-oriented news, that a news commentator used the word "nigger" on the air, and that the station broadcast White Citizens Council promotional advertisements.[29] Despite all this, the complaint was rejected because the FCC denied standing to the petitioners on the grounds that they did not show a direct causal relationship between the activities protested and tangible injury. Moreover, the FCC ruled that minority groups *per se* had no greater claim of injury than the public in general and, therefore, could not be given standing as a representative of the public interest.[30]

The United Church of Christ took the FCC to court and, on appeal, they obtained a favorable decision.[31] The Court of Appeals ruled against the FCC, and it forcefully declared that standing must be given not only to those with economic interests, but to the entire viewing public. The Court went on in its precedent-setting decision to invite "audience participation" in further FCC license-renewal hearings.[32] In the specific case of WLBT, reformers did not win a complete victory. The owners of the station (Lamar Life) did eventually lose their license in 1969, but after an

[29] William Greider, "TV Reform Slowing," *Washington Post*, July 17, 1973, p. A1.
[30] See "Public Participation in Federal Administrative Proceedings," pp. 756-757.
[31] *Office of Communication of the United Church of Christ v. FCC*, 359 F. 2d 944 (D.C. Cir. 1966).
[32] *Ibid.*

interim-management citizens group had integrated programming and staffing, the FCC awarded the license to a business concern strongly opposed by the reformers.[33]

Another key piece of litigation, filed at around the same time, involved the Scenic Hudson Preservation Conference and the Federal Power Commission (FPC). The Conference, an amalgam of conservation groups, brought suit against the FPC because it approved a proposal for a new power plant to be built by Consolidated Edison of New York. The Court of Appeals ruled that the Conference had standing for its noneconomic interests.[34] In its opinion, the Court declared that the FPC must consider aesthetic interests in its deliberations and that the Conference was a representative of this "special interest."[35] The Court remanded the case, ordering the FPC to consider the evidence presented by the petitioners.

The thrust of these decisions has been to expand significantly the right of participation in administrative proceedings of public interest and other citizen lobbies. Most essentially, the concept of "interest" has been broadened to include noneconomic concerns.[36] Although the decisions themselves will not guarantee that noneconomic groups will take advantage of their standing, they do offer the requisite legal access.

[33] See Greider, "TV Reform Slowing," and George Gent, "Church Group Seeks to Bar TV License," *The New York Times*, November 27, 1973, p. 74.

[34] In its decision, the court held that the Conference had standing for economic interests, but granted the standing to the petitioners on the basis of noneconomic interests. Consequently, the case should be considered in the context of public interest group standing. *Scenic Hudson Preservation Conference v. FPC*, 354 F. 2d 608 (2nd Cir. 1965).

[35] *Ibid.*

[36] In *Sierra Club v. Morton*, 405 U.S. 727 (1972), the Supreme Court placed some boundaries on who has the legal standing to speak for noneconomic interests. For one environmentalist's appraisal of this decision, see Joseph L. Sax, "Standing to Sue: A Critical Review of the Mineral King Decision," *Natural Resources Journal*, vol. 13 (January 1973), pp. 76-88.

Legal advocacy by public interest groups must be viewed in terms of the constraints and opportunities in each distinct policy area. The "law"—or its general judicial interpretation—makes some issues much more susceptible to legal tactics than others. The continuing presence of U.S. armed forces in Indochina, which was an issue with which many public interest groups were involved, was not one that was effectively influenced by court suits.[37] On the other hand, environmental questions have been particularly vulnerable to litigation. This potential for affecting decisions concerning the environment was dramatically increased by the passage of the National Environmental Policy Act (NEPA) of 1969.[38] NEPA requires government agencies to analyze the environmental impact of their projects, and their subsequent failure to do so has brought forth numerous important law suits filed by public interest lobbies.[39] In a third area, consumer groups have had some limited success with class action suits, but they need new

[37] The most notable failure among the legal efforts to stop the war was a suit brought by the ACLU in 1973 on behalf of Congressperson Elizabeth Holtzman (D., N.Y.) and four airmen, claiming that the bombing of Cambodia was unconstitutional. A federal district judge ruled in favor of the ACLU and its plaintiffs on the grounds that the bombing was, indeed, unconstitutional. Their victory was short-lived, however, as the decision was overturned by the Court of Appeals and the Supreme Court denied review. See Stephen Isaacs, "Judge Bars Bombing in Cambodia," *Washington Post*, July 26, 1973, p. A1; and Stephen Isaacs, "Bombing Ban Is Rejected," *Washington Post*, August 9, 1973, p. A1.

[38] Public Law 91-190.

[39] See Frederick R. Anderson, *NEPA in the Courts* (Baltimore: The Johns Hopkins University Press, 1973); Harold Levanthal, "Environmental Decisionmaking and the Role of the Courts," *University of Pennsylvania Law Review*, vol. 122 (January 1972), pp. 509-555; Richard A. Liroff, *A National Policy for the Environment* (Bloomington: Indiana University Press, 1976); and Walter A. Rosenbaum, "The End of Illusions: NEPA and the Limits of Judicial Review," in Stuart S. Nagel, ed., *Environmental Politics* (New York: Praeger, 1974), pp. 260-277. On strategies of influencing environmental issues in the courts beyond the NEPA requirements, see Joseph L. Sax, *Defending the Environment* (New York: Alfred A. Knopf, 1971).

legislation to expand and ensure their right to use class action as a tool of advocacy.[40]

There is evidence to suggest that lobbying through legal work is becoming an increasingly used strategy of influence. Not only have new groups that emphasize litigation and formal administrative intervention been formed, but some existing groups have moved to establish a legal advocacy capability within their own organizations.[41] The Public Citizen Litigation Group was started so that the Nader satellites, and Nader himself, could fortify their means of influencing government.[42] Nader had been doing some legal work before Public Citizen was started, but the primary lobbying was being done through the releasing of research results. Public Citizen, and the accompanying Litigation Group, gave Nader some additional tools and greater flexibility in his efforts.

The League of Women Voters, traditionally a legislative lobby, has also moved to include litigation as one of its available techniques of influence through the hiring of a legal staff for the the organization. This has been facilitated by a series of grants from the Ford Foundation. The initial $260,000 grant, in the words of one League representative, was aimed at "institutionalizing litigation as a tactic for the League." Ford contributed the money not only to give the League a legal staff in Washington, but also to enable the national office to undertake a campaign to educate state and local Leagues as to the potential of legal advocacy.[43]

[40] See Philip Schrag and Michael Meltsner, "Class Action: A Way to Beat the Bureaucracies Without Increasing Them," *Washington Monthly*, November 1972, pp. 55-61. A recent Supreme Court decision has seriously restricted the use of class action suits in consumer and environmental areas by requiring all plaintiffs in such litigation to have suffered individual damages in excess of $10,000. *Zahn v. International Paper Co.*, 414 U.S. 291 (1973).

[41] See Gordon Harrison and Sanford M. Jaffe, *The Public Interest Law Firm* (New York: Ford Foundation, 1973).

[42] See Theodore Jacqueney, "Nader Network Switches Focus to Legal Action, Congressional Lobbying," *National Journal*, June 9, 1973, pp. 840-849.

[43] For an overview of the evolution of public interest law, see Robert L. Rabin, "Lawyers for Social Change: Perspectives on Pub-

LOBBYING THROUGH CONSTITUENTS

Political Protest. Probably the most interesting finding
concerning political protests—street demonstrations, picket-
ing, and sit-ins—as a tactic is that almost a quarter of the
sample (24%) actually use them. It is not limited to the few
groups, such as the National Peace Action Coalition and
the Student Mobilization Committee, that use demonstrations as their principal means of advocacy. Although the
public interest groups hold protests for many different
reasons and in varying manners, their purpose is uniform:
to gain publicity for their cause. Whether the demonstrations are the only tactic a group uses or are used in conjunction with other techniques, the primary aim is to get
the media to cover the protest when it takes place.[44]

Not all protests are serious gatherings of partisans who
have come together to listen to speakers and shout emotional slogans. On occasion, histrionics will seem to offer a
better opportunity for press coverage. After President Nixon
permitted an American Ping-Pong team to travel through
the People's Republic of China, Dr. Carl McIntire, head of
the conservative March for Victory Committee, felt that
President Nixon should be informed that not all Americans
approved of détente with the Communists. In addition to
leading the March for Victory Committee, McIntire is pas-
tor of the Bible Presbyterian Church of Collingswood, New
Jersey, founder of Shelton College in Cape Canaveral,
Florida, minister of the air over 200 radio stations on the
20th Century Reformation Hour, and operator of a hotel in
Atlantic City.[45] As a protest against the move toward friend-

---

lic Interest Law," *Stanford Law Review*, vol. 28 (January 1976),
pp. 207-261.

[44] In Schattschneider's terms, they are trying to use the press to
expand the scope of the conflict. See E. E. Schattschneider, *The
Semisovereign People* (New York: Holt, Rinehart and Winston,
1960).

[45] McIntire's latest enterprise is a pirate radio ship, which he is
attempting to operate in defiance of the FCC and the fairness doc-

lier relations with mainland China, McIntire asked for permission to play ping-pong in front of the White House. When permission was denied, McIntire went to court and was then granted the right to play, but only as long as a table was not set up on the Pennsylvania Avenue sidewalk. The symbolic protest finally took place with four men holding the table and moving it up and down the sidewalk as the game progressed.

The use of political protests by public interest groups is, however, most associated with street demonstrations against the war in Vietnam. Within the antiwar movement, no consensus emerged concerning the efficacy of such demonstrations. There appear to be two major lines of thinking. One group of activists felt that the protests held around the country had a positive effect because they forced President Johnson out of office and mandated a deescalation of the war by President Nixon. The second set of opinions is that the demonstrations were largely a failure because the American involvement lasted for so long after the protests began in earnest subsequent to President Johnson's election in 1964.

Despite the differing evaluation of protests, both camps of thought indicated continued commitment to demonstrations as a tactic of political advocacy. This may seem contradictory, but it is less confusing if it is understood that this technique has not been adopted because it was initially considered to be highly effective. Rather, it was selected in the past because other alternatives were not perceived to be open and because it had great appeal to the student constituency of the antiwar movement.

The strategy behind demonstrations is threefold. First, protesters hope through press coverage to expand public awareness of an issue. Second, they anticipate that government officials will become more sensitive to and cogni-

---

trine. See Jules Witcover, "Pirate Radio Ship," *Washington Post*, September 7, 1973, p. A14.

zant of a particular point of view on an issue. Third, the expectation is that press coverage will strengthen the group's hand and give it more leverage in the political process.[46]

Finally, an interesting characteristic of organized protests is that they tend to be carried out by *ad hoc* coalitions of groups. Because protests require a significant expenditure of resources, there is a clear incentive to pool efforts. Another factor is that demonstrations, which as a rule are aimed at the press, generally decrease in newsworthiness the more they occur. This also acts as an incentive for cooperative behavior, because it is advantageous to decrease overlap among potentially similarly oriented protests. Nevertheless, it is also characteristic for a single group to take a distinct leadership role within the coalition.

Letter Writing. One of the most popular of all tactics of advocacy is letter-writing campaigns. Forty-seven percent of the groups view letter writing as an effective tool. On the other hand, fully 32% of the sample (practically all of which are nonmembership groups) do not use the tactic. Usually, letter-writing campaigns are aimed at Congress, but administrative agencies are occasional targets.[47] The rationale behind letter writing is very simple. Public interest representatives strongly believe that government officials are quite sensitive to the mail their offices receive and that

[46] See Michael Lipsky, "Protest as a Political Resource," *American Political Science Review*, vol. 62 (December 1968), pp. 1144-1158; and Paul D. Schumaker, "Policy Responsiveness to Protest-Group Demands," *Journal of Politics*, vol. 37 (May 1975), pp. 488-521.

[47] Verba and Nie report in their survey that 20% of the sample had contacted (wrote or spoken to) a local government official about an issue or a problem. Eighteen percent had contacted a state or national government official about a problem. Sidney Verba and Norman Nie, *Participation in America* (New York: Harper & Row, 1972), p. 31. See also Julien L. Woodward and Elmo Roper, "Political Activity of American Citizens," *American Political Science Review*, vol. 44 (December 1950), pp. 872-885.

members of Congress, in particular, really do listen to their constituents.[48]

Political scientists who have studied legislative lobbying have presented a mixed picture of congressional attitudes toward the mail. Basically, members of Congress are portrayed as being very much interested and concerned about issue sentiment expressed in letters, postcards, and telegrams. It has also been observed, however, that congressional offices are much less responsive to mail they regard as stimulated or produced by pressure groups. Writing of "manufactured" mail, Donald Matthews concluded, "This kind of thing fools nobody. It is expected, quickly recognized, and heavily discounted by the senators and their staffs."[49]

It is possible that Matthews and others have underestimated the attention paid to stimulated mail. If members of Congress discounted everything that was in some sense prompted by interest groups—as opposed to purely self-initiated correspondence—they would be ignoring a large part of their mail. What is primarily discounted is the most blatant and obvious of the manufactured mail, such as hundreds of nearly identically worded postcards received within a period of a few days.[50] But beyond that, it is probably fair to say that letters related to an organization effort are perceived with varying degrees of legitimacy, depending on the selective perception and initial predisposition of the individual Congressperson and his or her staff.[51]

[48] See Lewis Anthony Dexter, "What Do Congressmen Hear: The Mail," Public Opinion Quarterly, vol. 20 (Spring 1956), pp. 16-27; Dexter, The Sociology and Politics of Congress; and Mayhew, Congress: The Electoral Connection.

[49] Donald R. Matthews, U.S. Senators and Their World (New York: Vintage Books, 1960), p. 186.

[50] As James Rosenau points out, "our democratic beliefs lead us to value the volunteered, self-initiated acts of citizens more than those that are mobilized." See his "Mobilizing the Attentive Citizen," paper delivered at the annual meeting of the American Political Science Association, New Orleans, Louisiana, September 1973, p. 3.

[51] See Dexter, The Sociology and Politics of Congress. See also David M. Kreiger, "The Another Mother for Peace Consumer Cam-

There are three very general types of letter-writing campaigns stimulated by public interest groups. One such type is the mass appeal, which usually takes the form of a newspaper advertisement that urges people to write to their members of Congress or to a key committee chairperson. Sometimes these ads will contain a coupon-like letter that can be clipped, signed, and mailed to one's Representative or Senator. An example of this type of appeal is an advertisement the Committee for Humane Legislation placed in some important newspapers that encouraged people to write to their Senators and Representatives, Senator Warren Magnuson (Chairperson of the Commerce Committee), and Senator Ernest Hollings (Chairperson of the Subcommittee on Oceans and Atmosphere), telling them to strengthen a proposed bill to protect baby seals and other ocean mammals.

A second variety of organizational appeals is direct communication between the interest group and its members through the group's newsletter. Friends of the Earth's monthly newspaper, *Not Man Apart*, carries instructions at the end of many articles urging readers to write to particular members of Congress, agency heads, or even the President. The newspaper goes to all Friends of the Earth members, and each edition discusses a number of different environmental issues. A recent story on Mt. McKinley National Park ended with a request that members of the organization send letters to National Park Service Director George Hartzog informing him that they support his efforts to rid Mt. McKinley Park of private automobiles.

A third approach is for organizations to alert a specialized population of the membership. Quite often this is done through special legislative bulletins sent out prior to an important committee or floor vote. These alerts go to all members in certain key districts or states, or to known organizational activists and chapter leaders who can generally be

paign—A Campaign That Failed," *Journal of Peace Research*, vol. 8 (1971), pp. 163-166.

counted on to write letters and make phone calls. Most of the organizations that concentrate on Congress have their membership and/or activists broken down by district in a card file or, if they are well endowed, on computer tape. An illustration of this type of activity is a one-page alert sent out by the Society for Animal Protective Legislation to members in the states represented on the Senate Commerce Committee with regard to pending bills on predator control and use of leg-hold traps.

The letter-writing potential of public interest group members seems to be high. By their act of contributing money to their organization they may be said to belong already to an attentive public.[52] But as James Rosenau discovered in his study of the Americans for Democratic Action (ADA), there is within the attentive public of a group's membership a smaller, "mobilizable" public that is more likely to respond to requests (stimuli) from the organization to write letters.[53] As for the entire group membership, the letter-writing rate is impressive, as 81% of those in ADA write one to three letters a year to federal government officials.[54]

The letter writing of public interest group members should not be viewed merely as a response to organizationally induced stimuli. Issues may have salience independent of intraorganizational communications. On issues such as automobile traffic in Mt. McKinley National Park, it is likely that Friends of the Earth members knew about the problem only through the group's newspaper. At the other extreme are issues such as the 1964 Civil Rights Act, which was so salient that members of liberal groups such as ADA received a relatively small proportion of their information from group publications.

Stimuli for letter writing may come from unexpected

[52] Degree of political participation is, of course, significantly related to socioeconomic characteristics. See, generally, Lester W. Milbrath, *Political Participation* (Chicago: Rand McNally, 1965).

[53] Rosenau, "Mobilizing the Attentive Citizen," and *Citizenship Between Elections* (New York: The Free Press, 1974).

[54] Rosenau, "Mobilizing the Attentive Citizen," p. 17.

sources. An article in *Reader's Digest* concerning the disappearance of wild horses in the United States produced 45,000 letters addressed to Senator Henry Jackson (D., Wash.), Chairperson of the Interior and Insular Affairs Committee, who was mentioned by name in the piece. The 45,000-letter response was more than seven times the membership of the American Horse Protection Association, a group that was lobbying arduously at that time for the same bill specified in the *Reader's Digest* article.

The difficulty in ascertaining the actual impact of letter-writing campaigns on policy makers does not seem to deter its use as a tactic of advocacy. Although no public interest lobbyist would openly use the word "pressure," there is an assumption that the mail can sway uncommitted members of Congress or agency heads. At the very least, in the words of one public interest representative, "It creates a climate."

Influential Member. Using influential members or constituents to contact governmental policy makers is a surprisingly popular technique of advocacy for public interest groups. Although conventional stereotypes of lobbyists may lead one to believe that this behind-the-scenes type of activity may be more characteristic of private interest groups than of the press/publicity-oriented public interest lobbies, the tactic is commonly used by both.[55]

The purpose of these third-party contacts is to gain access to a member of Congress or agency official when other approaches do not seem open or advantageous.[56] But access cannot be divorced from influence. Obviously the individual group member or constituent who is doing the contacting is trying to persuade the target of a point of view. Even when the contact only amounts to the intermediary's getting an appointment for the professional staff lobbyist, there is still an implicit aspect of persuasion in the dynamics of the interaction.

[55] See Milbrath, *The Washington Lobbyists*, pp. 241-244.
[56] See David B. Truman, *The Governmental Process*, 2nd ed. (New York: Alfred A. Knopf, 1971), pp. 264-270.

Despite the fact that a fairly high proportion (34%) of the public interest lobbyists thought that this tactic was an effective one, the interviews also revealed that it is a tactic that is used infrequently. The reason for this is that organizational influentials can be asked to do this type of favor only so much. No old friend of a member of Congress or agency head wants to "wear out his welcome" by intervening too frequently. Professional staffers understand this and, thus, the tactic's usage is moderated. As a consequence, this tactic tends not to be part of the larger strategies of influence, but, rather, is used more on the spur of the moment as the occasion and individuals warrant.

INDIRECT LOBBYING

Campaign Money. Contributing campaign money is the least frequently used technique of influence for the public interest group sample. Only five of the organizations, the American Conservative Union, Americans for Constitutional Action, the Council for a Livable World, the League of Conservation Voters (an affiliate of the Environmental Policy Center),[57] and the National Committee for an Effective Congress (NCEC), raise and distribute campaign funds for congressional candidates. In 1972, these groups gave the following amounts: NCEC, $512,000; Americans for Constitutional Action, (approximately) $250,000; Council for a Livable World, $232,000; American Conservative Union, $110,000; and the League of Conservation Voters, $65,000 (including some contributions to nonfederal candidates). There are two reasons why interest groups give money to candidates. One is to put, or keep, people in Congress who

[57] The League of Conservation Voters was originally affiliated with Friends of the Earth. An internal conflict within Friends of the Earth resulted in the establishment of the Environmental Policy Center by some disgruntled staffers. The professional staff of the League of Conservation Voters went over to the Environmental Policy Center.

have the "right" policy positions. The second is to increase and ensure access to selected Senators and Representatives. For the NCEC and the Americans for Constitutional Action, the primary concern is clearly electing the "right" people. Aside from the mechanics of raising and distributing money and evaluating candidates, their advocacy efforts in other areas tend to be limited in scope. In contrast, for the American Conservative Union, the League of Conservation Voters (through the Environmental Policy Center), and the Council for a Livable World, there is more direct lobbying to supplement their electoral work.

Four of the groups give campaign money to candidates who are either distinctly liberal (NCEC and the Council for a Livable World) or distinctly conservative (American Conservative Union and Americans for Constitutional Action) in their political beliefs. Unlike many private interests— farm, labor, highway builders, etc.—public interest groups tend not to concentrate their giving to incumbents of key congressional committees. These four public interest lobbies take a broad view of a person's politics, and they have little use for middle-of-the-road candidates who may vote the right way on a single issue. Their desire is to elect ideologues on the correct side of the political spectrum.[58] The League of Conservation Voters has given considerably less than the other groups, but concentrated its $65,000 on 13 staunch conservationists in 1972, the majority of whom were challengers rather than incumbents. Seven of the 13 won their races, although one candidate supported for his primary lost the general election.

The linkage between the campaign contributions of public interest groups and the voting behavior of the recipients is impossible to determine in a valid manner. Most of the candidates who are given such money have strong, well-known predispositions before they even get to Congress. In

[58] On campaign finance generally, see Herbert E. Alexander, *Money in Politics* (Washington, D.C.: Public Affairs Press, 1972).

sum, this type of ideological money is given much more as a reward to candidates with the right views than as insurance of access and influence to certain members of Congress.[59]

One reason that more public interest groups do not use campaign contributions as a tactic is the requirements of 501(c)(3) tax status. The groups that possess 501(c)(3) status are absolutely forbidden to give contributions of any kind. Even for the remainder of the groups, however, contributing campaign funds is not viewed as a realistic alternative. Some respondents indicated that they did not think this was a proper activity for a public interest group. Most, however, talked in terms of available resources and the amounts of money necessary in the 1970s to fund campaigns adequately. The lobbyists, in effect, saw the tactic in terms of an either/or situation; they did not feel that the organization could afford to both contribute campaign money and continue to do the same amount of advocacy work in other areas.

Voting Records. The publishing of scorecards of congressional voting, or the reprinting of roll call votes from the *Congressional Record*, is a tactic that is used by one-third of the public interest groups. It is used almost exclusively by those groups that concentrate on Congress and do not have 501(c)(3) tax requirements.

The best known of the voting records are those put out by the Americans for Democratic Action (ADA) and the Americans for Constitutional Action (ACA). Each group constructs composite scores for each individual Representative and Senator and then publishes them after each session of Congress. The organizations choose issues of importance to them and, according to the group's political philosophy, they grade the members of Congress as voting either right

[59] This is not to say that these public interest groups are above using their money in an unsavory manner. Senator Gale McGee (D., Wyo.) was allegedly offered support by the Council for a Livable World in 1970 if he would drop his pro-administration position on the Vietnam War. See Joseph Alsop, "The 'Selling' of the Embassies," *Washington Post*, May 18, 1973, p. A31.

or wrong on each issue. The aggregate right and wrong votes are computed into percentages and scored in such a manner that the higher the percentage, the closer a Senator or Representative is to voting the way the organization wants him or her to.

The vote rankings of the ADA and ACA have become widely accepted and convenient indices of incumbent Congresspersons' liberalism or conservatism. Although the two groups do not use all the same votes, a Congressperson with a low ADA rating will invariably have a high ACA rating and vice versa. The ADA and ACA rankings have become so popular that they have become newsworthy in and of themselves. Local papers will often run stories such as "ADA Rates Adlai Perfect on Issues," or "Nine on Hill Given 100 by ACA," when the rankings are released.[60]

The popularity of the ADA and ACA ratings has encouraged other public interest groups to develop their own indices. The League of Conservation Voters grades members of Congress on their sensitivity to the environment. The American Security Council Index uses defense issues such as the B-1 bomber and the ABM system. The Consumer Federation of America and Public Citizen have scales that pull together consumer-related votes. The League of Women Voters has a Political Accountability Rating which emphasizes matters of social welfare, governmental reform, and foreign aid. The American Conservative Union felt that the ACA's rankings were inadequate measures of conservatism because they weighted all policy votes equally. Their ratings use a number of issues, but votes that bear on "central, crucial ideological issues from a conservative point of view" are statistically weighted to count more heavily in the overall scores.[61]

[60] For profiles of the ADA and ACA, see John L. Moore, "Americans for Democratic Action," pp. 1-33, and Andrew J. Glass, "Americans for Constitutional Action," pp. 35-68, in Judith G. Smith, ed., *Political Brokers* (New York: Liveright, 1972).

[61] *Battle Line*, August 1971, p. 1.

Rather than constructing their own organizational indices, more of the groups simply reprint the lists of those who voted yea or nay on key issues from the pages of the *Congressional Record*. The votes are published in the groups' newsletters for interested members to read.

In addition to the groups that contribute money, there are a few others that endorse candidates without any effort to raise campaign funds for them. It is probably fair to say, however, that the mere endorsement of a public interest group is of negligible consequence in determining election outcomes. If there is an exception to this, it might be Environmental Action's "Dirty Dozen." The 12 incumbent Representatives listed are judged to be those, in the words of the group's magazine, "who have legislatively contributed to the ecological problems that confront us today." They add, "You may feel free to hate them."[62]

Dirty Dozen members are picked primarily according to their records on the environment, but also with regard to their electoral chances. Not all Dirty Dozen members could be called marginal, but almost all are thought to have some potential of losing in the primary or the general election. In 1970, seven of the dozen were defeated. In 1972, five were defeated, but one, Wayne Aspinall (D., Colo.), was quite a prize, because he had long been considered an opponent of the environmental movement for his handling of the chair of the House Interior and Insular Affairs Committee.[63] After the 1974 election, 19 of the 31 Representatives targeted by Environmental Action since 1970 (some have been named more than once) had met defeat. It would be wrong to assume too much from the relative success of Environmental Action's "enemies list," as many other factors could be responsible for the defeat of Dirty Dozen Repre-

[62] *Environmental Action*, June 24, 1972, p. 13.

[63] The League of Conservation Voters gave Aspinall's Democratic primary opponent, Alan Merson, $16,300. This was by far the largest contribution the League gave, and it was one-fourth of the total amount they handed out. Merson beat Aspinall in the primary, but he lost the general election.

sentatives. Nevertheless, all but the safest of House members would be considerably agitated at their selection as one of the Dirty Dozen.

It is easy to understand why the public interest groups contribute money to campaigns. Money can aid congressional candidates, particularly nonincumbents, in their election races. The expenditure of resources to construct voting indices, though not defensible on the grounds that they have any real effect on elections, can be rationalized as useful because they generate publicity and esteem for the groups that provide them. Although endorsements without campaign money—Environmental Action being a possible exception—seem rather symbolic, they require so little in the way of time and money that they cannot really be considered a waste of resources. Reprinting roll call vote tabulations from the *Congressional Record* is hardly a powerful lobbying weapon, because only a few large groups could conceivably have enough "swing" voters in their state or district memberships actually to influence a congressional election. They are motivated by civic duty and by the simple belief that the more information a voter has, the better his or her decision will be on election day.

Releasing Research Results and Public Relations. Personal lobbying is probably best described as a process by which a group representative conveys information to a governmental official that the latter may not be aware of. There are occasions when lobbyists perceive that people in government are unwilling to listen, or that personally presenting arguments will not create the "pressure" necessary to catalyze action. In these instances lobbyists may try to take their case to the people, hoping that making the public, or a segment of it, aware of certain facts, will work to change the climate of opinion. They may do this by releasing research reports and results to the press, or by taking out advertisements in various media outlets.

Because some interviewees tended to view "public relations" as the process of publicizing research results, as well as advertising campaigns, it is best to discuss these two tactics together.[64] Both tactics relate to a larger question: how are resources best allocated for gaining effective publicity for the group's message?[65] One choice open to the lobbyists is to go directly to the press with information that may be newsworthy enough to warrant immediate coverage. There are three major methods, usually aimed at newspapers and newspaper reporters, used by public interest groups to transmit their news.

The first means of communication is the press release, which highlights the research or other information the group has available. Writing a good press release is somewhat of an art, where care must be placed in actually writing the story for the press. The first part of a press release should be written as if it were the lead paragraphs of a newspaper story. When the *Washington Post* reported in its May 7, 1973, edition that "The Center for Auto Safety said yesterday that an electrical relay in 1969 and 1970 Cadillacs constitutes a serious fire hazard," they were surely reprinting the first sentence of a Center press release.

The press release requires only moderate-to-small amounts of resources once the initial research has been completed. The potential payoff, newspaper coverage, is high, so they are good risks on issues of real importance to the organization. The news releases of national public interest groups are aimed at four particularly important outlets: the AP, the UPI, *The New York Times*, and the *Washington Post*. If any of these picks up a story, the public interest groups consider that the news has been legitimated and that it will be read by a sufficiently large audience, including people in govern-

[64] Thus, the percentage scores for the public relations category in Table VII-1 are not, unfortunately, an adequate measure of the perceived effectiveness of advertising campaigns.

[65] Again, there is the problem of expanding the conflict and appealing to the third party. See Schattschneider, *The Semisovereign People*; and Lipsky, "Protest as a Political Resource."

ment. Public interest groups have had substantially less success with TV, radio, and news magazines, although they remain highly desirable means of publicity.

The second method of communication is the press conference. Press releases are still given out at these events, but press conferences are a much less frequently used device. This is understandable. If a newspaper or TV station is going to cover a news conference, it must commit a reporter and a photographer or cameraman for most of a morning or afternoon. Consequently, a group must have a rather significant story before they can expect the media personnel to go to the trouble of coming to their conference.

There are only a few public interest groups that, independent of the issue, can be assured of drawing a respectable crowd to a press conference any time they want. One is Common Cause, whose chairperson, John Gardner, commands a great deal of respect both for himself and for his rather large organization. As a spokesperson for any of his satellite groups or associates, Ralph Nader is the most frequent "copy" of any public interest figure. Although a charge or a diatribe by Nader may not always make page 1, it will almost invariably make the wire services and the *Times* and the *Post.*

The fact that Nader will appear at a press conference makes the conference a recognized media event. One example is a jointly sponsored press conference with Friends of the Earth at which Nader accused the Atomic Energy Commission of negligence in nuclear power plant safety. Specifically, Nader said that research on the subject led them to believe that there are inadequate safeguards to prevent the type of loss-of-coolant accidents that can result in the melting of nuclear reactor cores and, thus, the releasing of lethal radiation. In conjunction with the press conference, a lawsuit was also filed against the AEC.[66]

[66] "Nader Sues to Close 20 A-Plants," *Washington Post,* June 1, 1973, p. D20.

This story not only got prominent newspaper play, but it even made the network TV news, a positive rarity for a group like Friends of the Earth. Had Friends of the Earth held the press conference on their own, it is quite unlikely that they would have received the publicity they did by operating in cooperation with Nader.

The third way in which groups may use the media directly to propagate research and other material is the cultivation of individual reporters. A sympathetic newspaper reporter is invaluable to a public interest group: it is a resource to be nurtured, cherished, and protected. The most prominent of the handful of reporters who have developed symbiotic relationships with people in the public interest movement are syndicated columnist Jack Anderson and *Washington Post* consumer correspondent Morton Mintz. Mintz is widely respected for his investigative reporting and in-depth analysis, whereas Anderson concentrates on tidbits of information aimed at embarrassing and exposing government officials. Anderson is constantly being fed potential stories by the Center for Science in the Public Interest, the Fund for Animals, the Nader people, and others; even if he devotes only a couple of lines in his column to an item, it serves the purpose of publicizing alleged malfeasance in government.[67]

The tactic of conducting and then publicizing research has been used to the greatest extent by Ralph Nader and his many associates. After he came into national prominence with his damning criticism of Chevrolet Corvairs, Nader commissioned a number of major studies in different consumer-related fields.[68] His idealistic, mostly college-aged assistants were popularly dubbed "Nader's Raiders," and

[67] On the value of the press to the consumer movement, see Mark V. Nadel, *The Politics of Consumer Protection* (Indianapolis, Ind.: Bobbs-Merrill, 1971), pp. 191-204.

[68] Nader's rise was unwittingly aided by General Motors, which had him investigated by private detectives. A great deal of controversy ensued when this became public. See McCarry, *Citizen Nader*, pp. 3-29.

within a few years the Nader Study Group Report became somewhat of an institution.[69]

Probably the most important of these early studies is *The Nader Report on the Federal Trade Commission*, written by Edward F. Cox, Robert C. Fellmeth, and John E. Schulz.[70] The report may not have been a best seller, but it was read within the FTC, and by President Nixon (Edward Cox's prospective father-in-law), who subsequently asked the American Bar Association to do an investigation of the FTC. The eventual rejuvenation of the FTC into a much more consumer-oriented agency must be, in part, credited to the initial charges made by Nader and the authors of the report, which were widely disseminated in the press.[71]

Since 1969, Nader's people have produced at least 25 major studies probing subjects as diverse as Volkswagen automobiles,[72] the influence of the DuPont family in Delaware,[73] old age homes,[74] and occupational health and safety.[75] The quality and design of these reports have not always been high. For example, *Who Runs Congress?*[76] was not well received because it had little to say that was new.

[69] See Julius Duscha, "Stop! In the Public Interest!" *The New York Times Magazine*, March 21, 1971, pp. 4ff; and Thomas Whiteside, "A Countervailing Force," *New Yorker*, October 8, 1973, pp. 50-111, and October 15, 1973, pp. 46-101. For some insights into Nader's view of what lies ahead, see Joe Klein, "Ralph Nader," *Rolling Stone*, November 20, 1975, pp. 54ff.

[70] Edward F. Cox, Robert C. Fellmeth, and John E. Schulz, *The Nader Report on the Federal Trade Commission* (New York: Baron, 1969).

[71] The change in the FTC is regarded as one of the real victories in the public interest movement. See Harrison Wellford, "How Ralph Nader, Tricia Nixon, the ABA, and Jamie Whitten Helped Turn the FTC Around," *Washington Monthly*, October 1972, pp. 5-13.

[72] *Small—On Safety* (New York: Grossman, 1972).

[73] James Phelan and Robert Pozen, *The Company State* (New York: Grossman, 1973).

[74] Claire Townsend, *Old Age: The Last Segregation* (New York: Grossman, 1971).

[75] Joseph A. Page and Mary-Win O'Brien, *Bitter Wages* (New York: Grossman, 1973).

[76] Mark J. Green, James M. Fallows, and David Zwick, *Who Runs Congress?* (New York: Bantam/Grossman, 1972).

Characteristically, however, Nader studies are well-researched tomes that, although sometimes tedious to read, deal with significant abuses in the corporate and public sectors.

Research reports, and the accompanying public relations, can serve two purposes. One is to draw direct attention to a particularly bad policy or to a poorly performing public servant, with the hope that there will be some immediate redress of the grievance. The second is to contribute to what public interest activists call "consciousness raising"—the process of gradually increasing the public's awareness and desire for needed change.[77] Often the same research effort can have both the long- and short-term components by attacking a single part of a problem while going to lengths to document the larger issues at hand.

In terms of actually influencing public policy, the limitations of just releasing and publicizing research results are substantial. Unless the research contains some really dramatic findings, there will be little follow-up by the press after the initial denials and rebuttals by corporate or government officials. Therefore, for research to have an impact, it usually must be accompanied by other tactics such as litigation, legislative lobbying, or administrative intervention.[78]

The inadequacy of releasing research results as an isolated tactic had been recognized by its most frequent user, Ralph Nader. In the past few years, Nader has tried to create a "second strike" capability to back up his numerous study groups. The first move in this direction was the establishment of the Public Citizen Litigation Group, which does advocacy work before the courts on behalf of the Nader satellites and on issues initiated within the group itself. Another effort by Nader was his founding of Congress

[77] The term derives from Charles Reich's prescription for social change. Reich writes that revolution will come through changes in states of "consciousness." *The Greening of America* (New York: Random House, 1970).

[78] It should be reiterated that the operational definition of a public interest group required that the organizations be advocacy groups rather than pure research institutions.

Watch, a lobbying group that is concentrating on consumer affairs issues.[79]

Congress Watch is, in fact, a follow-up to Nader's Congress Project, a research group whose purpose was to build a comprehensive body of knowledge on the legislative process. There was only lukewarm reception to the Project's first major effort, 20-40 page profiles of all incumbents seeking reelection, which were released during the 1972 campaign period.[80] Another publication, the *Who Runs Congress?* paperback, raised badly needed cash to support the Project, but it was hardly a catalyst for congressional reform.[81] Although more substantive research reports were to follow, Nader realized that the Congress Project and his other study groups needed a lobbying arm on Capitol Hill to back them up, and in early 1973 he started Congress Watch.[82]

Finally, "public relations" should be discussed within the context of pure media campaigns. In this type of public relations endeavor, the interest group may communicate directly with its audience rather than having to have its "news" interpreted and capsulized, or not covered at all, by reporters. Activities of this sort might include advertising (paid or public service), personal appearances (speeches, forums, TV and radio talk shows), and self-produced movies or TV and radio programs.

The key difference between the tactic of releasing and

[79] Jacqueney, "Nader Network Switches Focus to Legal Action, Congressional Lobbying." See also Ben Bagdikian, "Congress and the Media: Partners in Propaganda," *Columbia Journalism Review*, vol. 12 (January/February 1974), pp. 8-10.

[80] Mary Russell, "Nader's Profiles of 485 Members of Congress Unveiled," *Washington Post*, October 22, 1972, p. A20.

[81] See Mary Russell, "Nader's Book on Congress No Eye-Opener," *Washington Post*, October 8, 1972, p. A16.

[82] On the problems of the Congress Project, see Paul L. Leventhal, "Political Reaction Overshadows Reform Aim of Massive Nader Congress Study," *National Journal*, September 23, 1972, pp. 1483-1495. Nader later referred to the Congress Project as "my C-5A," a reference to the problem-ridden cargo plane. "Public Interest Lobbies: Nader and Common Cause Become Permanent Fixtures," *Congressional Quarterly*, May 15, 1976, p. 1200.

publicizing research results and pure public relations is that a number of groups commit considerable resources for research purposes while few groups allocate more than a marginal amount for advertising, electronic media presentations, and the like. The primary reason for the low resource commitment is the sheer costs involved in public relations. It is simply too expensive for most groups to use to any significant degree. Its utility seems to be perceived more for consciousness raising than for short-term problems, although there are some notable exceptions, such as the newspaper ads against the Central Arizona Project which were placed by the Sierra Club and which generated considerable controversy.[83]

The use of public relations for short-term issues is, however, characteristic of *ad hoc* public interest groups. Quite often *ad hoc* groups will depend on newspaper advertisements for fund raising. These ads may also be ends in and of themselves, as many *ad hoc* groups are nothing more than a small number of people who wish to make a symbolic statement of protest ("we the undersigned . . .") in the Sunday *New York Times* or other outlet, but who have no other advocacy plans.

ADDITIONAL TACTICS

In addition to endless variations and combinations of the tactics already summarized, two tactics that were not listed on the interview card should be noted briefly. Although they relate to aspects of tactics already discussed, they need to be identified as distinct techniques of advocacy.

Shareholders' Actions. Shareholders' actions are aimed directly at private corporations rather than at government. These actions are efforts by public interest groups to persuade individuals and institutional shareholders to vote their proxies in favor of group-sponsored proposals for cor-

[83] See the discussion of the Sierra Club and its tax problems in Chapter III.

porate reform at the annual open meeting of the targeted corporation. The most notable of these actions is "Campaign GM," which was initiated by the Project on Corporate Responsibility.[84]

In terms of short-term corporate reforms, Campaign GM and other earlier undertakings were, by everyone's admission, failures. Although there was certainly some positive contribution in the form of consciousness raising, the proposals themselves never received more than a few percent of the proxies cast.[85] Moreover, management has tended to act hostilely toward the groups that have sponsored the confrontations. At least for the Project on Corporate Responsibility, the limits of shareholders' actions have become evident. In the words of one staffer, "we feel more can be gained now by litigation and research."[86]

Whistle-Blowing. Public interest groups sometimes act as outlets for disgruntled bureaucrats or corporate officers who are frustrated by what they perceive as irresponsible policy positions by the institution they work for. To combat this, the individual may release information to which he has access that is being covered up by his superiors and that is also potentially embarrassing to them.[87]

When an individual "blows the whistle" and goes public

[84] See Donald E. Schwartz, "The Public-Interest Proxy Contest: Reflections on Campaign GM," *Michigan Law Review*, vol. 69 (January 1971), pp. 421-538.

[85] See David Vogel, "Contemporary Criticism of Business: The Publicization of the Corporation," paper delivered at the annual meeting of the American Political Science Association, New Orleans, Louisiana, September 1973, pp. 31-32.

[86] Public interest and various other public-spirited organizations have seen some progress in the use of shareholder actions since the initial Campaign GM effort. Partisans cite both an increase in the votes received for floor resolutions and in the number of negotiated settlements resulting in the withdrawal of resolutions. See Marilyn Bender, "3% Vote Delights Corporate Critics," *The New York Times*, June 5, 1974, p. 65.

[87] See, generally, Charles Peters and Taylor Branch, *Blowing the Whistle* (New York: Praeger, 1972); and Ralph Nader, Peter Petkas, and Kate Blackwell, eds., *Whistle Blowing* (New York: Grossman, 1972).

with his data, he or she invites punishment or even dismissal from his or her job.[88] Some individuals prefer to act in secret to leak information to a sympathetic member of Congress or newspaper reporter. Alternatively, the whistle-blower may covertly hand over his material to a public interest group which will act as an intermediary for the purposes of releasing or leaking the information to the press. As a consequence, public interest groups are careful to protect as well as cultivate sources in government bureaucracies.

[88] Such was the case with Pentagon cost analyst A. Ernest Fitzgerald, who exposed $2 billion in cost over-runs in the C-5A cargo plane during congressional testimony. Fitzgerald was later fired, but the American Civil Liberties Union took his case before the U.S. Civil Service Commission and won his reinstatement. See Peters and Branch, *Blowing the Whistle*, pp. 207-221. See also Joann S. Lublin, "Disclosing Misdeeds of Corporations Can Backfire on Tattlers," *Wall Street Journal*, May 21, 1976, p. 1.

CHAPTER IX

... And the Strategies of Influence

THE tactics of interest group advocacy have been described as a set of alternative actions open to staff lobbyists. Each tactic has unique costs and benefits associated with its utilization. Explaining the actual choice of lobbying tactics is no easy task, however, for there is much more that needs to be considered than just the individual tactics themselves. An attempt will be made here to try to relate the choice of tactics to the organizational and environmental variables that affect lobbying decisions. The framework to be developed is intended to synthesize the findings of the previous chapters into a coherent portrait of organizational behavior.

One further piece of analysis must precede the final elaboration of this decision-making model. Tactics are inextricably tied to strategies of influence. Earlier, strategies were defined as more general, long-range approaches to lobbying, whereas tactics were said to be the immediate, day-to-day activities of an interest group attempting to influence government. There are two aspects of lobbying strategy that must be examined. *Cooperative strategy* pertains to the relationship of an interest group to other, sympathetic organizations during an extended lobbying campaign. A public interest group must often decide if it will enter into a working arrangement with other organizations or if it will go it alone on an issue. If it chooses to work cooperatively, it can be said to be a member of an interest group coalition. In the following discussion, emphasis will be placed on distinguishing the different types of public interest coalitions and upon understanding the rationale behind coalition participation.

The *advocacy strategies* of public interest groups are the underlying theories of influence that guide an organization's choice of lobbying tactics. These strategies must also be fitted into the decision-making framework because they are so important in a group's determination of how to expend its resources most effectively. The model will be completed after the advocacy strategies are each identified and examined in relation to their tactical options.

The subject of strategies of influence quite logically leads to the question of interest group efficacy. Because the research for this study was conducted from the viewpoint of public interest activists, the present work is not well suited for an in-depth treatment of public interest group effectiveness. Research addressed directly to measuring interest group efficacy must take into account the views not only of lobbyists, but of all actors who participate in particular policy conflicts. Consequently, it is only the lobbyists' perceptions of their influence that may be explored at this point.

COALITIONS

The first thing that may be said in terms of cooperative strategy is that coalitions are extremely popular among public interest lobbies. Coalitions, defined as explicit working relationships among groups for the purpose of achieving a public policy goal, are not only popular, but are seemingly easy to form as well. Public interest activists were asked to evaluate "joint activity with other organizations," and an overwhelming proportion (76%) responded that they considered it "important" or "very important" (see Table IX-1). The popularity of coalitions is clearly evident. The question to be answered now is why it is advantageous for groups to join forces.

Most of the reasons public interest lobbyists gave for their positive attitude toward coalitions are fairly obvious. There are natural incentives to share costs when an advo-

TABLE IX-1

Coalition Activity

Very important	52%	(43)
Important	24%	(20)
Important, but with qualifications	7%	(6)
Not important	17%	(14)
	100%	(N = 83)

cacy effort is beyond the means of a single group. When two or more groups are working in the same area, they will usually want to share information if they are ideologically compatible. Most significantly, though, the representatives saw it as a means by which their organization could overcome some of their inherent limitations.[1] Some sample responses illustrate:

With our size, it is the only way to have an impact.

Nothing is done by itself in Washington.

Extremely important for a small office like this. It would be presumptuous of us to tell members that *we* really are having an impact on public policy here in Washington. We have to do what we can with the other groups.

In conservation circles, everybody has to cooperate.

[1] Truman writes of legislative lobbying, "Although a group may easily enjoy advantages in position and in the size and disposition of the public concerned with its claims, rarely can any single group achieve its legislative objectives without assistance from other groups." David B. Truman, *The Governmental Process*, 2nd ed. (New York: Alfred A. Knopf, 1971), p. 362. In her research on women's lobbies in Washington, Anne N. Costain found that representatives of 14 out of 15 organizations surveyed described joint activity as "very important." See "A Social Movement Lobbies: Women's Liberation and Pressure Politics," paper delivered at the annual meeting of the Southern Political Science Association, Nashville, Tennessee, November 1975, p. 16.

I don't think we have an unrealistic view of what one group can do in terms of impact on public policy. I don't think we can have a naive view of what a coalition can do either. But we do know how to maximize our impact and this is how we can do it.

The advantages and disadvantages of coalition formation can be better understood if the different kinds of coalitions are distinguished. Although it is generally true that coalitions form because lobbyists wish to maximize their strength, there are more subtle explanations to be made for each of the types of coalitions. Coalitions appear to be structured along two dimensions. Such cooperative arrangements differ in the extent of participation by member organizations and the extent to which they are able to involve their supporters. A second dimension is the degree of permanence of the organization. At one extreme, the coalition may be nothing more than an occasional meeting of some of the members; at the other extreme, the coalition may operate with a professional staff of its own in an office distinct from the headquarters of any of the member groups.

The coalitions actually observed tend to fall into three general categories. *Dependent* coalitions are those where one group dominates in both active participation and resource commitment. Other groups will act in concert with the dominant group during major lobbying efforts, but their participation in the coalition's decision making tends to be of a secondary nature.

Most typically, dependent coalitions are good ideas that never quite fulfill their promise. An entrepreneur in an individual public interest group attempts to attract members to a proposed coalition. There is enough initial favorable reaction for the entrepreneur to get the backing of his own organization to "start up" the coalition. The dependency condition arises when the hoped-for financial support never materializes and the parent organization, because it is deeply committed to the cause of the incipient coalition, continues to maintain it. Because it is always possible that the dependent coalition will eventually find enough outside support to sustain itself, the coalition structure may be kept intact, or allowed to wither naturally.

An example of the dependent coalition is the Highway Action Coalition, which was founded by Environmental Action. The purpose of the Highway Action Coalition is to persuade Congress to divert money from the Highway Trust Fund to mass transit projects. Although all environmental groups support "busting the trust," the Highway Action Coalition could not get its member groups to put up much cash to support the organization. Members include such highly esteemed groups as the Sierra Club, Common Cause, and the League of Women Voters, and the Coalition has received significant lobbying assistance from some of the affiliated organizations. Still, the Coalition and its director, John Kramer, have been dependent on Environmental Action, which houses the Coalition and continues to be its primary means of support.[2]

A second type of organization is the *participatory* coalition. In a participatory coalition, no one group is dominant, although a single member group may have a major leadership or coordinating role. At least two organizations are highly active and supportive of a participatory coalition. Although it is possible for the coalition to include some nominal members, it is more likely that all members will be committing significant resources.

The earlier case study of the Women's International League for Peace and Freedom (WILPF) traced the development of a participatory coalition between WILPF, the Indochina Resource Center, the Friends Committee on National Legislation, Women's Strike for Peace, Amnesty

[2] The efforts of Kramer and others who worked to bust the trust finally came to fruition in the 93rd Congress when a highway act was passed that, for the first time, allows money to be taken from the trust to fund mass transit projects. The bill was a compromise, and actual funding for mass transit could not begin until 1975. Public Law 93-87.

International, and Members of Congress for Peace Through Law. These groups cooperated in sponsoring and arranging the Washington tour of Jean-Pierre Debris and Andre Menras, two former political prisoners in South Vietnam. The New York office of Amnesty International provided most of the financial sustenance, but the other groups expended a great deal of staff time over a three-week period.[3]

Most frequently, participatory coalitions are *ad hoc* working arrangements that do not lend themselves to institutionalized or permanent arrangements. It is something quite different to have groups share significant resource costs over an indefinite period rather than for a relatively short time, no matter how urgent the cause.

A third classification is the *independent* coalition. These coalitions tend to have a much greater permanence than participatory coalitions, as well as an independent staff and a distinct identity from any member group. One such organization is the Coalition on National Priorities and Military Policy. It was started in 1969 as a response to the Vietnam War. It was not designed to be an anti-Vietnam group; its purpose is to prevent future Vietnams from happening by fighting to curb the power of the military. Since its inception, the group has concentrated on matters pertaining to the military budget and arms control.

The Coalition on National Priorities was begun by church groups and other liberal, peace-oriented lobbies. The 39 member groups do not, individually, have to contribute a great deal of money to support the small Coalition staff. Among them, they provide only a little over $10,000 per year. The Coalition receives the other two-thirds of its annual budget from direct mail and a few large donors. The member groups are, however, expected to allocate considerable staff time to the workings of the Coalition to aid it in its ongoing advocacy efforts. In practice, this amounts

[3] In this case the WILPF and, secondarily, the Indochina Resource Center took more of a leadership responsibility than the others, but all were active participants. See Chapter VI.

to attending biweekly meetings and participating in coordinated lobbying efforts a couple of times a year.

With this brief description of the three basic kinds of coalitions complete, it is now possible to examine the factors that encourage and discourage their formation. It is the independent coalition that is hardest to form. Even if member groups do not have to contribute a great deal in the way of cash, the financial requirement is still a real inhibition to potential members. A contribution of just $100 a year is enough to make group directors think twice about joining a coalition. And unless there are outside sources of income, or a parent organization that is willing to carry the coalition, the number of member groups needed for financial purposes is quite high.[4]

Making matters more difficult, there always exists a great deal of competition for prospective coalition members. The average public interest group already belongs to one or two coalitions.[5] The entrepreneur must convince those he or she wants to join that it is worthwhile to spend even more in the way of resources for coalition activity and, conversely, less on his or her organization's own projects.[6]

Most dependent coalitions are, of course, prospective independent coalitions that never fully succeed.[7] It may seem

[4] Much has been written by formal theorists on the size principle of coalitions. Operationally, there is no such thing as a minimum winning coalition for public interest groups. They will always be trying to expand membership so as to increase what they consider to be inferior resources. See, generally, William H. Riker, *The Theory of Political Coalitions* (New Haven, Conn.: Yale University Press, 1962).

[5] For example, liberal groups could very well already belong to the Leadership Conference on Civil Rights, the Coalition on National Priorities and Military Policy, or the Coalition for Human Needs and Budget Priorities, among other possibilities.

[6] On competition by entrepreneurs for individual interest group members, see Norman Frohlich, Joe A. Oppenheimer, and Oran R. Young, *Political Leadership and Collective Goods* (Princeton, N.J.: Princeton University Press, 1971).

[7] Independent coalitions may, of course, be formed by new entrepreneurs, rather than by staff personnel of existing groups. Dependent coalitions may evolve out of participatory coalitions when

rather irrational for a parent group to underwrite a coalition when other, sympathetic organizations are willing to only provide nominal support. From another perspective, this type of behavior is not so foolish. Entrepreneurs do not enter these arrangements naively. When an organization tries to spin off another, it is doing so because the people in the group feel that there is an urgent need for action in a particular area. It is something they are willing to support and, for any additional support they can attract through the coalition, it is a case of so much the better.

Nominal participation in a dependent or independent coalition may be induced by social or peer group pressure.[8] Although a group's staff may realize that their joining will make only a marginal contribution to the coalition's success and that they have no intention of working hard for the coalition, they may still join because their absence would be noticed by the other members. Broken down by subfield and specialization, the world of public interest groups, and the private interest groups with which they sometimes work in concert, is a small one. Nominal participation in coalitions, therefore, is a way around the problem of being perceived as selfish and disloyal to the cause by one's peers.[9]

It is possible that participatory coalitions are the easiest to form, but they are likely to come together only in certain

an interim goal is reached and one partner is decidedly more interested in keeping the arrangement going than are others.

[8] This discussion follows the lines of Mancur Olson's argument concerning "small" groups in *The Logic of Collective Action* (New York: Schocken Books, 1968).

[9] In his study, *Cooperative Lobbying*, Donald Hall found that groups were very conscious of not entering into coalitions that included groups with bad images. If they associated with such a coalition, it was possible that the bad image might rub off on them. Hall also found that groups sometimes did not cooperate because they feared adverse press reaction, or because they needed to operate in secrecy. None of these factors was ever mentioned by public interest groups. Hall's study focused primarily on private interest groups. See *Cooperative Lobbying—The Power of Pressure* (Tucson: University of Arizona Press, 1969).

types of situations. When an issue or subissue is not so enduring that a long-term arrangement is necessary, and
where one group does not have, or does not choose to allocate, the resources for a solitary effort, it is obviously advantageous to enter into a participatory coalition. Another
situation that may stimulate a participatory coalition is
when two or more groups begin working independently on
an issue and subsequently become aware of the others' efforts. Cooperation becomes increasingly feasible as overlap
develops.

One factor that operates against cooperative endeavors
is the desire of staff personnel to enhance organizational
esteem. Regardless of how worthy the cause, if they work
with other groups, they must share an identity with them.[10]
All groups, quite naturally, want to "make a name for themselves." Consequently, they will want to devote the bulk
of their resources toward efforts that are most likely to add
to their own reputation as being expert and influential in
specific areas.[11] This not only hinders initial formation of
coalitions, but it also acts to impede nominal participation
from developing into fuller participation, and against *ad
hoc* participatory coalitions from developing into more permanent structures.[12]

[10] Herbert Simon summarizes the conflict: "When it is recognized
that actual decisions must take place in some such institutional setting,
it can be seen that the 'correctness' of any particular decision may be
judged from two different standpoints. In the broader sense it is 'correct' if it is consistent with the general social value scale—if its consequences are socially desirable. In the narrower sense, it is 'correct' if it
is consistent with the frame of reference that has been organizationally
assigned to the decider." *Administrative Behavior*, 2nd ed. (New York:
The Free Press, 1957), p. 199.
[11] For a case study of organizational "egos" getting in the way of a
natural alliance, see Lucius J. Barker and Donald Jansiewicz, "Coalitions in the Civil Rights Movement," in Sven Groennings, E. W. Kelley,
and Michael Leiserson, eds., *The Study of Coalition Behavior* (New
York: Holt, Rinehart and Winston, 1970), pp. 192-208.
[12] The term "coalition" has been used here to refer to the process by
which one public interest group acts in cooperation with other interest
groups. In reality, of course, a working coalition in the legislative or
administrative process also includes government officials and their

STRATEGIES AND INTEREST GROUP BEHAVIOR

Before commenting upon the strategies of influence of public interest groups, it may be best to begin by outlining the decision-making model that will help to tie together the forces that influence the choices of strategy and tactics. For the purposes of analysis, the selection of advocacy strategy and tactics can be conceived of as the final steps in an interest group's decision-making process. The model below attempts to show the pattern by which internal organizational capabilities and external opportunities affect the choices of specific strategies and tactics.

As was the case with understanding the choice of new issues by public interest groups, the best place to begin is with organizational goals, capabilities, and constraints. These variables act to structure a group's behavior independent of any situational variables that change from issue to issue. These factors can, of course, change (e.g., a non-membership group can decide to go public), but alterations of this sort are related to the more general evolution and adaptation of organizational goals and not to an advocacy effort on any particular issue. As listed in Figure IX-1, these basic characteristics are the amount of financial and staff resources, tax status, membership, legal advocacy capability, expertise of the staff, group goals, and issue priorities.

Much has already been written about these variables, and there is little need for extensive elaboration on them. The tremendous range of staff and financial resources among the sample has been detailed in full. The more resources available to a group, the more alternatives open to it in choosing lobbying strategy and tactics. A critical resource, of course, is the capability to carry out legal advo-

---

staffs. See, for example, Stephen K. Bailey, *Congress Makes a Law* (New York: Columbia University Press, 1950); and Eric Redman, *The Dance of Legislation* (New York: Simon and Schuster, 1973).

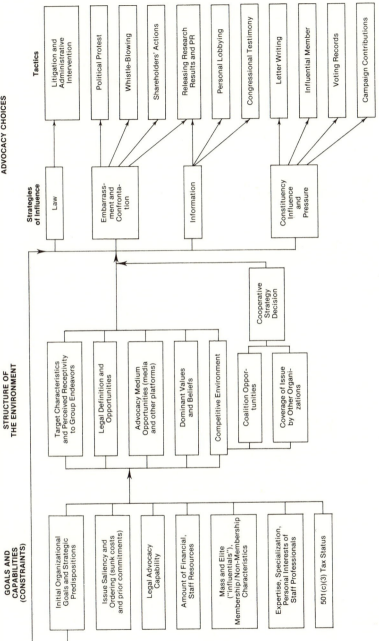

FIGURE IX-1

Strategies and Tactics: A Decision-Making Framework

cacy through in-house counsel or outside attorneys. Whether or not an organization has 501(c)(3) status is of paramount significance in determining the group's utilization of campaign contributions, endorsements of candidates, personal legislative lobbying, and other direct forms of legislative advocacy.

The initial goals of a group have important implications for what may be termed the "strategic predispositions" of the organization. Many public interest groups are set up to perform their advocacy work in a particular manner, such as an antiwar protest group, a public interest law firm, a consumer research center, or a citizens' legislative lobby. Consequently, from the day of their inception, most organizations are inclined toward some strategies and tactics and away from others. A closely related factor is a group's ongoing primary issue commitments, which may reserve more costly tactics (e.g., litigation) for high-priority issues while permitting less costly resource expenditures (e.g., nominal coalition participation) on issues of somewhat lesser urgency.

The expertise and specialization of professional staffs is obviously relevant to whether or not an organization depends on more highly skilled tactics, such as litigation or certain types of original research. The more experienced, more professional lobbyists may also be able to make greater use of influential members or personal lobbying as a means of influencing government. Lastly, the membership (and its qualities) of an organization is a vital resource for advocacy endeavors. Groups with no formal memberships are not as readily able to conduct letter-writing campaigns or use electoral endorsements. Other public interest lobbies may have members, but lack a substantial body of elites who can intervene on their behalf before government.[13]

---

[13] James Rosenau distinguishes between attentiveness and mobilizability in an interest group membership. One could say the higher degree of mobilizability, the greater value of the membership as an organizational resource. See Rosenau, *Citizenship Between Elections* (New York: The Free Press, 1974).

A second set of factors are those that must be viewed in a more situational context. For a given issue, what are the coalition opportunities? Which officials or institutions of government will be most receptive to a group's efforts? What are the opportunities for exposure through the media or other outlets? How well is an issue being covered by other sympathetic lobbies? What are the barriers or opportunities for legal advocacy? Given the basic characteristics of the organization, these factors further structure behavior according to the issue and the day-to-day realities of Washington politics.

Again, only brief mention needs to be made of most of these variables. The legal definition of an issue refers to the manner in which the law facilitates or inhibits legal intervention through the requirements of standing or through statutes that affect participation, such as the National Environmental Policy Act. Advocacy medium opportunities pertain to the chances a group's staff perceive of other actors being sufficiently concerned with an issue to assist the organization by providing a forum for a lobbying effort. Will the newspapers and wire services cover a press conference? Is Congress likely to hold hearings in the near future? Do people care enough to come and demonstrate in front of the Capitol? The comparative opportunities of various forums and platforms must always enter into any calculations concerning the use of various tactics.

Similarly, interest groups must evaluate the receptivity of different governmental institutions to any planned lobbying activities. Organizations will often be faced with particular agencies or congressional committees that are less than sympathetic to the group's policy objectives. If an agency is clearly hostile to a lobby's goals, that organization may want to forego any personal lobbying with its officials and rely instead on litigation or initiatives in the Congress.[14]

[14] On the attitudes of governmental officials toward lobbies and lobbyists, see Betty Zisk, *Local Interest Politics: A One-Way Street*

The competitive environment, as defined earlier in the analysis of issue decision making, is the coverage of issues by like-minded organizations and the opportunities for coalition participation. It is clear that groups are often faced with the decision of whether or not they should join a newly forming coalition when they begin to work on an issue. Strategic cooperative decisions have been distinguished from strategic advocacy decisions. If a public interest group makes the decision to join a coalition, then it must share in collective decision making on coalition strategies and tactics.

One must add to all this the dominant value and belief systems of the polity. Traditions, symbols, and generally accepted political values work to give legitimacy to certain types of participation, such as letter writing, while casting other activities, such as protests or campaign contributions, in a more negative light. Although a societal belief system does not really change on an issue-to-issue basis as do the other variables discussed here, it is part of the external environment within which interest groups must operate.[15]

The Strategies of Influence. The strategies of influence have been spoken of in the abstract, but have yet to be adequately identified. The model depicts strategy decisions as being structured by organizational goals and capabilities and by environmental variables that are largely determined by the issue at hand. It has also been noted, however, that public interest lobbies often have pronounced strategic predispositions and, thus, "choice" of a strategy of influence may be largely predetermined. The four strategies may be

---

(Indianapolis, Ind.: Bobbs-Merrill, 1973); John C. Wahlke, Heinz Eulau, William Buchanan, and LeRoy C. Ferguson, *The Legislative System* (New York: Wiley, 1962); and Andrew M. Scott and Margaret A. Hunt, *Congress and Lobbies* (Chapel Hill: University of North Carolina Press, 1965).

[15] See L. Harmon Zeigler and G. Wayne Peak, *Interest Groups in American Society*, 2nd ed. (Englewood Cliffs, N.J.: Prentice-Hall, 1972), pp. 28-63.

labeled as law, embarrassment and confrontation, information, and constituency influence and pressure. Few groups limit themselves to using only one of these general strategies, and, likewise, few are able to utilize all four.

1. Law. There is a dichotomy that may be made between those groups, such as the Environmental Defense Fund and the Public Citizens' Litigation Group, that view law as their primary means of influence, and those, such as Common Cause and the Sierra Club, that consider law as an important, but secondary, means of advocacy. For the former type of lobby, the law is thought of as a way to work within the system without having to "stoop to politics." The representatives of these groups would have one believe that they are, in some sense, on a higher level than other interest groups because their primary purpose is to see to it that the law is enforced.

For the groups that rely primarily on legal advocacy, there is great faith in the fairness of the law. There is no doubt, however, that the lobbyists for these organizations accord much greater legitimacy to the federal court system than they do to administrative agencies. For the most part, administrative agencies were viewed by interviewees as politically loyal subunits of the Nixon White House and, therefore, basically hostile to change-oriented public interest groups. Despite the fact that the courts have not always agreed with the interpretations of the law by public interest legal groups, the courts are revered by these same lobbyists.

For the remainder of the groups that use legal advocacy, law tends to be a back-up strategy. It is an alternative that can be used when all else fails. For these groups, long-range strategy may incorporate legal advocacy as an available tool that can be used if needed, or if the issue warrants, as the basic resource in an enduring policy fight.[16]

[16] It should be obvious that as operationalized plans of attack, the strategies identified here are not always completely discrete. In practice they may sometimes appear as mixed types.

2. Embarrassment and Confrontation. The underlying premise of this strategy is that sufficient exposure of bad policy will act to stimulate governmental officials to change such policy. Lobbyists whose tactics are guided by this strategy strongly believe that if a minimum of publicity can reveal what people in government are doing, those same people will find themselves under a new set of circumstances for future actions in that their behavior will be critically scrutinized. This strategy corresponds closely with Schattschneider's notion that a disadvantaged interest group must try to expand a conflict, bring in new participants and spectators, if it is to improve its chances of achieving its policy preferences.[17]

Publicity cannot be simply equated with true "expansion" of a conflict. The Center for Auto Safety can leak the major findings of a study on the mobile home industry to Jack Anderson and have a story in print the next day, but this does not guarantee continued oversight on the issue. What a group is really attempting to do by using this strategy is to create a continuing controversy.

One means of sustaining controversy is to try to put an official on the defensive. Painting a man as a villain, making him the focal point of attention, embarrassing him if possible, may make a combatant out of him or, in other words, make him respond to the group's charges. By fighting his adversaries, a bureaucrat or member of Congress helps to breathe life into a potential adversary.

The more a group sees itself, because of its policy views, in an adversary position toward governmental institutions, the more likely it is to adopt this strategy as its *modus operandi*. Groups imbued with this strategy have a rather hos-

---

[17] Schattschneider writes, "*Private conflicts are taken into the public arena precisely because someone wants to make certain that the power ratio among the private interests most immediately involved shall not prevail.*" E. E. Schattschneider, *The Semisovereign People* (New York: Holt, Rinehart and Winston, 1960), p. 38.

tile, untrusting view of government.[18] Of the variables previously discussed, the one that is probably most important in pushing a group toward this strategy is the perceived receptivity of targets. Groups adopting this strategy have long accepted that they are not going to be institutionalized into the policy-making process. Rather, they must force people in government to listen to them through protests, news leaks, whistle-blowing, and other similar tactics.

3. Information. The groups that use this strategy base their efforts on the opinion that government operates the way it does, in part, because of imperfect information. The key to achieving influence is providing useful data to policy makers. This philosophy encompasses a less hostile and cynical attitude toward government and considers a good number of people in government to be open-minded and approving of the group's work. It is much more an "inside" strategy—one that depends on the good will of officials and their staffs. Sympathetic people in government are expected to fight for the "right" policies in a conflictual, but reasonable, political arena.

An unstated assumption of this strategy is that there is marginal attention on most political issues. Consequently, it is the role of the groups to stimulate awareness of certain information, thus enabling policy makers to reach more rational decisions. This strategy of information places groups in less of a permanent adversary position. Although they have not been coopted by the policy makers with which they deal, they have established themselves as eager participants in cooperative activity with staff and officials.

4. Constituency Influence and Pressure. This is a strategy of indirect influence. Washington lobbies act as catalysts to activate rank-and-file, and individual "influentials," so that they may lobby key members of Congress and bureau-

[18] See William Gamson's treatment of "alienated" groups and the implications for efforts to influence government. *Power and Discontent* (Homewood, Ill.: Dorsey Press, 1968).

crats. Although professional staffers also engage in direct lobbying, they see grass roots activity as a prerequisite for overall group effectiveness.[19]

Organizations characterized by this strategy may come closest to fitting the image of a "pressure" group. This is much more a strategy of persuading than informing. The "pressure" aspect of this strategy is more evident because the groups' sanctions are more conspicuous. Most of the lobbies that rely on this strategy are primarily concerned with the Congress. The potential of negative information about individual legislators supplied to group members of a man's constituency is an explicit sanction to which members of Congress are thought to be quite sensitive.

Although it is not usually the case that a public interest group can influence enough votes in a district or state to decide an election, members of Congress do not like to take chances. In a close election, one additional unfriendly organization could be the difference between victory and defeat. It can be said that there is a component of cynicism in this strategy. Policy makers are seemingly thought of as people who can be pushed one way or another on issues for which they have no strong predispositions. Alternatively, it could be argued that this strategy is one that acts to enforce democratic norms by making officials responsive to their constituents.[20]

The model of public interest group behavior, as presented in Figure IX-1, is, admittedly, a simplification of an extremely complex decision-making process. If all the individual relationships among the numerous variables were drawn in

[19] On constituency influence versus lobbyist/interest group influence, see John W. Kingdon, *Congressmen's Voting Decisions* (New York: Harper & Row, 1973), pp. 139-168.

[20] On the relationship between members of Congress and constituents, see Warren E. Miller and Donald E. Stokes, "Constituency Influence in Congress," *American Political Science Review*, vol. 57 (March 1963), pp. 45-56; Roger H. Davidson, *The Role of the Congressman* (New York: Pegasus, 1969); and David R. Mayhew, *Congress: The Electoral Connection* (New Haven, Conn.: Yale University Press, 1974).

with appropriate lines and arrows, one fears that all would be obscured in a hopelessly tangled maze. Although sacrificing comprehensiveness for clarity is defensible, some caveats are still in order. The model as it is graphically outlined, presents advocacy decision making as if it takes place in logical, sequential steps. It may appear that first groups evaluate their goals and capabilities, subsequently assess the current political environment, then make their cooperative strategy decision, advocacy strategy decision, and tactical decisions in that order. This is, of course, idealized, and the entire process is much more dynamic and interdependent in the real world. Furthermore, this framework should not be mistakenly identified as a causal model. Organizational goals and capabilities do not cause change in the nature of the external issue environment. In short, the model tries to show how advocacy decisions are structured and shaped by organizational and environmental variables.

Finally, some general conclusions about strategy may be made. The first thing that must be stressed is that the most important decision on a given issue is not the selection of strategy or choice of tactics, but the decision to become active on the issue in the first place. Because the decision to use a specific strategy is strongly influenced by organizational characteristics and situational variables, the most critical step a lobby takes is when it moves to take on a new issue and commit significant organizational resources to such efforts. The decisions regarding strategy and tactics are intertwined with the decision as to the amount of resources to be allocated.

There is, of course, a strong assumption on the part of the lobbyists that they are, in fact, choosing the most effective strategies and tactics among those that are practically available to them. This is primarily a relative assessment on their part. Lobbyists feel that in terms of strategies and tactics, they are doing the best they can within the limitations of their resources.

There is also a great deal of uncertainty on the part of

lobbyists as to how effective their chosen strategies and
tactics are in terms of actually influencing policy. It is understandable that they tend to utilize what they perceive
to have been effective in the past. This is not so simple a
process; it is quite difficult to distinguish ineffective tactics
from lack of resources. When a group fails to achieve its
goals during a policy struggle, it is far more likely to evaluate its lack of success as a function of not being "powerful"
enough, having to fight government officials who had already made up their minds, or being outspent by adversary interest groups.

The subjectivity in the lobbyists' own appraisal of their
advocacy efforts and the emphasis on situational variables
in decision making suggest that there is a great deal of im-
precision in this model of interest group behavior. It is not
possible, unfortunately, to create a fully predictive model
of organizational decision and choice. The effort here has
been to try to bring about a greater understanding of the
way in which different variables affect a lobby's activity on
issues of concern to it. This explanation of the process may
not enable one to predict decision outcomes, but it should
distinguish the factors that push groups toward certain patterns of behavior and away from others.

INFLUENCE

The inevitable question arises as to the efficacy of public
interest groups. Beyond the various strategies and specific
tactics, what can be said of the general impact of public interest groups upon governmental policy making? It is tempt-
ing to dodge the question by merely stating that it all
depends—some groups are more influential than others. Indeed this is true, but to leave the matter at this may be less
than a satisfactory solution. It is also true, however, that
political scientists have not progressed very far in developing highly powered generalizations on the nature of interest
group influence.

As noted earlier, it was beyond the scope of this project to engage in a full-scale examination of public interest influence. The self-appraisals of their organizations' influence by public interest lobbyists is, without question, an insufficient base for such an endeavor.[21] Any objective study of public interest group influence would have to include interviews with governmental officials, private interest lobbyists, and neutral observers.[22] The remarks here, therefore, will be restricted to the *perceptions* of influence on the part of the lobbyists. With the limitations of the data in mind, it will be useful to try to ascertain how lobbyists evaluate their own organization's performance.

Before describing the difficulty public interest lobbyists have in measuring their influence, a brief overview of how political scientists have dealt with this subject may place the problem in perspective. The obstacles in evaluating what properly constitutes interest group "influence" or "power" are, to say the very least, quite formidable.[23] On its most basic level, "power,"[24] in Robert Dahl's words, can

[21] On self-appraisals of interest group influence, see Harry M. Scoble, *Ideology and Electoral Action* (San Francisco: Chandler Publishing, 1967), pp. 180-184.

[22] This is not to suggest that interviewing *per se* is the proper methodological approach to this problem. Interviewing is probably better applied to analysis of specific policy conflicts rather than to general assessments of influence asked of survey respondents. Milbrath's survey of members of Congress and lobbyists, for example, is a very unpersuasive measure of actual interest group influence. See Lester W. Milbrath, *The Washington Lobbyists* (Chicago: Rand McNally, 1963).

[23] Graham Wootton writes of trying to measure influence, "This is where we need a sure-footed guide with a large lantern to see us through the treacherous bog." *Interest-Groups* (Englewood Cliffs, N.J.: Prentice-Hall, 1970), p. 76.

[24] "Power" can be differentiated as a form of influence characterized by coercive sanctions. See Harold D. Lasswell and Abraham Kaplan, *Power and Society* (New Haven, Conn.: Yale University Press, 1950). To avoid semantic confusion, the term "influence" will be used here. Dahl's definition of influence is that "A influences B to the extent that he changes B's behavior in some way." See Robert A. Dahl, *Modern Political Analysis*, 2nd ed. (Englewood Cliffs, N.J.: Prentice-Hall, 1970), p. 17.

274 Lobbying for the People

be defined in the following manner: "A has power over B
to the extent that he can get B to do something that B would
not otherwise do."[25] This seems straightforward enough, but
as Martha Derthick points out, operationalizing the concept
is not as easy as abstractly defining it:

> A fundamental difficulty is that of proving that B would
> not have done what A wanted him to do even in the ab-
> sence of A's efforts to exert power. Although we can dis-
> cover that A wanted B to take a certain action, and we
> can observe that A has certain resources of potential
> power and used the available means to bring them to
> bear on B, and we can observe that B took the action
> that A intended, we still cannot be sure that B would
> not have taken the action without A's efforts.[26]

The crux of the issue, therefore, is actually "proving"
that the interest group *caused* government officials to
change their behavior in some manner. How is one actually
to know that it was an interest group that caused an observed change in behavior on the part of a governmental
policy maker?[27] It is not overly cynical to suspect that people in government will be less than candid in admitting to
being influenced by an interest group. As one of Ralph
Nader's aides put it, "The administrators just won't ac-
knowledge that they act because of us." However, it is
probably not so much a case of officials wanting to hide
something as it is the selective perception that leads them
to believe that their decisions were based on other factors.

Given what seems to be an insurmountable methodologi-

[25] Robert A. Dahl, "The Concept of Power," *Behavioral Science*,
vol. 2 (July 1957), pp. 202-203.

[26] Martha Derthick, *The National Guard in Politics* (Cambridge,
Mass.: Harvard University Press, 1965), p. 7. This passage is cited
in Wootton's discussion of this question. *Interest-Groups*, p. 74.

[27] Another aspect of this problem is that interest groups do not
necessarily have to make observable, concrete actions to be exerting
real influence. See Peter Bachrach and Morton S. Baratz, "Two Faces
of Power," *American Political Science Review*, vol. 56 (December
1962), pp. 947-952.

cal problem, it is not surprising that the work on the measurement of interest group influence has not progressed very rapidly. A few brave souls, such as William Gamson,[28] Robert Dahl,[29] and Graham Wootton,[30] have ventured forth with conceptual schema that, ostensibly, can be used in measuring the influence of lobbies in policy conflicts. Without going into a detailed review of their efforts, a general criticism that can be made of them is that they still require *inferring* influence on the basis of a governmental actor's changing a policy position subsequent to an organization's advocacy effort. The authors, of course, recognize the operational difficulties, and the actual application of any of these measuring scales still remains to be done on a meaningful basis.

It is clear that there is little consensus concerning the best approach to measuring interest group influence. The case studies that have recorded government-interest group interaction have not used common criteria and, consequently, their validity must be judged upon the overall quality of the research.[31] To ask for more rigorous methods in this area may be going beyond the capabilities of contemporary political science.

Perceptions of Influence. Given the difficulty that political scientists have in measuring influence, it could be expected that there are no standards for criteria for effectiveness accepted by the lobbyists themselves. Groups that might seem the most ineffective to the outside observer have fully rationalized their role in the policy-making process. Public interest lobbyists in many such groups seemed to feel that

[28] Gamson, *Power and Discontent.*
[29] Dahl, *Modern Political Analysis*, pp. 14-34.
[30] Wootton, *Interest-Groups*, pp. 73-95.
[31] For some recent examples, using various approaches, see Harry Brill, *Why Organizers Fail* (Berkeley: University of California Press, 1971); John Hall Fish, *Black Power/White Control* (Princeton, N.J.: Princeton University Press, 1973); August Meier and Elliott Rudwick, *CORE: A Study in the Civil Rights Movement* (New York: Oxford University Press, 1973); and Bruce Ian Oppenheimer, *Oil and the Congressional Process* (Lexington, Mass.: Lexington Books, 1974).

it was a bit unfair to ask them about short-term victories, and they stressed the long-term nature of their work. For example, lobbyists in the liberal peace-arms groups, where successes seem to have been relatively infrequent, appeared to have no illusions about their impact on government. At the same time, however, they would reject criticism that they are spinning their wheels. To them, admitting their ineffectiveness was not an acknowledgment of their organizations' failures, but a reaffirmation of their commitment to the cause.

The "no easy victories" emphasis of some public interest representatives is an attempt to place lobbying efforts in perspective. One public interest lobbyist for a church group summarized many of his colleagues' sentiments:

> I've always believed that public interest lobbying is a very ineffective thing. You can't point to something and say "We did that." But if you didn't do the work, it would be so much the worse.

Issues such as more liberal welfare policies or nuclear disarmament, for which public interest groups find entrenched opposition, are regarded as being susceptible to influence only when the "climate" changes and public opinion forces policy makers to act. Thus, lobbyists believe that they are doing their best to be "effective" by engaging in long-range consciousness raising while hoping that it will not take too long for public opinion to crystallize in the right direction.

Not all self-appraisals of lobbying impact are so pessimistic. In the interviews, most representatives were able to cite shorter-term issues on which they felt they had had some definite influence. In analyzing the lobbyists' discussions of the issues on which they had success, what is most striking is their resignation to the fact that they operate in incremental policy systems.[32] Although preliminary answers were

[32] On incrementalism, see Charles E. Lindblom, "The Science of Muddling Through," *Public Administration Review*, vol. 19 (Spring 1959), pp. 79-88.

couched in black/white terms (e.g., "we got the bill passed"), the more detailed responses revealed that the lobbyists really saw their impact at the *margins* of policy decisions (e.g., "we strengthened the one amendment").

For the public interest lobbyists, partial victories are a way of life. Getting the "whole loaf," instead of half a loaf, is something that happens rarely. Surely, some victories are of greater magnitude than others. But for the most part, policy outputs (court decisions, legislation, etc.) are thought of as only small steps down a long road. Every public interest lobbyist knows that a step forward may soon be followed by two backwards. A representative of one of the poverty-civil rights groups told of her personal frustrations:

> Take the question of day care. Now the regulations were pretty good, but they were not being effectively implemented. At the time of H.R. 1, welfare reform [in the 92nd Congress] an effort began within the administration to rewrite federal standards and regulations. They wanted to lower the costs of federally supported day care centers. We mobilized a lot of activity and spent a lot of time fighting them. They would have been promulgated, except for the outside pressure that was brought to bear. So now it has been taken out of the Office of Child Development in HEW and the regulations are now being written by OMB. The regulations we'll get will be worse than they would have if we hadn't made the effort we did.

The incremental nature of the policy fights in which the lobbyists find themselves is also well illustrated by the survey data. After the interviewees were asked to give two or three examples of specific issues where their organization had been effective in influencing policy, they were asked to name two or three issues where they had been *ineffective*. Somewhat unexpectedly, 43% of the public interest representatives mentioned the exact same issue as they had spoken of under effective advocacy efforts.

In analyzing what they admitted to be ineffectiveness in certain issues, the lobbyists did not associate their organization's lack of success with any personal mistakes on their part. Few mentioned strategic or tactical mistakes in such a way as to leave the impression that they had any individual responsibility for the failure on a particular issue. Although it is natural for people not to want to dwell on the errors they make in their day-to-day work, there is more to these depersonalized answers than that. There is also a sincere modesty concerning the abilities of any one lobbyist to move the government one way or the other. Even when talking about group successes, the public interest representatives tended to talk much more in terms of what the organization did rather than of their own efforts.

Policy defeats are usually seen as being beyond the control of the lobbyist's group or the public interest movement in general. If they lose, it is because they were overwhelmed by superior resources on the "other side." For the lobbyists, it is not so much a case of "If only we had done this instead" as "They were going to get us no matter what." As with the account of the day care regulations, the point the lobbyist was trying to make was not that the fight should not have been made, but that the Nixon administration was going to get what it wanted one way or another.

In the battle of resources, public interest groups—regardless of how much they have—see themselves in a David and Goliath struggle where Goliath is often the winner. Sometimes this "other side" is composed of private interest groups. If the private interests prevail, the public interest lobbyists usually see greater resources (money, contacts, etc.) at work.[33] In discussing their disappointment with pesticide legislation on which they had worked, environmental activists saw resources, not comparative lobbying

[33] It is common for lobbyists to assume that their opponents have much more resources than they do. Bauer, Pool, and Dexter found that the people to whom they talked consistently overestimated the amounts of money at the disposal of their foes. Raymond A. Bauer, Ithiel de Sola Pool, and Lewis Anthony Dexter, *American Business and Public Policy* (New York: Atherton, 1963), pp. 341-345.

skills, as the reason for a weak bill emerging from the Congress:

> We fought tooth and nail on the pesticides bill. I don't know if it's a step backwards or not. We don't have the clout that the chemical industry does.

> The bill which passed is not a good bill because the agri-chemical industry has a lot more clout than we do plus the administration screwed us.

> On the pesticide bill we have evidence from the EPA that pressure has been felt.

The strongest adversary in the minds of the public interest representatives is the federal government. The government was spoken of at times as if it were impenetrable or was simply a hopeless cause. Certainly much of the frustration and anger was directed at the ideology of the Nixon administration, and a more liberal regime might have drawn less negative marks. Nevertheless, the lobbyists had a more than healthy respect for the Nixon administration's ability to defy its critics and pursue its own course. This attitude, quite naturally changed from issue to issue. If the administration had compromised on an issue, it was because the public interest groups, the media, and public opinion had forced them to. If the administration had largely stood its ground, it was because they had made up their minds and there was nothing public interest groups could do about it.[34]

---

[34] These general remarks are most applicable to legislative and administrative lobbying, and less so to advocacy before the federal courts. The courts, of course, are not subject to the same type of political influence as are the other institutions. It is sometimes easier to assess interest group influence in a court decision; the plaintiff is always clear, and cause-and-effect relationships can be inferred from the filing of a suit. Legal rulings should still be viewed from an incrementalist perspective. The court decisions are not the final policy output, and any proper evaluation of group influence would want to take into account their efforts in terms of subsequent litigation, and the administration and implementation of the policy changes intended by the first, successful suit.

To summarize briefly, it has been found that public interest lobbyists perceive their groups as being more or less effective depending on the issue, but rarely as being wholly ineffective. Even if the government is moving in a direction diametrically opposed by a group, there is the feeling that things would be worse without their efforts. On most issues, however, the lobbyists discern positive incremental changes in the development of policy that are, in part, a result of the advocacy efforts of their organizations. When the resources of their opponents are so much greater that "holding the line" on a policy is the best they can hope for, there is always the rationalization that they must engage in long-term consciousness raising before the time for change will come. As one consumer lobbyist noted, "If you fail, you can say you educated people."

Access Through Information. The lobbyists' self-appraisals of their influence have offered some insight into how they view their relationship with government. Up to this point, the entire analysis of public interest advocacy has been conducted from the perspective of how interest groups approach government. Mention should also be made of communication between government and these organizations that is initiated by a government official.[35] It is quite common for people in government to try to influence interest groups or, more likely, to solicit their assistance. Furthermore, it is possible to conceive of this second channel of communication as a means of access by which public interest groups have the opportunity to exert influence through an information-type strategy.

There are three basic reasons why government officials and their staffers will take the first step in contacting an interest group. First, interest groups may be the target of efforts to enlist them as supporters of a particular policy position. A member of Congress or an agency head may feel

[35] Bauer, Pool, and Dexter found that the lobbies they observed were more likely to be "service bureaus" to sympathetic members of Congress than "pressure groups" that tried to influence uncommitted legislators. *American Business and Public Policy*, pp. 350-357.

that a policy he is pushing is not receiving the backing it should from the private sector. Consequently, he may try to persuade representatives of interest groups to become more active on behalf of the cause.[36]

A second reason why interest groups may be approached is that they often are valuable sources of political intelligence. Most important, they can provide information concerning the lobbying activities of all other interest groups, pro and con, on the issue at hand. Generally, they can act as another set of eyes and ears for their friends in government.

Third, people in government may come to interest groups for the purpose of obtaining substantive data with regard to an issue. Congressional and agency staffs rarely have the time to gather on their own all the information they need. Interest groups can be particularly useful in situations where information is needed right away, when there is no time to put the Library of Congress research service to work or to allow staff social scientists to prepare a report. Not only can interest groups offer documentation of the "facts" on an issue, but they can also offer the "facts" that support a particular point of view.

It is probably every group's desire to become a known, trusted source of pertinent data. It is "cheaper" in resources expended to have people come to solicit their views than for them to have to attract the attention of those they want to influence through various lobbying tactics. It is not, of course, an either/or matter; groups will still try to lobby those who do not solicit their views.

To measure the extent of government-initiated contacts with public interest groups, respondents were asked how often their views on policy matters are solicited by officials and their staffs.[37] To get an idea of how much this type of

[36] See Francis E. Rourke, *Bureaucracy, Politics, and Public Policy* (Boston: Little, Brown, 1969), pp. 11-37.

[37] Interviewees were reluctant to quantify the number of contacts on a per-week or per-month basis because contact tended strongly to go in spurts as issues came to the forefront. Therefore, the responses have been coded to their more general evaluation.

contact is a function of the groups' abilities to offer useful data to policy makers, the individual public interest lobbies were each evaluated for their research/data capability. A distinction—albeit a crude one—was made between those groups with a "high" information capability and those with a "low" capability. To rate "high," a lobby had to have at least one person who concentrated on collecting data and putting together research reports, or it had to put out a regular publication or special memoranda that carried research that was sufficiently sophisticated to be of use to officials and their staffs.[38] Roughly two-thirds of the sample met at least one of these criteria.

A very strong pattern emerges when research and data capability is cross-tabulated with frequency of solicitation (see Table IX-2). Washington representatives of public interest groups are much more likely to be called on by people in government if their group has a "high" research capa-

TABLE IX-2

Information Capability

Frequency of Solicitation	Capability High		Low		Total	
Never, very infrequently	6%	(3)	39%	(11)	17%	(14)
Infrequently	7%	(4)	18%	(5)	11%	(9)
Sometimes	11%	(6)	18%	(5)	13%	(11)
Frequently	24%	(13)	11%	(3)	20%	(16)
Ongoing	41%	(22)	11%	(3)	30%	(25)
NA	9%	(5)	4%	(1)	7%	(6)
DK	2%	(1)	—		1%	(1)
Total	100%	(54)	101%[a]	(28)	99%[a]	(N = 82)

[a] Rounding error.

[38] The organization's staff researcher did not necessarily have to be in the Washington office as long as the person's research and data were readily available to, and frequently utilized by, the Washington representative of the group.

bility.[39] The research capability of the groups is, of course, related to the financial and staff resources of the lobbies. Each group, however, must decide how much of its resources it will devote to informational activities. Those that have decided to emphasize such endeavors appear to profit by it.

It seems logical that interest groups are approached because they have something to offer. It is possible that a group's information capability is a much more important factor for gaining access to decision makers than is the independent skill of its lobbyists.[40] The more frequently a group is contacted by people in government, the more likely it is to become "institutionalized" into the policy-making processes. When government officials solicit information from interest group representatives on a regular basis, they may be incorporating those groups' positions into their decision making.

Many observers have criticized the manner in which interest groups become too institutionalized into government policy making, especially that which takes place in administrative agencies. Political scientists, such as Theodore Lowi, have argued that agencies of government do not serve the public interest because they become the agents of particular interests or "clients."[41] Thus, when an agency begins to

[39] The frequency of solicitation of public interest groups compares favorably with the frequency for private interet lobbyists as recorded by Milbrath. Thirty percent of the public interest groups were approached by government on an "ongoing" basis. Of those private interest representatives Milbrath interviewed, 14% said that they were consulted as an ongoing activity. Another 18% of his sample reported 11-25 contacts per year, the category directly below "ongoing." Because some of Milbrath's sample were lawyers on retainer, and not full-time employees, the figures are not strictly comparable. Milbrath, *The Washington Lobbyists*, p. 341.

[40] On lobbyist-government interaction, see, generally, Harmon Zeigler and Michael Baer, *Lobbying* (Belmont, Calif.: Wadsworth, 1969), pp. 146-197.

[41] Theodore J. Lowi, *The End of Liberalism* (New York: Norton, 1969). See also, Marver H. Bernstein, *Regulating Business by Independent Commission* (Princeton, N.J.: Princeton University Press, 1955); and Paul Sabatier, "Social Movements and Regulatory Agen-

institutionalize interest groups into its policy making, it runs the risk of being captured by them.

It is difficult to determine where institutionalization of interest group opinion for the purpose of facilitating government responsiveness to the needs of citizens stops, and where the domination by a client interest group begins.[42] For the public interest groups in the sample, however, there is no evidence that any of those that are consulted regularly by governmental agencies come even close to being a paramount influence on agency behavior. There is considerable difference between a group's being frequently solicited for information and its being a major source of real influence in policy making.[43]

A more precise assessment of actual institutionalized influence exerted by public interest groups must await further research. But if it is true, as David Truman notes, that access is "the facilitating intermediate objective of political interest groups," it may be concluded that at least half of the organizations have achieved this goal to some significant degree.[44] Certainly, if a group is approached on a frequent or ongoing basis, there exists an open channel for communicating their ideas, preferences, and data. At the same time, few groups believe that they have sufficient access to the most important decision makers in the relevant area of government. It is likely that no interest group is satisfied with any position short of dominance in their policy domain.

cies: Toward a More Adequate—and Less Pessimistic—Theory of 'Clientele Capture,' " *Policy Sciences*, vol. 6 (September 1975), pp. 301-342.

[42] It is Lowi's argument in *The End of Liberalism* that "interest group liberalism," rationalizes the latter by justifying it as the former. For a more sanguine view of close interest group-government interaction, see Wallace S. Sayre and Herbert Kaufman, *Governing New York City* (New York: Russell Sage Foundation, 1960), pp. 481-515. See also, Harry Eckstein, *Pressure Group Politics* (Stanford, Calif.: Stanford University Press, 1960).

[43] It should be noted that although the rate of solicitation is high among the public interest groups, more of this contact is with congressional offices than with administrative agencies.

[44] Truman, *The Governmental Process*, p. 264.

CONCLUSION

The model of public interest group decision making presented in this chapter has attempted to tie together the many interrelated factors that influence the advocacy choices made by staff lobyists. It is intended to provide a summary picture of the dynamics of public interest group lobbying. It "explains" no more than the analytical material that preceded it. This framework has, hopefully, illuminated some of the sets of circumstances that lead public interest groups toward specific courses of action.

The other major focus of this chapter has been public interest group influence. The evaluation of their efficacy was limited by the scope of this research project. Any attempt at evaluation, however, is limited by the methodological difficulties to be encountered in trying to operationalize the concept of influence. The problems of distinguishing the influence of interest groups upon policy makers, as distinct from other influences such as the press, general public opinion, and other political elites, remain rather substantial.

Despite the lack of an accepted measuring instrument, the influence of public interest groups must remain a focus of continued research. Their impact has been real and significant in numerous policy areas. A starting point for such research is examination of the role of public interest groups in individual policy conflicts. This type of inquiry should emphasize both the influence of public interest groups in drawing attention to new issues and their effect on policy at subsequent decision points in the political process. In helping to create the necessary awareness to push issues onto the political "agenda," public interest groups may have a long-term influence on public policy that cannot be adequately measured by analysis of specific issues that have already reached the stage of formal consideration by the Congress, agencies, or the courts.

CHAPTER X

Public Interest Groups and the Governmental Process

INDIVIDUALS who belong to public interest groups have strong public policy sentiments to the degree that they are willing to "do something" about them. Beyond their votes in elections, this "something" includes, at a minimum, financial support of an advocacy organization that is actively trying to influence governmental actions in a particular policy area. Their support, depending on the organization to which they belong and their own personal commitment, may extend to letter writing, participation in political protests, or even volunteer work in a local chapter of the group. Given the diversity of the organizations in the sample, it is difficult to speak of the constituency for public interest groups in singular terms. What can be said in general, however, is that the supporters of these groups form a segment of the population that is highly attentive and deeply concerned about the actions of government in formulating various public policies. Moreover, they believe that they are capable of influencing public policy outcomes through their collective endeavors.

The data for this work have been drawn primarily from the 83 public interest groups that could be identified as operating in Washington, D.C., during 1972-1973. Twenty-five of these organizations had no memberships at the time, and seven more were coalitions made up of other groups. One may wonder how extensive this supporting constituency of public interest group sympathizers is for the 51 noncoalition membership organizations. A rough estimate of the collective membership of the 51 organizations is

three and one-half million people.[1] Because there are overlapping memberships, the real number of individuals who
belong to one or more of these groups is somewhat lower.
At the same time, this number does not include national
organizations that operate without a Washington office.
Even more important, this figure does not take into account
all the people who belong to local organizations that have
no relation to a national group. One study puts the number
of voluntary environmental organizations alone at around
20,000.[2] Surely not all of these are public interest groups,
but clearly the scope of participation outside of the national
groups in this study is quite substantial.

By any measure, the combined memberships of local,
state, and national public interest groups is a significant
portion of our population. For their members, their larger
constituencies, and society as a whole, what can be said
of the roles played by these organizations? Of what value
are these groups to the functioning of the political system?

The contributions of public interest groups to American
political life fall into a number of different areas. By helping
to bring new issues to the fore, they influence the shape
of political agendas. Through their utilization of litigation,
administrative intervention, and other tactics, public interest
groups often perform a law enforcement function in obtaining new rulings or exacting compliance with old ones.

[1] This figure includes only the 600,000 people who pay dues directly to the National Wildlife Federation by virtue of one or more
magazine subscriptions. It does not count the 800,000 people who
buy the wildlife stamps each year or the million and one-half people
who belong to local organizations that are affiliated with state wildlife
federations. Nor does this estimate include all the 2 million or so sub-
scribers to *Consumer Reports*. Using Consumers Union's definition of
their membership, only those who return a yearly ballot (around
350,000) are counted.

[2] David Horton Smith and Burt R. Baldwin, "Voluntary Associations
and Volunteering in the United States," in David Horton Smith, ed.,
Voluntary Action Research: 1974 (Lexington, Mass.: Lexington Books,
1974), p. 286.

Public interest groups also act in an educational capacity. Their publications, their lobbying campaigns, and media coverage of their advocacy efforts all work to expand the public's knowledge of various political issues.

In addition to what they accomplish through their lobbying, public interest groups also play an important role in facilitating the political participation of their members and related attentive publics. The organizations not only activate supporters and constituents, but they provide meaningful channels through which participation can be directed. For an individual, participating in a group endeavor seemingly increases the likelihood that their message will not only be received by government, but it will be "heard" as well.

The most important function of public interest groups is, of course, to represent the policy preferences of their constituents. Like all interest groups, public interest lobbies form a linkage element between citizens and governmental elites. In their lobbying they articulate what they perceive to be the issue positions of certain sectors of society. What is particularly noteworthy about the advocacy work of public interest groups is that they represent constituencies that have been chronically unrepresented or underrepresented in American politics.

If public interest groups have come to represent an expanding array of societal interests and constituencies over the past decade or so, their increased prominence stands in contrast to the development of the two-party system over the same period of time. Partisan identification has decreased dramatically since 1964. The proportion of the population that identifies with either party has declined, and those who do identify themselves as Republicans or Democrats are less likely now to be strong partisans.[3] At the same time, there is evidence that issue voting has in-

[3] See Norman H. Nie, Sidney Verba, and John R. Petrocik, *The Changing American Voter* (Cambridge, Mass.: Harvard University Press, 1976).

creased, and the drop in partisanship cannot be explained simply as a decrease in interest or awareness of public policy questions.[4] Public interest groups did not cause this decline in partisanship, but they have surely benefited from the disillusionment and alienation that are at the roots of party disaffection. As more and more people become disenchanted with the parties, the opportunities for public interest groups to attract those concerned about matters of government increases. Party support and public interest group membership are not mutually exclusive, but public interest groups do represent an alternative channel for individual political involvement.

What public interest groups accomplish may not be adequately described by a review of the roles that they play. What may be said on a more general level is that these organizations are slowly changing the overall environment within which governmental officials formulate public policy. In numerous policy areas, public interest groups have been consistent and enduring actors, aggressively trying to influence governmental decision makers. They are not a countervailing force in that they are always an equal power to those they must influence or compete with, but they do possess significant resources and public support. The opinion they can arouse, the bad publicity they can generate, the law suits they can file, are all factors that are relevant to the deliberations of those who must make policy decisions. The potential influence of public interest groups varies considerably according to issue—they have surely had more impact on power plant sitings than they have had on the purchasing of weapons systems. Nevertheless, in an increasing number of issue areas, public interest groups have become part of the political environment and thus part of the equation that explains public policy outcomes.

Although the value of public interest groups may seem incontrovertible, this study has identified many instances

[4] *Ibid.*, pp. 156-173.

in which the actions of government have worked to circum-
scribe the participation of public interest groups in the
political processes. The institutions of government have
many different ways of facilitating or inhibiting the lobbying of all types of interest groups. Public interest groups
have not always found their participation structured and
regulated to their maximum advantage.

One glaring abuse of government regulation has been
the highly capricious and arbitrary behavior of the Internal
Revenue Service in dealing with public interest groups.
The IRS holds life-and-death power over 501(c)(3) groups,
and those organizations that hold the favored status are
clearly constrained by it. Reforms that are currently being
considered by Congress would be a substantial improvement in this area. The rights of participation for public
interest groups are also deeply affected by the legal rulings
of the courts. The ability of public interest and citizen
groups to participate in formal administrative proceedings
has been expanded by decisions in cases such as *Scenic
Hudson* and *United Church of Christ*. Although the requirements of standing have been liberalized in this area, the
Supreme Court has moved in the opposite direction on class
action suits. It is now much more difficult for a public
interest group to sue on behalf of many plaintiffs with individually small claims. This is certainly a serious setback for
consumer and environmental organizations. The Supreme
Court has also severely restricted the prerogative of federal
courts to award fees to public interest groups that, through
successful litigation, act to enforce the law as private attorneys general. This will not only make it more difficult for
existing public interest legal units to sustain themselves, but
it will also make it that much more difficult for new groups
of this sort to arise.

In the laws that it writes, the Congress also acts to structure the role of all citizen advocacy groups in the governmental process. By creating grievance procedures, mandat-
ing advisory boards, and the like, Congress enlarges the
formal opportunities for citizen participation in public

policy making. Administrative agencies play the same role as they devise the means for eliciting citizen input into program development and implementation. Overall, it can be said that although all organizations and citizens have the constitutional right of petition, the privileges to present these "petitions" vary across political institutions and policy areas.

It has been argued that public interest advocacy is beneficial to the political system. Further, it is the position here that governmental policy should manifest a positive view toward the political participation of all types of citizens' groups. This positive attitude should extend not only to the formal regulation of participation, but also to the informal government-interest group communication that characterizes the legislative and administrative processes. This is not to say that all government rules regarding access should be changed to permit unlimited participation by the private sector in all government proceedings. Rather, it is only contended that whereas efficiency and speed are important in governmental deliberations, the first priority of all rules of access should be to maximize the participation of all relevant parties that seek to represent significant interests.

If it is common sense to assume that interest groups are a necessary ingredient of our present political system, it is also common sense to realize that public interest groups are not the savior of that system. Giving the views of public interest groups greater credence, or tailoring public policy more closely to what they advocate, will not necessarily make the governmental decisions more reflective of the national will. Nor is representation through interest groups *per se* an adequate supplement to elected representatives in government. The fact that 30% of the public interest groups in the sample have no real membership attests to the problems of organizing individuals around certain interests that they ostensibly share. The current constellation of interest groups simply leaves too many sectors of society inadequately represented.

But given that ours is an imperfect system and that

interest groups will never reflect all the political interests of the polity, it is still important for government to encourage and ease the participation of those groups that are organized. Public interest groups often represent views that are contrary to established public policy, and special care should be taken to ensure the inclusion of their opinions when government is considering the views of any outside interest groups. This call for special attention to the participation of public interest groups is most applicable to the courts and administrative agency proceedings, where the financial costs can be a greater hindrance to them than any legal barriers.

The lobbying activity of public interest groups is no more legitimate than that of their private interest counterparts. In the last analysis, it remains the function of government to weigh the conflicting interests of both the organized groups and the unorganized citizenry. Critics and opponents of public interest groups have often pointed out that these organizations frequently have goals that place the comfort and well-being of a minority over that of a majority. For example, most people probably prefer the convenience of cars and highways, despite the air pollution that they cause, to mass transit and bicycles. Yet this will never deter the environmentalists, who see clean air as an absolute necessity, regardless of the changes that must be made. Can one then say that public interest groups are elitist, where what they consider as "right" takes precedence over what is commonly preferred? There is no doubt that public interest activists believe that they know what is best. This is a sin, however, of which all lobbyists and interest groups are guilty. "Self-righteous" might be a more accurate description of these groups. Their selectively nonmaterial, philanthropic basis of organization cannot help but make members and activists feel at times that they really do represent the common good. But if this is the worst that can be said about them, then the positive side of the scale will certainly be the heavier one.

APPENDIX A

Interview Schedule*

Date _____ Time _____ to _____
Interviewee:
Job Title:
Organization:
Address:
General Location:
Description of Building, Business Offices, and Individual
   Office:
Attitude of Interviewee:
General Comments on Interview:

1. I'd like to begin by getting some background on your organization. Could you briefly describe how this organization originated?
   a. (If N) in what year did the organization start?
2. How would you describe the general goals of this organization?
3. Since the founding of this organization, have the goals or objectives stayed relatively consistent, or have they changed significantly?
4. How many people work in your Washington office?
   a. Of these employees, how many are full-time, paid professionals?
   b. How much volunteer labor do you use, if any?
5. Could you tell me the current membership of this organization?
6. (If A) generally speaking, what is the relationship between the Washington office and the membership? How much influence do they have in the policy making of the organization?

* In the text of the questions, "If N" stands for "if necessary": "If A" stands for "if appropriate."

7. Does this organization have any state or local chapters?
   a. Is there a national headquarters outside of Washington?

8. In addition to representing their interests on matters of public policy, does the organization perform any other services for the membership?

9. Do you have a newsletter or other means of regular communication with your membership besides your appeals for dues or contributions?
   a. (If yes, probe for frequency.)

10. When this organization has made efforts to influence public policy, who or what has usually been the target of your activities?

11. How is this organization supported financially?
    a. (If A) how much are the dues?
    b. (If A) do those contributions include any foundation donations or grants?
    c. Is this organization tax exempt?
    d. Are contributions tax deductible?

12. Could you give me a rough estimate of this organization's annual budget?
    a. (If there's a headquarters outside of the Washington office) what is the annual budget of the Washington office?

13. Now I'd like to turn my attention to you and to your role in the organization. How would you describe your specific job in this organization?

14. Is this a full-time job for you?
    a. (If no) what are your other activities? What percentage of your time do you devote to this job?

15. In what year were you born?

16. How much formal education have you had?

17. One of the things I'm most interested in is how people get into this type of work. Could you summarize your occupational history since the completion of your formal education?

a. (Probe for career training if not discerned from #16 or #17.)

b. (If N) when and how did you happen to come into your present position?

18. Would you like to continue in this type of work for the rest of your professional career?

a. (If yes and if N) why?

b. (If no and if N) what would you like to do after this?

19. (Full-time employees only) I'd like to get an idea of how much this organization pays you on an annual basis. Using the letters on this card could you tell me within what range your salary falls? (Hand card #1 to R.)

20. Are you now or have you ever been active in a political party? (If yes and if N) when and where were you active?

21. Do you usually think of yourself as a Republican, a Democrat, an Independent, or what?

a. (If Independent) do you think of yourself as closer to the Republican or Democratic party?

b. When you compare your own political views with those of other Americans, how would you classify yourself?

22. How does this organization decide on which specific issues it will become active upon?

a. (Probe for role of executive board if A) could you tell me a little about the executive board? Who sits on it? What is its relationship with the professional staff? (If A and if N probe for conflict resolution.)

23. When it is decided that the organization is going to become active on an issue, how is the strategy on the specific problem developed?

24. How important is joint activity with other organizations? (If no and if N, probe for why not.)

25. A number of possible techniques that can be used in trying to influence a governmental decision maker are listed on this card. Which of these techniques has your organization used in the past? It would also be helpful if you

could evaluate the effectiveness of those techniques which you have used. (Hand card #2 to R.)

    Court Suit:

    Cong. Hearing:

    Voting Records:

    Research Results:

    Contributing Money:

    Personal Presentation:

    Letter Writing:

    Political Protest:

    Public Relations:

    Influential Member:

    Other:

26. Could you give me two or three examples of specific issues where you think your organization has been effective in influencing the course of public policy during the past few years?

27. Could you give me two or three examples of specific issues where you think your organization has been *ineffective* in trying to influence the course of public policy during the past few years?

28. How often do public policy makers—by that I mean members of Congress or agency heads or their staffs—come to you to solicit your views on a policy matter? (Probe for example.)

29. Over the next five years, what role do you expect your organization to play in the political process?

Can you think of anything else about your organization that I should know about?

Card No. 1

Select the letter which corresponds to your annual salary.

    a. Volunteer. No salary.

    b. Less than $5,000

    c. $5,000–$7,499

    d. $7,500–$9,999

    e. $10,000–$14,999

f. $15,000–$19,999
g. $20,000–$24,999
h. $25,000+

Card No. 2

A number of possible techniques that can be used in trying to influence a governmental decision maker are listed below. Which of these techniques has your organization used in the past? It would also be helpful if you could evaluate the effectiveness of those techniques which you have used.

1. Filing a court suit.
2. Testifying at a congressional hearing.
3. Publicizing voting records of Congressmen.
4. Releasing research results.
5. Contributing money to political campaigns.
6. Personal presentation of argument to Congressmen, agency heads, or White House personnel.
7. Instigating a letter-writing campaign.
8. Organizing political protests.
9. Public relations campaigns.
10. Having an influential member or constituent of the organization contact the governmental decision maker.
11. Other.

Sample of Public Interest Groups Used in the Study

Agribusiness Accountability Project
American Baptist Churches, USA
American Civil Liberties Union
American Conservative Union
American Horse Protection Association
American Security Council
Americans for Constitutional Action
Americans for Democratic Action
Arms Control Association
Aviation Consumer Action Project
Center for Auto Safety
Center for Defense Information
Center for Law and Social Policy
Center for National Policy Review
Center for Science in the Public Interest
Center for the Study of Responsive Law
Children's Foundation
Church of the Brethren
Citizens Advocate Center
Citizens Committee on Natural Resources
Citizens Communication Center
Clergy and Laity Concerned
Coalition on National Priorities and Military Policy
Coalition to Stop Funding the War
Committee for a Free China
Committee for Congressional Reform
Committee for Humane Legislation
Committee for National Health Insurance
Common Cause

Consumer Federation of America
Consumers Union
Corporate Accountability Research Group
Council for a Livable World
Defenders of Wildlife
Environmental Action
Environmental Defense Fund
Environmental Policy Center
Fishermen's Clean Water Action Project
Friends Committee on National Legislation
Friends of the Earth
Fund for Animals
Humane Society of the United States
Indochina Resource Center
Institute for Public Interest Representation
Izaak Walton League
Joint Washington Office for Social Concern
Lawyers' Committee for Civil Rights Under Law
League of Women Voters
Liberty Lobby
Media Access Project
Mennonite Central Committee
National Audubon Society
National Committee for an Effective Congress
National Consumers League
National Council of Churches
National Council to Repeal the Draft
National March for Victory Committee
National Peace Action Coalition
National Wildlife Federation
Natural Resources Defense Council
Peace Alert USA
Population Crises Committee
Project on Corporate Responsibility
Public Citizen Litigation Group
Sane
Sierra Club

Society for Animal Protective Legislation
Stern Community Law Firm
Student Advisory Committee on International Affairs
Student Mobilization Committee to End the War in
  Southeast Asia
Tax Analysts and Advocates
Trout Unlimited
United Church of Christ
United Methodist Church
United Presbyterian Church
Washington Peace Center
Washington Research Project
Wilderness Society
Woman's Christian Temperance Union
Women's International League for Peace and Freedom
World Federalists, USA
Young Americans for Freedom
Zero Population Growth

A Note on Research Methods

THE basic structure of the research methodology for this study was set forth in Chapter I. This appendix has been added for those readers who desire a more detailed explanation of the survey and case studies.

As noted earlier, one of the most difficult aspects of this whole enterprise was to construct the list of public interest groups for the survey. Because there is no real body of scholarly literature on public interest groups, I was initially dependent on the press for much of my information at the outset of this project. The Capital's morning paper, the *Washington Post*, with exemplary coverage of national politics, is the best source of news on these groups. The *Wall Street Journal*, *The New York Times*, and the *Washington Star-News* supply less total coverage, but were generally useful. The *National Journal* has included a number of public interest groups in its profiles of "Washington Pressures." *Congressional Quarterly*, the *Encyclopedia of Associations*, and the *Conservation Directory* were also utilized. One invaluable source of information was the subjects of the first round of interviewing. These people, some showing unusual interest in the study, provided a great deal of information about groups that had yet to be identified or about which little was known.

The self-constructed list of organizations was, by necessity, an expanding one, and groups were added as they could be identified throughout the interviewing stages of the research. It was initially thought that as many as 100 to 120 groups would eventually be confirmed as public interest. Because 80 to 100 interviews were planned, it was anticipated that sampling from the residual list would take care of any "surplus" that developed. As it turned out, there was no surplus, and the list was exhausted within a week of the pre-set June 1, 1973, deadline for the completion of the interviews. Interviewing began in mid-September 1972.

Again, although the list was completely used up by the end of the interviewing period, it is not suggested that this "sample" of groups is really a census of the public interest organizations that existed at the time. I suspect, though, that the number of groups I never learned of or the ones I wrongly disqualified as not being public interest without doing an interview, is a modest one. There is no way, of course, of actually confirming this. It should also be mentioned that some of the Ralph Nader organizations were left out of the sample on purpose. Because almost all of the satellite groups are financially dependent on his fund raising, it seemed wrong to consider each of them as distinct organizations. It was decided to try to do interviews at half of the Nader-related groups that existed in Washington at the time and were considered potentially eligible within the definition. Interviews were completed at seven organizations affiliated with the Nader complex, although one of the groups was subsequently disqualified under the operational definition.[1]

Efforts were made to reduce potential bias in the sample. In a number of cases where a preliminary judgment as to whether a group was public or private could not be made, an interview was conducted anyway. Although this was inefficient—six interviews (organizations) had to be thrown out—the process did lead to the inclusion of a few groups that might not otherwise have made it. Of the six groups disqualified after an interview, three were removed because they were evaluated as pursuing significant amounts of private interest lobbying. Two others were discarded because they exceeded the 20% limitation of government funding in

[1] For a line chart that explains the entire Nader empire as it then existed, see Theodore Jacqueney, "Nader Network Switches Focus to Legal Action, Congressional Lobbying," *National Journal*, June 9, 1973, p. 846.

their annual budgets. One group turned out to be a purely educational unit and not an advocacy organization.

The interviewees were, on the whole, extremely receptive, and there was little trouble in arranging interviews. There were only three refusals of interviews. Because one of these refusals was for a supplementary interview, there are just two organizations that were approached but that do not appear in the sample. The subjects were sent a letter of introduction that gave a brief description of the research project prior to their being contacted by telephone. The interview sessions lasted an average of an hour each. Most interviewees appeared to enjoy the experience, and many seemed gratified to be able to tell their "story." Subjects were told, both in the letter of introduction and before the first question was asked, that their remarks were not for personal attribution. Copious notes were taken in my own shorthand during each interview. Between my shorthand and "filling in" the interviews immediately after each session, very little of what was said was missed.[2] All transcriptions (done the day of the interview) and coding of the interviews were done solely by the author.

Although the standardized interview schedule was used for each of the primary interviews, the supplementary interviews were done on a somewhat different basis. The portion of the standardized format that dealt with the personal background of each lobbyist was used in the supplementary interviews, and these responses were included in the summary statistics in Chapter IV (see Appendix A). The remaining questions were developed before each interview, and they pertained specifically to the organization at hand.

At each of the interview sessions, additional data were gathered by asking for any available printed information on the organization. As it turned out, the respondents often volunteered this material before it was requested. The

[2] Practitioners differ over whether or not notes should be taken during elite interviews. See Lewis Anthony Dexter, *Elite and Specialized Interviewing* (Evanston, Ill.: Northwestern University Press, 1970).

printed matter collected, varying from group to group, consisted of samples of their magazines and newsletters, reproductions of collected press clippings, research reports, congressional testimony, intraoffice memoranda, pamphlets for prospective members, fund-raising brochures, and grant applications for foundation support.

The two case studies that were done offer a distinct contrast to the carefully planned survey. Prior to doing them, I went out of my way not to think about what I should be looking for or how they should be written up. During my work in the two groups, I did not want to be conscious of trying to fit my observations into some preconceived research design. It was impossible, however, to enter the case studies without some strong ideas about how public interest groups operate. The first study was done after months of research on the entire project and after a third of the interviews; and the second case study commenced after 30 more interviews. Moreover, there are biases in the method itself that are hard to escape. Paul Diesing expands upon some of these intrinsic problems:

> every scientist must be active with his subject matter in some fashion and must therefore change it as he studies it. Even the act of singling somebody out for attention has an effect on him, as we have long known. But the participant observer is more thoroughly and more continuously active than practitioners of other methods. He cannot take the detached, neutral pose of the experimenter and the survey researcher, but must actively involve himself in his subject matter emotionally, cognitively, and behaviorally. He must accept and work within the belief systems of the people he studies, take the roles that are offered to him if possible, and form genuine, not feigned, attachments. But any such socialization process is transactional, with influence coming from socialized as well as socializer.[3]

[3] Paul Diesing, *Patterns of Discovery in the Social Sciences* (Chicago: Aldine-Atherton, 1971), pp. 279-280.

Although it is difficult to assess how my presence affected the subjects, it is possible to discuss some of the personal biases that may have influenced my observations. First, I am sympathetic to the goals and policy objectives of both the Fund for Animals and the Women's International League for Peace and Freedom. Although I was never previously an activist on behalf of either cause, I went to work with an initially favorable attitude toward the groups. Second, as could be expected, strong friendships developed over time. Objectivity was sought throughout, but it is possible that these "biases" tempered the arguments in the two studies.

No two public interest groups could be representative of all the groups. A number of formal criteria were used, however, in choosing the two organizations. Most important, because time was limited, it was decided to study only small groups. One of the primary purposes of the case studies was to observe all facets of an organization's activities. This would not be possible in a large organization during a five-week period. In addition to large groups, conservative groups were excluded because I disagree with them ideologically and it would not have been fair to them to have a worker who was less than enthusiastic about their goals. Offices that are operated as public interest law firms were not approached because I have no legal training. The final selection was made from among those groups where I felt an immediate rapport with the interview subject and where I found the group's work to be interesting.

Both organizations were, of course, fully informed of my research intentions. I worked without remuneration, and my role was roughly similar to that of a college intern, although I was probably given more responsibility than an undergraduate would have received. Workers in both groups understood that I was free to write up whatever I saw. In a few instances, I did not use the names of certain people with whom the organizations had dealings so as not to embarrass either the Fund for Animals or the WILPF. After I had written first drafts of the case studies, I asked the staff members of each group to read my manuscript and to make comments on it. Lewis Regenstein and Marian Newman of the Fund for Animals spotted a number of small factual errors (since corrected), but had no disagreements with any of my interpretations. At the WILPF, Rosalie Riechman and Bill Samuels were somewhat taken aback by what they believed to be overstated criticism of their effectiveness. They felt that I did not see the WILPF's objectives as they saw them. In subsequent drafts of Chapter VI, I do not think I have changed the basic thrust of my argument, but I have tried to incorporate their perspective into the text.

The purpose of these case studies was not to draw out concrete generalizations from the two groups to the larger universe of public interest groups. Rather, the basic goal was to illustrate the day-to-day operations of these lobbies. It was hoped that some of the subtleties of public interest group behavior, such as the working habits of the lobbyists, the utilization of resources, and the intricacies of daily decision making, would be well brought out by the in-depth coverage that the case studies allowed.

BIBLIOGRAPHY

BOOKS AND MONOGRAPHS

Adams, James L. *The Growing Church Lobby in Washington.* Grand Rapids, Mich.: William B. Eerdmans, 1970.

Alexander, Herbert E. *Money in Politics.* Washington, D.C.: Public Affairs Press, 1972.

Amory, Cleveland. *Man Kind?* New York: Harper & Row, 1974.

Anderson, Frederick R. *NEPA in the Courts.* Baltimore: The Johns Hopkins University Press, 1973.

Bailey, Stephan K. *Congress Makes a Law.* New York: Columbia University Press, 1950.

Bailis, Lawrence Neil. *Bread or Justice.* Lexington, Mass.: Lexington Books, 1974.

Banfield, Edward C. *Political Influence.* New York: The Free Press, 1965.

Barber, James D. *The Lawmakers.* New Haven, Conn.: Yale University Press, 1965.

Bauer, Raymond A., Ithiel de Sola Pool, and Lewis Anthony Dexter. *American Business and Public Policy.* New York: Atherton, 1963.

Bernstein, Marver H. *Regulating Business by Independent Commission.* Princeton, N.J.: Princeton University Press, 1955.

Blau, Peter M. *Exchange and Power in Social Life.* New York: Wiley, 1964.,

Brill, Harry. *Why Organizers Fail.* Berkeley: University of California Press, 1971.

Brown, Holmes, and Don Luce. *Hostages of War.* Washington, D.C.: Indochina Mobile Education Project, 1973.

Buckhorn, Robert F. *Nader: The People's Lawyer.* Englewood Cliffs, N.J.: Prentice-Hall, 1972.

Campbell, Angus, Philip E. Converse, Warren E. Miller, and Donald E. Stokes. *The American Voter.* New York: Wiley, 1964.

Cobb, Roger W., and Charles D. Elder, *Participation in American Politics: The Dynamics of Agenda Building.* Boston: Allyn and Bacon, 1972.

Cox, Edward F., Robert C. Fellmeth, and John E. Schulz, *The Nader Report on the Federal Trade Commission.* New York: Baron, 1969.

Dahl, Robert A. *Modern Political Analysis,* 2nd ed. Englewood Cliffs, N.J.: Prentice-Hall, 1970.

————, and Charles E. Lindblom. *Politics, Economics, and Welfare.* New York: Harper Torchbooks, 1963.

Davidson, Roger H. *The Role of the Congressman.* New York: Pegasus, 1969.

Deakin, James. *The Lobbyists.* Washington, D.C.: Public Affairs Press, 1966.

Derthick, Martha. *The National Guard in Politics.* Cambridge, Mass.: Harvard University Press, 1965.

Detzer, Dorothy. *Appointment on the Hill.* New York: Henry Holt, 1948.

DeVries, Walter D. *The Michigan Lobbyist.* Unpublished Ph.D. dissertation, Michigan State University, 1960.

Dexter, Lewis Anthony. *Elite and Specialized Interviewing.* Evanston, Ill.: Northwestern University Press, 1970.

————. *How Organizations Are Represented in Washington.* Indianapolis, Ind.: Bobbs-Merrill, 1969.

————. *The Sociology and Politics of Congress.* Chicago: Rand McNally, 1969.

Diesing, Paul. *Patterns of Discovery in the Social Sciences.* Chicago: Aldine, Atherton, 1971.

Eckstein, Harry. *Pressure Group Politics.* Stanford, Calif.: Stanford University Press, 1960.

Ehrlich, Paul. *The Population Bomb.* New York: Ballantine, 1968.

Ehrmann, Henry W., ed. *Interest Groups on Four Continents.* Pittsburgh: University of Pittsburgh Press, 1958.

Esposito, John C. *Vanishing Air.* New York: Grossman, 1970.

Etzioni, Amitai. *A Comparative Analysis of Complex Organizations.* New York: The Free Press, 1961.

Eulau, Heinz, and John D. Sprague, *Lawyers in Politics.* Indianapolis, Ind.: Bobbs-Merrill, 1964.

Fanning, Odom. *Man and His Environment: Citizen Action.* New York: Harper & Row, 1975.

Fish, John Hall. *Black Power/White Control.* Princeton, N.J.: Princeton University Press, 1973.

Friedrich, Carl J., ed. *The Public Interest.* New York: Atherton, 1962.

Frohlich, Norman, Joe A. Oppenheimer, and Oran R. Young, *Political Leadership and Collective Goods.* Princeton, N.J.: Princeton University Press, 1971.

Gamson, William. *The Strategy of Social Protest.* Homewood, Ill.: Dorsey Press, 1975.

————. *Power and Discontent.* Homewood, Ill.: Dorsey Press, 1968.

Gorey, Hays. *Nader and the Power of Everyman.* New York: Grosset and Dunlop, 1975.

Goulden, Joseph C. *The Superlawyers.* New York: Dell, 1973.

Green, Mark J. *The Other Government.* New York: Grossman, 1975.

————, James J. Fallows, and David Zwick. *Who Runs Congress?* New York: Bantam/Grossman, 1972.

Greenstone, J. David, and Paul E. Peterson. *Race and Authority in Urban Politics.* New York: Russell Sage Foundation, 1973.

Guide to the Congress of the United States. Washington, D.C.: Congressional Quarterly, 1971.

Hall, Donald R. *Cooperative Lobbying—The Power of Pressure.* Tucson: University of Arizona Press, 1969.

Harrison, Gordon, and Sanford Jaffe. *The Public Interest Law Firm.* New York: Ford Foundation, 1973.

Held, Virginia. *The Public Interest and Individual Interests.* New York: Basic Books, 1970.

Holbert, Robert L. *Tax Law and Political Access.* Beverly Hills, Calif.: Sage Professional Papers in American Politics, 1975.

Holtzman, Abraham. *The Townsend Movement.* New York: Bookman, 1963.

Homans, George. *Social Behavior.* New York: Harcourt, Brace, & World, 1961.

Jaffe, Sanford. *Public Interest Law: Five Years Later.* New York: Ford Foundation/American Bar Association, 1976.

James, Marlisle. *The People's Lawyers.* New York: Holt, Rinehart and Winston, 1973.

Key, V. O., Jr. *Politics, Parties, & Pressure Groups,* 5th ed. New York: Crowell, 1964.

————. *Public Opinion and American Democracy.* New York: Alfred A. Knopf, 1961.

Kingdon, John W. *Congressmen's Voting Decisions*. New York: Harper & Row, 1973.

Lasswell, Harold D., and Abraham Kaplan. *Power and Society*. New Haven, Conn.: Yale University Press, 1950.

Law and Taxation. Washington, D.C.: The Conservation Foundation, 1970.

Lazarus, Simon. *The Genteel Populists*. New York: Holt, Rinehart and Winston, 1973.

Liebow, Elliot. *Talley's Corner*. Boston: Little, Brown, 1967.

Lipset, Seymour Martin, Martin Trow, and James Coleman. *Union Democracy*. Garden City, N.Y.: Anchor Books, 1956.

Liroff, Richard A. *A National Policy for the Environment*. Bloomington: Indiana University Press, 1976.

Lowi, Theodore J. *The Politics of Disorder*. New York: Basic Books, 1971.

———. *The End of Liberalism*. New York: Norton, 1969.

Lutzker, Paul. *The Politics of Public Interest Groups: Common Cause in Action*. Unpublished Ph.D. dissertation, The Johns Hopkins University, 1973.

McCarry, Charles. *Citizen Nader*. New York: Saturday Review Press, 1972.

McFarland, Andrew S. *Public-Interest Lobbies: Decision-Making on Energy*. Washington, D.C.: American Enterprise Institute, 1976.

McPhee, John. *Encounters with the Archdruid*. New York: Farrar, Straus & Giroux, 1971.

March, James G., and Herbert A. Simon. *Organizations*. New York: Wiley, 1958.

Matthews, Donald R. *U.S. Senators and Their World*. New York: Vintage Books, 1960.

Mayhew, David R. *Congress: The Electoral Connection*. New Haven, Conn.: Yale University Press, 1974.

Mech, L. David. *The Wolf*. Garden City, N.Y.: Natural History Press, 1970.

Meier, August, and Elliott Rudwick. *CORE: A Study in the Civil Rights Movement*. New York: Oxford University Press, 1973.

Michels, Robert. *Political Parties*. Glencoe, Ill.: The Free Press, 1958.

Milbrath, Lester W. *Political Participation*. Chicago: Rand McNally, 1965.

——. *The Washington Lobbyists*. Chicago: Rand McNally, 1963.

Miller, Robert W., and Jimmy D. Johnson. *Corporate Ambassadors to Washington*. Washington, D.C.: The American University, 1970.

Nadel, Mark V. *The Politics of Consumer Protection*. Indianapolis, Ind.: Bobbs-Merrill, 1971.

Nader, Ralph, Peter Petkas, and Kate Blackwell, eds. *Whistle Blowing*, New York: Grossman, 1972.

——, and Donald Ross. *Action for a Change: A Student's Guide for Public Interest Organizing*, 2nd ed. New York: Grossman, 1972.

Nie, Norman H., Sidney Verba, and John R. Petrocik. *The Changing American Voter*. Cambridge, Mass.: Harvard University Press, 1976.

Nielsen, Waldemar. *The Big Foundations*. New York: Columbia University Press, 1972.

Olson, Mancur, Jr. *The Logic of Collective Action*. New York: Schocken, 1968.

Oppenheimer, Bruce Ian. *Oil and the Congressional Process*. Lexington, Mass.: Lexington Books, 1974.

Page, Joseph A., and Mary-Win O'Brien. *Bitter Wages*. New York: Grossman, 1973.

Pateman, Carole. *Participation and Democratic Theory*. Cambridge: Cambridge University Press, 1970.

Peabody, Robert L., Jeffrey M. Berry, William G. Frasure, and Jerry Goldman. *To Enact a Law: Congress and Campaign Financing*. New York: Praeger, 1972.

Peters, Charles, and Taylor Branch. *Blowing the Whistle*. New York: Praeger, 1972.

Phelan, James, and Robert Pozen. *The Company State*. New York: Grossman, 1973.

The Pressure Groups. Washington, D.C.: National Journal, 1971.

Prewitt, Kenneth. *The Recruitment of Political Leaders*. Indianapolis, Ind.: Bobbs-Merrill, 1970.

Redman, Eric. *The Dance of Legislation*. New York: Simon and Schuster, 1973.

Regenstein, Lewis. *The Politics of Extinction*. New York: Macmillan, 1975.

Reich, Charles. *The Greening of America*. New York: Random House, 1970.

Riker, William H. *The Theory of Political Coalitions.* New Haven, Conn.: Yale University Press, 1962.

Rosenau, James N. *Citizenship Between Elections.* New York: The Free Press, 1974.

Ross, Donald. *A Public Citizen's Action Manual.* New York: Grossman, 1973.

Rourke, Francis E. *Bureaucracy, Politics, and Public Policy.* Boston: Little, Brown, 1969.

Sanford, David. *Me and Ralph: Is Nader Unsafe for America?* Washington, D.C.: New Republic Book Company, 1976.

Sax, Joseph L. *Defending the Environment.* New York: Alfred A. Knopf, 1971.

Sayre, Wallace S., and Herbert Kaufman. *Governing New York City.* New York: Russell Sage Foundation, 1960.

Schattschneider, E. E. *The Semisovereign People.* New York: Holt, Rinehart and Winston, 1960.

Schlesinger, Joseph A. *Ambition and Politics.* Chicago: Rand McNally, 1966.

Schubert, Glendon. *The Public Interest.* Glencoe, Ill.: The Free Press, 1960.

Scoble, Harry M. *Ideology and Electoral Action.* San Francisco: Chandler Publishing, 1967.

Scott, Andrew M., and Margaret A. Hunt. *Congress and Lobbies* Chapel Hill: University of North Carolina Press, 1965.

Selznick, Philip. *TVA and the Grass Roots.* New York: Harper & Row, 1966.

Sills, David. *The Volunteers.* New York: The Free Press, 1957.

Simon, Herbert A. *Administrative Behavior,* 2nd ed. New York: The Free Press, 1957.

Small—On Safety. New York: Grossman, 1973.

Smith, Judith G., ed. *Political Brokers.* New York: Liveright, 1972.

Sundquist, James L. *Dynamics of the Party System.* Washington, D.C.: Brookings Institution, 1973.

Thompson, Dennis F. *The Democratic Citizen.* Cambridge: Cambridge University Press, 1970.

Townsend, Claire. *Old Age: The Last Segregation.* New York: Grossman, 1971.

Truman, David B. *The Governmental Process,* 2nd ed. New York: Alfred A. Knopf, 1971.

Tucker, Marna. *The Private Law Firm and Pro Bono Publico Programs: A Responsive Merger.* Washington, D.C.: American Bar Association, 1972.

Verba, Sidney, and Norman H. Nie. *Participation in America.* New York: Harper & Row, 1972.

Wahlke, John C., Heinz Eulau, William Buchanan, and LeRoy C. Ferguson. *The Legislative System.* New York: Wiley, 1962.

The Washington Lobby. Washington, D.C.: Congressional Quarterly, 1971.

Wertheimer, Fred. *The Common Cause Manual on Money and Politics.* Washington, D.C.: Common Cause, 1972.

Wilensky, Harold. *Organizational Intelligence.* New York: Basic Books, 1967.

Wilson, James Q. *Political Organizations.* New York: Basic Books, 1973.

——————. *The Amateur Democrat.* Chicago: University of Chicago Press, 1962.

Wootton, Graham. *Interest-Groups.* Englewood Cliffs, N.J.: Prentice-Hall, 1970.

Zeigler, L. Harmon, and Wayne G. Peak. *Interest Groups in American Politics,* 2nd ed. Englewood Cliffs, N.J.: Prentice-Hall, 1972.

——————, and Michael Baer. *Lobbying.* Belmont, Calif.: Wadsworth, 1969.

Zinger, Clem L., Richard Dalsemer, and Helen Margargle. *Environmental Volunteers in America.* National Center for Voluntary Action's Environmental Project. Washington, D.C.: Environmental Protection Agency, 1973.

Zisk, Betty. *Local Interest Politics: A One-Way Street.* Indianapolis, Ind.: Bobbs-Merrill, 1973.

Zurcher, Arnold J., and Jane Dustan. *The Foundation Administrator.* New York: Russell Sage Foundation, 1972.

ARTICLES AND UNPUBLISHED PAPERS

"Awarding Attorney and Expert Witness Fees in Environmental Litigation." *Cornell Law Review* 58 (1973).

"Awarding Attorneys' Fees to the 'Private Attorney General': Judicial Green Light to Private Litigation in the Public Interest." *Hastings Law Journal* 24 (1973).

Bachrach, Peter, and Morton S. Baratz. "Two Faces of Power." *American Political Science Review* 56 (1962).

Bagdikian, Ben. "Congress and the Media: Partners in Propaganda." *Columbia Journalism Review* 12 (1974).

Barker, Lucius J., and Donald Jansiewicz. "Coalitions in the Civil Rights Movement," in *The Study of Coalition Behavior*, Sven Groennings, E. W. Kelley, and Michael Leiserson, eds. New York: Holt, Rinehart and Winston, 1970.

Berlin, Edward, Anthony Roisman, and Gladys Kessler. "Public Interest Law." *George Washington Law Review* 38 (1970).

Berry, Jeffrey M. "On the Origins of Public Interest Groups: A Test of Two Theories." *Polity* (forthcoming 1977).

————, and Jerry Goldman. "Congress and Public Policy: A Study of the Federal Election Campaign Act of 1971." *Harvard Journal on Legislation* 10 (1973).

Bishop, Joseph W. "Politics and ACLU." *Commentary* (December 1971).

Cahn, Edgar, and Jean Camper Cahn. "Power to the People or the Profession?—The Public Interest in Public Interest Law." *Yale Law Journal* 79 (1970).

Clark, Peter B., and James Q. Wilson. "Incentive Systems: A Theory of Organizations." *Administrative Science Quarterly* 6 (1961).

Clarke, Duncan L. "Congress, Interest Groups, and the U.S. Arms Control and Disarmament Agency." Paper delivered at the annual meeting of the International Studies Association, New York, March 1973.

Cochran, Clarke E. "Political Science and the 'Public Interest.'" *Journal of Politics* 36 (1974).

Cohen, Richard E. "Public Interest Lawyers Start Looking Out for Their Own Interests." *National Journal* (June 19, 1976).

————. "Ineffective Reporting Law Likely to Be Toughened, Extended." *National Journal* (April 19, 1975).

Corrigan, Richard. "Public Interest Law Firms Win Battle with IRS over Exemptions, Deductions." *National Journal* (November 21, 1970).

Costain, Anne N. "A Social Movement Lobbies: Women's Liberation and Pressure Politics." Paper delivered at the annual meeting of the Southern Political Science Association, Nashville, Tennessee, November 1975.

"Court Awarded Attorney's Fees and Equal Access to the Courts." *University of Pennsylvania Law Review* 122 (1974).

Crampton, Roger. "The Why, Where and How of Broadened Public Participation in the Administrative Process." *Georgetown Law Journal* 60 (1972).

Dahl, Robert A. "The Concept of Power." *Behavioral Science* 2 (1957).

Dawson, John P. "Lawyers and Involuntary Clients in Public Interest Litigation." *Harvard Law Review* 88 (1975).

Dawson, Paul. "On Making Public Policy More Public: The Role of Public Interest Groups." Paper delivered at the annual meeting of the American Political Science Association, New Orleans, Louisiana, September 1973.

Dexter, Lewis Anthony. "The Representative and His District." *Human Organization* 16 (1957).

⸻. "What Do Congressmen Hear: The Mail." *Public Opinion Quarterly* 20 (1956).

Downs, Anthony. "Up and Down with Ecology—The 'Issue Attention Cycle.'" *Public Interest* 28 (1972).

Drew, Elizabeth. "Conversation with a Citizen." *New Yorker* (July 23, 1973).

Duscha, Julius. "Stop! In the Public Interest!" *The New York Times Magazine* (March 21, 1971).

Gamson, William. "Stable Unrepresentation in American Society." *American Behavioral Scientist* 12 (1968).

Gellhorn, Ernest. "Public Participation in Administrative Proceedings." *Yale Law Journal* 81 (1972).

Goldberg, Steven S., and Joel Cohen. "Does Higher Authority than IRS Guidelines Exist for Public Interest Law Firms?" *Journal of Taxation* 34 (1971).

Goldsmith, Richard N. "The IRS Man Cometh: Public Interest Law Firms Meet the Tax Collector." *Arizona Law Review* 13 (1971).

Gordon, C. Wayne, and Nicholas Babchuk. "A Typology of Voluntary Associations." *American Sociological Review* 24 (1959).

Greenwald, Carol S. "The Use of Litigation by Common Cause: A Study of the Development of Campaign Finance Reform Legislation." Paper delivered at the annual meeting of the American Political Science Association, San Francisco, California, 1975.

Halpern, Charles R., and John M. Cunningham. "Reflections on the New Public Interest Law: Theory and Practice at the Center for Law and Social Policy." *Georgetown Law Journal* 59 (1971).

Jacob, Herbert. "Initial Recruitment of Elected Officials in the U.S.—A Model." *Journal of Politics* 24 (1962).

Jacqueney, Theodore. "Common Cause Lobbyists Focus on the Structure and Process of Government." *National Journal* (September 1, 1973).

————. "Nader Network Switches Focus to Legal Action, Congressional Lobbying." *National Journal* (June 9, 1973).

Klein, Joe. "Ralph Nader." *Rolling Stone* (November 20, 1975).

Kovenock, David. "Influence in the U.S. House of Representatives: A Statistical Analysis of Communications." *American Politics Quarterly* 1 (1973).

Kreiger, David M. "The Another Mother for Peace Consumer Campaign—A Campaign That Failed." *Journal of Peace Research* 8 (1971).

Levanthal, Harold. "Environmental Decisionmaking and the Role of the Courts." *University of Pennsylvania Law Review* 122 (1974).

Leventhal, Paul L. "Political Reaction Overshadows Reform Aim of Massive Nader Congress Study." *National Journal* (September 23, 1972).

Lindblom, Charles E. "The Science of Muddling Through." *Public Administration Review* 19 (1959).

Lipsky, Michael. "Protest as a Political Resource." *American Political Science Review* 62 (1968).

Luttbeg, Norman R., and Harmon Zeigler. "Attitude Censensus and Conflict in an Interest Group: An Assessment of Cohesion." *American Political Science Review* 60 (1966).

McClosky, Herbert, Paul J. Hoffman, and Rosemary O'Hara. "Issue Conflict and Consensus Among Party Leaders and Followers." *American Political Science Review* 54 (1960).

Messinger, Sheldon L. "Organizational Transformation: A Case Study of a Declining Social Movement." *American Sociological Review* 20 (1955).

Mezey, Michael L. "Ambition Theory and the Office of Congressman." *Journal of Politics* 32 (1970).

Miller, Warren E., and Donald E. Stokes. "Constituency Influence in Congress." *American Political Science Review* 57 (1963).

Mitnick, Barry M. "A Typology of Conceptions of the Public Interest." *Administration & Society* 8 (1976).

"The New Public Interest Law." *Yale Law Journal* 79 (1970).

Orren, Karen. "Standing to Sue: Interest Group Conflict in the Federal Courts." *American Political Science Review* 70 (1976).

Page, Joseph A. "The Law Professor Behind ASH, SOUP, PUMP, and CRASH." *The New York Times Magazine* (August 23, 1970).

Patterson, Samuel C. "The Role of the Lobbyist: The Case of Oklahoma." *Journal of Politics* 25 (1963).

Pratt, Henry J. "Bureaucracy and Interest Group Behavior: A Study of Three National Organizations." Paper delivered at the annual meeting of the American Political Science Association, Washington, D.C., 1972.

"Private Attorney General Fees Emerge from the *Wilderness*." *Fordham Law Review* 43 (1974).

"Public Interest Lobbies: Nader and Common Cause Become Permanent Fixtures." *Congressional Quarterly* (May 15, 1976).

"Public Participation in Federal Administrative Proceedings." *University of Pennsylvania Law Review* 120 (1972).

Rabin, Robert L. "Lawyers for Social Change: Perspectives on Public Interest Law." *Stanford Law Review* 28 (1976).

Rosenau, James N. "Mobilizing the Attentive Citizen." Paper delivered at the annual meeting of the American Political Science Association, New Orleans, Louisiana, September 1973.

Rosenbaum, Walter. "The End of Illusions: NEPA and the Limits of Judicial Review," in *Environmental Politics*, Stuart Nagel, ed. New York: Praeger, 1974.

Sabatier, Paul. "Social Movements and Regulatory Agencies: Toward a More Adequate—and Less Pessimistic—Theory of 'Clientele Capture.'" *Policy Sciences* 6 (1975).

Salisbury, Robert H. "An Exchange Theory of Interest Groups." *Midwest Journal of Political Science* 13 (1969).

Sax, Joseph L. "Standing to Sue: A Critical Review of the Mineral King Decision." *Natural Resources Journal* 13 (1973).

Schell, Jonathan. "The Time of Illusion—II" *New Yorker* (June 9, 1975).

Schrag, Philip, and Michael Meltsner. "Class Action: A Way to Beat the Bureaucracies Without Increasing Them." *Washington Monthly* (November 1972).

Schulman, Paul R. "Nonincremental Policy Making: Notes Toward an Alternative Paradigm." *American Political Science Review* 69 (1975).

Schumaker, Paul D. "Policy Responsiveness to Protest-Group Demands." *Journal of Politics* 37 (1975).

Schwartz, Donald E. "The Public-Interest Proxy Contest: Reflections on Campaign GM." *Michigan Law Review* 69 (1971).

Seligman, Lester G. "Political Parties and the Recruitment of Political Leaders," in *Political Leadership in Industrial Societies*, Lewis Edinger, ed. New York: Wiley, 1967.

Shor, Edgar. "Administrative Representation for the Under-Represented." Paper delivered at the annual meeting of the American Political Science Association, Washington, D.C., 1972.

"The Sierra Club, Political Activity, and Tax Exempt Charitable Status." *Georgetown Law Journal* 55 (1967).

Simon, Herbert A. "On the Concept of Organizational Goal." *Administrative Science Quarterly* 9 (1964).

Smith, David Horton, and Burt R. Baldwin. "Voluntary Associations and Volunteering in the United States," in *Voluntary Action Research: 1974*, David Horton Smith, ed. Lexington, Mass.: D.C. Heath, 1974.

Sorauf, Frank J. "The Public Interest Reconsidered." *Journal of Politics* 19 (1957).

Swanston, Walterene. "Consumer Federation of America Waging Spirited Battle for Survival." *National Journal* (July 8, 1972).

"Symposium: The Practice of Law in the Public Interest." *Arizona Law Review* 13 (1971).

"The Tax-Exempt Status of Public Interest Law Firms." *Southern California Law Review* 45 (1972).

Vogel, David. "Contemporary Criticism of Business: The Publicization of the Corporation." Paper delivered at the annual meeting of the American Political Science Association, New Orleans, Louisiana, 1973.

Vose, Clement E. "Litigation as a Form of Pressure Group Activity." *Annals of the American Academy of Political and Social Science* 319 (1958).

Wellford, Harrison. "How Ralph Nader, Tricia Nixon, the ABA, and Jamie Whitten Helped Turn the FTC Around." *Washington Monthly* (October 1972).

White, Orion. "The Dialectical Organization: An Alternative to Bureaucracy." *Public Administration Review* 29 (1969).

Whiteside, Thomas. "A Countervailing Force—I." *New Yorker* (October 9, 1973).

———. "A Countervailing Force—II." *New Yorker* (October 15, 1973).

———. "Annals of Advertising." *New Yorker* (December 19, 1970).

Woodward, Julien L., and Elmo Roper. "Political Activity of American Citizens." *American Political Science Review* 44 (1950).

Wright, Charles R., and Herbert H. Hyman. "Voluntary Association Memberships of American Adults." *American Sociological Review* 23 (1958).

Zald, Mayer. "The Power and Functions of Boards of Directors." *American Journal of Sociology* 75 (1969).

———, and Roberta Ash. "Social Movement Organizations: Growth, Decay, and Change." *Social Forces* 44 (1966).

INDEX

Abzug, Bella, 171-72
Adams, James L., 198n
Addams, Jane, 141
AFL-CIO, 10
Agribusiness Accountability
  Project, 75
Agriculture Department, 216
Alexander, Herbert E., 239n
Alsop, Joseph, 240n
*Alyeska Pipeline Service Co. v.
  Wilderness Society et al.*, 76-77
American Bar Association, 75n,
  247
American Civil Liberties Union,
  13, 35, 61, 68, 184, 200,
  229n, 252n
American Civil Liberties Union
  Foundation, 50
American Conservative Union,
  66, 238-39, 241
American Horse Protection
  Association, 237
American League to Abolish
  Capital Punishment, 8
American Security Council, 191,
  241
Americans for Constitutional
  Action, 66, 96n, 238-39, 241
Americans for Democratic Action,
  63, 68, 236, 240-41
Amnesty International, 156,
  159n, 257-58
Amory, Cleveland, 110-20, 122,
  134n, 140
Anderson, Frederick R., 229n
Anderson, Harold E., 127
Anderson, Jack, 54n, 129, 138,
  164, 246, 268
Anderson, Wendell, 126, 130
Anderson, William, 166n
AP (Associated Press), 129, 244
Arms Control Association, 74
Arnold and Porter, 70

Ash, Roberta, 198n
Aspinall, Wayne, 49, 242
Atomic Energy Commission
  (AEC), 245
Augustus, Amy, 164
authority, *see* organizational
  decision making

Babchuk, Nicholas, 35n
Bach, Richard, 115
Bachrach, Peter, 190n, 274n
Baer, Michael, 11-12, 83, 84n,
  86-87, 89n, 99, 106n, 213n,
  215, 283n
Baez, Joan, 150
Bagdikian, Ben, 249n
Bailey, Stephen K., 6, 262n
Bailis, Lawrence Neil, 22n
Baily, Ed, 167-69
Baldwin, Burt R., 65n, 287n
Banfield, Edward C., 207-209
Banzhaf, John, 88n
Baratz, Morton S., 190n, 274n
Barber, James D., 79n
Barker, Lucius J., 261n
Barth, Roger V., 54
Bauer, Raymond A., 59, 91, 92n,
  207, 209, 216n, 217, 222,
  278n, 280n
Bender, Marilyn, 251n
Berlin, Edward, 69n
Bernstein Foundation, 73n
Bernstein, Marver, H., 283n
Berry, Jeffrey M., 27n, 67n, 197n,
  200n, 225n
Biden, Joseph, 161
Bishop, Joseph W., Jr., 184n
Black Panthers, 143
Blackwell, Kate, 251n
Blake, Amanda, 134n
Blau, Peter M., 21n
Bohlen, E. U., 132
Bourassa, Robert, 125-26

Zeehandelaar, Fred, 135
Zeigler, L. Harmon, 11-12, 83,
    84n, 86-87, 89n, 99, 106n,
    193n, 194, 213n, 214-15, 225n,
    266n, 283n
Zero Population Growth, 32, 50

Zero Population Growth Fund,
    50
Zinger, Clem L., 65n
Zisk, Betty, 217n, 265n
Zurcher, Arnold J., 92n
Zwick, David, 247n

Library of Congress Cataloging in Publication Data

Berry, Jeffrey M   1948-
    Lobbying for the people.

    Bibliography: p.
    Includes index.
    1. Lobbying—United States.   2. Pressure groups—
United States.   3. Public interest—United States.
I. Title.
JK1118.B4   322.4'3'0973   77-71973
ISBN 0-691-07588-3
ISBN 0-691-02178-3 pbk.

	DATE DUE		
FEB 21 92			
MAY 20 93			
JUN 28 93			

LOBBYING FOR THE PEOPLE